ESSENTIAL CENTRAL GOVERNMENT 2002

RON FENNEY

The recommended textbook for the examinations of the
National Council for the Training of Journalists

First published 1988 as Central Government for Journalists
Second Edition 1993
Third Edition 1995
Fourth Edition 1997
Fifth Edition 2000
Sixth Edition 2002

© Copyright LGC Information
All rights reserved. No part of this publication may be reproduced, stored in a retrieval system, or
transmitted in any form or by means, electronic, mechanical, photocopying, recording, or otherwise,
without prior permission in writing from the publisher.

Price £15.95
ISBN 1-904009-06-9

Published by
LGC Information
part of EMAP Public Sector Management,
Greater London House, Hampstead Road,
London NW1 7EJ
Telephone: 020 7347 1828
Fax: 020 7347 1815
Website: www.lgcnet.com

RON FENNEY

Contents

LGC· Information

Preface

The National Council for the Training of Journalists (NCTJ) Public Affairs Board devises the Council's syllabus and sets its exams. Part of the assistance which the NCTJ gives to students is to arrange for the publication of this book and its companion, *Essential Local Government*, by LGC Information.

This is the sixth edition of this book and it is a revised and extended version of the third, fourth and fifth editions, which I wrote in 1995, 1997 and 2000, respectively. A lot has happened since then — the New Labour government has entered its second term in office. In addition, the European dimension continues to grow and devolution is now firmly on the UK scene, albeit a little shaky in Northern Ireland and still in preparation for England. I have tried to make the book readable and at the same time to include more detail to explain how organisations work and the context in which events have taken place. I hope that my background as a local government solicitor is not betrayed too often by the prose style!

As for previous editions of this and the companion book, *Essential Local Government*, I should like to acknowledge the invaluable help of Mandy Ball of Sheffield College who, as a member of the NCTJ Studies Board, was well placed to let me know if I was straying away from what might be of interest to students. Mandy also very helpfully reviewed my draft text and, if any errors remain, they are entirely mine.

Although this book is primarily written for students studying Part II of the NCTJ Public Affairs Syllabus, I have also tried to write it as a general reference guide for anyone with an interest in having a plain person's guide to central government.

The pace of change seems to be unremitting but I had to stop writing at some point — in this instance at the beginning of February 2002. Where change seems likely, I have mentioned it in the text. I hope that readers will bear that in mind and take the trouble to check for themselves that things are still as written here. In the present age of e-government, the most up-to-date information is to be found on the Internet and, for the first time, I have included in the body of the text the more relevant website addresses for those with a more inquisitive inclination. The best portal for UK central and local government information is *www.ukonline.gov.uk* (not to be confused with *www.ukonline.co.uk* which is an ISP!) which then leads to other websites; the corresponding portal for the EU is *www.europarl.eu.int*

Ron Fenney
February 2002, Leicester

1   The Constitution

The UK Constitution — the Rule of Law — the separation of powers — the sovereignty of Parliament

The United Kingdom — a democracy

The United Kingdom consists of Great Britain (England, Wales and Scotland) and Northern Ireland. The introduction to the chapter on *Devolution* explains the historical context in which the various parts of the UK came together. The country's proper title is the *United Kingdom of Great Britain and Northern Ireland*. The Isle of Man and the Channel Islands are not, strictly speaking, part of the UK, since they are Crown dependencies having a special relationship with the UK but having legislative, fiscal and judicial autonomy. The UK is also one of the 15 Member States of the European Union.

The essential feature of a democracy is a competitive election at fairly frequent and regular intervals, in which the whole of the adult population is entitled to vote — a competition in which there is a genuine choice between at least two political parties with different ideologies and policies.

The UK is a *unitary*, as opposed to *federal*, democratic state — that is, a country where the power of government resides in a single national authority elected by its people. As a matter of principle this is still true, even though devolution in Scotland, Wales and Northern Ireland might suggest otherwise.

Given the size of the UK population (or, indeed, the population of any country), it is not really practical for the people to exercise that power directly themselves, and so it is exercised through elected representatives — a *representative democracy*. Anyone

2

searching for an example of a representative democracy in action need look no further than the outcome of the UK 1997 and 2001 General Elections.

In addition, unlike some representative democracies which are republics, the UK also has a monarchy and can also be called a *monarchical democracy* — albeit a monarchy whose powers have been progressively reduced over the past few hundred years (as will be seen later in this and the next chapter).

The Constitution — rigid or flexible

Any democracy would be expected to have a *Constitution*, that is, a system of laws, customs and conventions which defines the way in which the country is to be governed and which regulates relations between the various arms of government and between the government and the individual citizen. The Constitution is particularly important in describing any limits imposed on any person or organisation exercising power of government.

Constitutions are sometimes to be found in a single document — long (India's has 395 articles and 11 schedules) or relatively short (USA's has seven articles). The 55 delegates who wrote the American Constitution during the summer of 1787 did not, for obvious reasons, want to use the British Constitution as a precedent. So, they based their document on their practical experience of the way in which their country had been run since independence had been declared in 1776. They could not foresee how their society would develop and it has been necessary to amend the original American Constitution on 27 occasions since its ratification in 1788. The first 10 amendments collectively ratified in 1791 amounted to the American Bill of Rights and later amendments reflected the changes in USA society (for example, the 19th Amendment in 1920 granted suffrage to women).

The American Constitution is regarded as 'rigid', because proposals to amend it either must be supported by a two-thirds majority vote in both the House of Representatives and the Senate, or must arise out of a national convention followed by ratification by three-quarters of the state legislatures or state conventions.

But even then, the American Constitution as a document itself is not the complete story — the Supreme Court and Acts of Congress are extensively used to 'interpret' the Constitution and apply it to modern-day issues. For example, in 1954 the Supreme Court declared that the 14th Amendment (1868 — no state shall deny the equal protection of its laws) had the effect of outlawing racial segregation in USA schools.

The UK's constitution is different. It is regarded as 'flexible' because all of its constitutional institutions and rules can be abrogated or modified by an Act of Parliament. It is often described, wrongly, as an 'unwritten' constitution — in reality it is part unwritten and part written. The written part of it is not to be found in a single document — instead, it is derived from a variety of sources.

So, constitutions can be written, unwritten or a combination of both. The advantages of a written constitution can nearly always be regarded as being the disadvantages of an unwritten constitution — and *vice versa*.

A written constitution has the major benefit of being certain — that is, the people whom it is designed to regulate will know what it contains and the limits on their behaviour and on the power of the State. This means that they should be able to have confidence that they will know beforehand whether their actions will stray beyond the boundaries of their rights and obligations within the constitution. This certainty should also make it clearer whether any challenges of theirs to the actions of the State have a guaranteed chance of success. However, even a written constitution may not provide adequate guarantees if the Executive of the day does not respect the other elements of the Separation of Powers, the Judiciary and the Legislature; as can be seen in Zimbabwe. The disadvantages of a written constitution also derive from its certainty — this time, presented as rigidity and unresponsive to the changing needs of society, unless it contains mechanisms for change, through a predefined process which has democratic credibility and safeguards.

On the other hand, an unwritten constitution is inherently flexible, precisely because it is unwritten. It can readily be changed as society evolves and the rights and obligations of the people can be aligned more easily with current conditions and expectations. The State can change it through action promoted in the legislature and the courts, provided, of course, that the power to modify the constitution is not used gratuitously and for inappropriate or undemocratic purposes. Because the boundaries are not fixed, the people can themselves modify them by promoting their own actions in the courts if they believe that the State has exceeded its powers or that the limits of their rights or obligations, as they understand them (because they are not written down in a constitution), should be changed. On the other hand, the lack of a written definition could make it that much more difficult to be absolutely confident of success in the courts.

The remainder of this Chapter may help to form an opinion on whether a written constitution is likely to be preferable to an unwritten one.

Where the UK Constitution is to be found

There are five main sources of the UK Constitution:

- *Statute* — originally made by the Sovereign, starting with Magna Carta (1215); but then made by the Sovereign to a lesser extent — the Bill of Rights (1689) and the Act of Settlement (1701); and, more recently, by various Acts of Parliament (the Parliament Acts 1911 and 1949, the Representation of the People Acts and other less obvious ones, such as the Race Relations Act 1968) and the mass of delegated legislation authorised by Parliament; and, even more recently, the Human Rights Act 1998, the Government of Wales Act 1998, the Northern Ireland (Elections) Act 1998, the Scottish Parliament Act 1999 and the House of Lords Act 1999;

- *Common Law* — a continually evolving body of law made by judges in court decisions in interpreting and reviewing the royal prerogative powers of the Crown and the law and practice of Parliament;

- *Conventions* — precepts and practices which have never themselves been codified into a single document and are not directly enforceable in a court of law, but which, nonetheless, are regarded as having binding force by those who operate the Constitution (such as the privilege claimed by Parliament and the resignation of a government which loses a vote of confidence);

- *Works of authority or treatises* — influential works which have been written to offer guidance in clarifying uncertain areas of the Constitution, which have powerfully persuasive, rather than binding, authority — such as Fitzherbert's *Abridgement* (1516), Coke's *Institutes of the Law of England* (1628-44), Erskine May's *Parliamentary Practice* (1844), and Dicey's *An Introduction to the Study of the Law of the Constitution* (1885); and

- *European Treaties and law* — the transition of the European Community (EC) from just an economic partnership to a much closer union (EU) has brought into the UK constitutional equation the supra-national influence of the EU institutions. For example, in a 1990 ruling (the *Factortame* case), the European Court of Justice (ECJ) 'disapplied' UK legislation because it did not comply with EC law — declaring unlawful a UK government policy banning Spanish fishermen from fishing in UK waters and giving rise to significant compensation claims by Spanish fishermen against the UK government. Increasingly, UK domestic courts and tribunals are referring questions to the ECJ on the interpretation of EU Treaties and Directives before reaching final decisions on the cases before them — as Leeds Industrial Tribunal did in July 1999 in a case arising out of the contraction of the coal mining industry *(Allen v ACC Co.)*.

As explained, the UK Constitution can be amended by an Act of Parliament or by general agreement to create, vary or abolish a convention. In this way, it is said that the UK Constitution can be adjusted more easily to changing political conditions and ideas.

The Constitution — developments — the Human Rights Act

An illustration of this ease of amendment is the Human Rights Act 1998 which came into effect in England and Wales on 2 October 2000 — heralded in the first Queen's Speech following the New Labour General Election win in 1997. The Act incorporates into UK domestic law 'the main provisions' of the European Convention on Human Rights — in particular, Articles 2 to 13 and the First and Sixth Protocols (usually known as 'Convention Rights'). Article 1 of the Convention requires the country's domestic courts to provide effective remedies, which make it unnecessary for the individual to have to go to the European Court of Human Rights (ECHR) in the first instance — the rôle of the ECHR is then to ensure that the domestic courts are performing properly in enforcing the Convention Rights. The preface to every Bill now presented to Parliament must contain a formal statement from the relevant Secretary of State to the effect that he or she is satisfied that the provisions of the Bill are compatible with the Convention Rights.

The Convention Rights are:

Article 2	Right to life
Article 3	Protection from torture and inhuman or degrading treatment or punishment
Article 4	Protection from slavery and forced or compulsory labour
Article 5	Right to liberty and security of person
Article 6	Right to a fair trial
Article 7	Protection from retrospective criminal offences
Article 8	Protection of private and family life
Article 9	Freedom of thought, conscience and religion
Article 10	Freedom of expression
Article 11	Freedom of association and assembly
Article 12	Right to marry and found a family
Article 13	Freedom from discrimination

First Protocol:

Article 1	Right to property
Article 2	Right to education
Article 3	Right to free and fair elections

Sixth Protocol:

Articles 1 & 2	Abolition of death penalty in peacetime

The Human Rights Act will strengthen the ability of ordinary people to challenge, in the UK and EU courts, the actions of the various institutions of government. The Act is particularly relevant in disputes between the individual and the State or a public body of some kind — the courts may be reluctant to apply its provisions to disputes which concern only individuals. Its implications are far-reaching and with, as yet, unknown consequences. The ambit of this new area of Constitutional Law will emerge as the courts are asked to use the Act's provisions to protect the rights of the individual against the State.

There is a limitation period — claims have to be brought against the State or public body within one year of the 'act' about which the complaint is made. The Convention Rights are not absolute — they can be breached in accordance with the laws of the country or in the following circumstances: in the interests of national security, public safety or the country's economic well-being; for the prevention of crime and disorder; the protection of health or morals; and to protect the freedom and rights of others. A recent example of this was the Anti-terrorism, Crime and Security Act 2001 passed in December 2001 in response to the events of 11 September 2001 and which allowed the detention and deportation, without trial, of people with suspected terrorist links.

In relation to Scotland, where the 1998 Act came into effect in advance of England, the consequences started to emerge earlier. In November 1999, the High Court declared unlawful the appointment of 129 temporary sheriffs, who act as judges in the Scottish criminal courts, because they had been hired by the Lord Advocate, the member of the Scottish Executive responsible for prosecutions — a clear conflict with the principles of the separation of powers.

In the UK generally, one of the more significant consequences may be the eventual repeal of the Act of Settlement 1701, because it discriminates against non-Protestants by prohibiting them from succeeding to the Throne and is thus inconsistent with the Human Rights Act. Such a move could have the knock-on effect of disestablishing the Church of England, because a Catholic sovereign could hardly be its Head. The practice of the eldest son (rather than daughter) succeeding to the Throne might also be regarded as inconsistent with the Human Rights Act.

All of this may be some years away but, in the meantime, there is a more immediate aspect. For some time now the *Guardian* has been campaigning for the repeal of the Act of Settlement and has raised for debate the issue of the possible abolition of the Monarchy as an institution. There is, however, a problem about this — the Treason Felony Act 1848 makes it a criminal offence to advocate the abolition of the Monarchy, even by peaceful means. The maximum penalty for this offence is life imprisonment, although the last prosecution was in 1883 and it is unlikely that one would be brought in the modern context. However, to make the point, the *Guardian* tried to obtain a High Court declaration that the 1848 Act was incompatible with Article 10 of the Human Rights Act 1998. The court decided that it was not prepared to play the *Guardian's* game, deciding that the refusal of the Attorney General to give immunity to the *Guardian's* Editor was not an 'act' of the State and, therefore, there was nothing on which the *Guardian* could base a claim.

The Constitution — developments — referenda — devolution
The main feature of a representative democracy is that political issues are usually decided by the elected representatives, rather than directly by the voters. As explained later in this Chapter, although the voters are informed about a political party's intentions by means of the election manifesto, the party, if elected, is not committed to following that manifesto. As also explained later, the political sovereignty of the people *vis-à-vis* Parliament really works only after the event — at the next General Election.

There is another mechanism for settling political issues, using, instead, direct consultation with the people — a *referendum*. (The strict plural of referendum is referend*a*, although the alternative, less strict, version, referend*ums*, seems to be favoured by the government). The use of referenda is more common outside the UK and has been adopted within the UK only recently and then only to settle a major political issue. One of the key features of a referendum is how the question is phrased — if there is to be confidence in the validity of the referendum then the question needs to be put in neutral terms. The clear implication is that the government will regard itself as bound by the outcome of a referendum, unless it can demonstrate that a low turnout suggested that the result was an unreliable indicator of overall public opinion.

The use of a referendum in the UK on a national basis was unknown before 1975 (whether the UK should stay in the EC) and some would argue that referenda are inconsistent, as a matter of principle, with a representative democracy. There have been referenda on only two other occasions and then on a country basis: Northern Ireland (1973 — the border with Eire) and Scotland/Wales (1979 — devolution).

The Queen's Speech which followed New Labour's 1997 General Election victory contained proposals for two further referenda, canvassing the possibility of a devolved Parliament in Scotland and an Assembly in Wales. These referenda led to the Scottish Parliament and the Welsh Assembly which are discussed in more detail in the chapter on *Devolution*. This time, not only the issue itself but also the way it was handled (the use of referenda) represented changes in the constitution.

The latest Scottish and Welsh referenda will not be the last. The entry of the UK into European Monetary Union (EMU) and the UK's participation in the single unit of EU currency, the euro (€), will be the subject of a further referendum — this time on a UK-wide basis. At the time of writing (February 2002), the government is still unclear about when it proposes to put this issue to the people. The factors involved are discussed in a little more detail in the section about the euro in the Chapter on the *European Union*. However, as the UK population sees the effects of the introduction of the euro on 1 January 2002 in the 12 Euroland countries, this will increase UK familiarity with the euro which, in turn, should quicken the pace towards a referendum on UK participation. Indeed, at the end of December 2001, both the CBI and the TUC were calling for the government to reach a decision on the euro referendum.

As a consequence of the Political Parties, Elections and Referendums Act 2000, the new *Electoral Commission*, established on 30 November 2001, has the statutory duty to conduct national referendums. The other duties of the Electoral Commission are described in the later Chapter on *Elections*.

The Rule of Law

The Rule of Law is generally accepted as one of the essential features of a free democratic society.

Defining what is meant by *The Rule of Law* is rather more difficult. One definition might be that it is the doctrine that the arbitrary exercise of power by, say, a government is made subordinate to well-defined and impartial principles of law. The key words in the previous sentence are 'arbitrary', 'subordinate', 'well-defined' and 'impartial'. The ideas underlying this are best illustrated by quotations from some eminent commentators on constitutional issues:

One of the classic definitions was put forward in 1885 by A.V. Dicey in his *An Introduction to the Study of the Law of the Constitution* when he described the protection available through ordinary legal processes: *"When we say that the Supremacy or the Rule of Law is a characteristic of the English Constitution, we generally include under one expression at least three distinct though kindred conceptions. We mean, in the first place, that no man is punishable or can be made to suffer in body or goods except for a distinct breach of law established in the ordinary legal manner before the ordinary courts of the land..."* The key word in this quotation is 'ordinary'.

Lord Justice Hewitt put a more modern gloss on the concept, as he believed it to be operating in the UK context, in his *The New Despotism* published in 1929: *"What is meant here by the 'Rule of Law' is the supremacy or dominance of law, as distinguished from mere arbitrariness, or from some alternative mode, which is not law, of determining or disposing of the rights of individuals"*.

The purpose of the Rule of Law for the proper functioning of a modern society like the UK is illustrated by T.D. Weldon's 1953 *Vocabulary of Politics*. Although he was talking about associations, the principles also hold good for countries: *"Strictly speaking, there is nothing difficult or impressive about the 'Rule of Law'. It is merely a convenient way of referring to the fact that associations have rules and that unless those rules are pretty generally kept and enforced, the association breaks down and the activity which it was designed to promote becomes impracticable"*.

The rights of the individual can also be protected by the way in which the power of government is conferred on the state's institutions — especially if there is a degree of separation in the way in which that power is allocated. The American Constitution and Bill of Rights provides a useful example of a more explicit description of the protections enjoyed by a citizen under the Rule of Law — including forbidding retrospective laws (cf Article 7 of the Human Rights Act 1998, mentioned earlier); and guaranteeing the writ of *habeas corpus,* a fair procedure for people accused of crime, a speedy and public trial by a local impartial jury before an impartial judge and representation by counsel (cf Article 6 of the Human Rights Act 1998). For example, the Fifth Amendment (1791) to the American Constitution stated: *"... nor shall any person be subject for the same offense to be twice put in jeopardy of life and limb; nor shall be compelled in any criminal case to be a witness against himself, nor be deprived of life, liberty, or property, without due process of law".*

The Separation of Powers — USA

It is argued that the separation of the legislative, executive and judicial functions of government between different and independent bodies limits the possibility of excessive and arbitrary government — in other words, a system of checks and balances. The way in which the doctrine of the separation of powers is reflected in constitutional documents varies considerably. Again, the American and UK Constitutions provide a useful contrast.

In a federal state, such as the USA, the separation is achieved by splitting power between the national and state levels. Power at national level in the USA is further split between Congress, the President and the Supreme Court. This separation of powers at national level is structural within the American Constitution and the concentration of power is further precluded by staggering the terms of office of the key elements of government. John Adams, apart from being one of the authors of the Declaration of Independence, the first Vice-President and second President, was also an influential political theorist and wrote: *"It is by balancing each of these powers against the other two, that the efforts in human nature toward tyranny can alone be checked and restrained, and any degree of freedom preserved in the constitution".*

- Article I of the American Constitution vests all *legislative* powers in the bicameral (two chamber) Congress — the House of Representatives and the Senate. Bills must pass both houses and be signed by the President before they can become law — the President can veto a Bill but his veto can be overturned by a two-thirds vote of both houses. Congress's powers also include levying taxes, borrowing money and declaring war.
- Article II vests *executive* power in the President: chief executive, making treaties, commander-in-chief of the armed forces, Head of State, proposing legislation to Congress and formulating foreign

policy. Any appointments which the President intends to make to assist him in the exercise of his powers are subject to the 'advice and consent' (a majority vote in favour) of the Senate. The President can be impeached by Congress.

● Article III vests *judicial* power in the hands of the courts, both state and federal under the supervision of the US Supreme Court. Judicial power has included, since a case in 1803, the power of judicial review and interpretation of the Constitution itself.

The Separation of Powers — UK

The separation of powers in the UK is less clear-cut. The UK is a unitary state, so the separation is achieved at national level only, although somewhat modified by devolution to Scotland.

The various parts of government in the UK are, in theory, essentially separate:

● *The Legislature*, which consists of the *Queen in Parliament,* is the supreme legislative authority.

● *The Executive;* or Government, which consists of:

— the *Cabinet and other Ministers of the Crown*, responsible for initiating and directing national policy;

— *government departments,* mostly under the control of Ministers, responsible for administration at national level; and

— *public agencies* or bodies responsible for the administration of specific services and subject to Ministerial control to a varying extent.

● *The Judiciary*, which determines the *Common Law* and interprets statutes and is independent of both the Legislature and the Executive.

The impact of devolution in Scotland, Wales and Northern Ireland on the Legislature, Executive and Judiciary is discussed in the Chapter on *Devolution*.

However, it might be argued that complete separation could lead to less efficient government, as the various elements wielded their own exclusive power without regard to the others. So, in the UK the elements often overlap, and interconnect with, one another. In this way there is a system of checks and balances to prevent excessive exercise of power by any one element, but it can lead to confusion.

The overlaps include, for example:

● *The Queen* is Head of the Executive and Judiciary and has a rôle in the working of the Legislature.

● *The Lord Chancellor* presides over the House of Lords part of the Legislature, manages the Judiciary on behalf of the Queen and is also part of the Executive through his membership of the Cabinet; however, this has been the subject of increasing the criticism on grounds of conflict of interest (the Lord Chancellor sitting in judgment in cases against the Executive of which he is a member) and may be ruled to be unlawful by the European Court in a case involving a similar arrangement in Guernsey.

- *The Cabinet*, by its very nature, represents an overlap of the Executive and Legislature.
- *The House of Lords* is part of the Legislature and is also part of the Judiciary in its rôle as the ultimate domestic court of law.
- *The Judiciary,* through its judgments at the various levels of the legal process, interprets the will of the Legislature when determining the proper application of Acts of Parliament and also reviews the actions of the Executive in administrative law cases brought by individuals aggrieved at the effect of the actions of the Executive upon them.

The Sovereignty of Parliament

Parliament (which consists of the Queen, the House of Commons and the House of Lords) is the supreme legislative authority. Parliament can legislate for the UK as a whole or for one or more of its constituent countries. This is now subject to the arrangements approved by Parliament for devolution in Scotland, Wales and Northern Ireland.

Because there are no limitations imposed by an entirely written Constitution, Parliament, at least in theory, can legislate how it likes. Laws can be made, repealed or amended. Something which was unlawful before can be made lawful; something which was lawful before can be made unlawful.

Amongst other things, this ability to rewrite laws enables Parliament to reverse decisions of the Judiciary on the present state of the law which Parliament finds to be inconsistent with its real intentions. For its part, the Judiciary will always work on the assumption that there is no theoretical limit on the ability of Parliament to legislate, when interpreting Acts of Parliament in individual cases. In interpreting the intentions of Parliament, judges will now refer to *Hansard* as a source of information. However, the Judiciary will also have regard to relevant EU law, brought to bear through the UK's membership of the EU.

As a consequence of the Parliament Act 1911, Parliament usually has a life of not more than five years — the limit was seven years prior to 1911. However, Parliament can even prolong its own life without consulting the electorate first, if Parliament believes that the circumstances justify that course of action. For that to happen, the three components of Parliament have to agree and this has only happened twice —

during the two World Wars. Some people suspect that a reformed second chamber in place of the Lords, especially if wholly or mainly appointed, would make it too easy for Parliament to extend its life beyond the five year term and thus avoid a General Election.

Conventions and Parliamentary Privilege

Conventions, which are an important part of the Constitution, can be eliminated by Parliament or can be converted into binding law, enforceable in the courts.

A recent example of Parliament eliminating a convention was the insertion of section 13 into the Defamation Act 1996 during its passage in the House of Lords. Section 13 had the effect of removing one of the provisions of the 1689 Bill of Rights — specifically to enable Neil Hamilton MP to continue (and then subsequently abandon) defamation proceedings against the *Guardian* in the 'cash for questions' case. The Bill of Rights included: *"That the freedom of speech and debates or proceedings in Parliament ought not to be impeached or questioned in any court or place out of Parliament"*.

This is normally taken to mean that anything said in Parliament cannot result in defamation proceedings — called *absolute privilege* (similar to that which applies to the courts of law). The reverse was also declared to be true on a strict interpretation of the 1689 wording — that no defamation proceedings could arise out of a report alleging wrongdoing in Parliament by an MP — effectively stalling Hamilton's case against the *Guardian*. He lobbied for the right to pursue the *Guardian* and section 13 was inserted in the 1996 Act to enable him to waive Parliamentary privilege to do so.

In 1999, it was argued before the Joint Committee on Parliamentary Privilege that the implications of section 13 were not thought through at the time and its insertion as a short-term expedient to meet the personal needs of an individual MP was mistaken as a matter of principle. In November 1999, the Joint Committee reported its conclusion that only the whole House should have the power to permit privilege to be waived, rather than an individual MP. The Leader of the Commons confirmed that the government broadly supported these recommendations and that the law would be changed — at some time.

Parliament and the Executive

There are various ways in which Parliament (particularly the House of Commons) exercises control over the Executive — which can be quite effective if used skilfully by the Opposition and by the government's own back-benchers. The mechanisms which are particularly useful include: Question time; Motions for the Adjournment of the House; Standing and Select Committees and Motions connected with the supply of money.

However, the size of the New Labour majority in the Commons following the 1997 and 2001 General Elections, together with the government's perceived preoccupation with spin, discipline and 'control-freakery', and Tony Blair's style of Premiership, is regarded by some as creating a climate in which New Labour back-bencher questioning of government activity is not encouraged.

For example, the government whips determine the nominations for membership of Select Committees and these were being reappointed after the 2001 General Election. The Select Committees appoint their own chairmen but that is largely academic if the whips decide not to reappoint the likely candidates to the committee. The whips might try to do this if the activities of a particular chairman of a Select Committee are a little too challenging for the government's taste. This is what happened in July 2001 — Hilary Armstrong, the government's Chief Whip, decided to tell Gwyneth Dunwoody and Donald Anderson that they would not be re-appointed to their respective Select Committees. When this became known, Betty Boothroyd, former Speaker, decided to intervene:

> "It seems that the government is manipulating Parliament. Select
> Committees are not an arm of government. They are a mechanism to
> scrutinise government. It is outrageous that the government cannot stand
> the heat of a bit of criticism. This is what their jobs should be about — to
> speak out when there is a need to speak out".

She invited the backbench MPs in Parliament to disregard Hilary Armstrong and reappoint Mrs Dunwoody and Mr Anderson to the committees. Mr Anderson summarised the position well:

> "I guess that there will be an enormous temptation just to roll over and let
> the Executive do what they will. Parliament is in a unique position to say,
> are we effectively a rubber stamp for the Executive, do we allow the
> Executive to appoint its own committees and chairmen, or do we stand
> now and say enough, no more, no further?"

In the event, the Leader of the House, Robin Cook, was forced to distance himself from what Hilary Armstrong had done and conceded that backbenchers and Ministers could have a free vote — the result was the reinstatement of both Mrs Dunwoody and Mr Anderson.

The Executive is, in law, *Her Majesty's Government,* and the Ministers of the government exercise *royal prerogative powers* on the Queen's behalf in governing the country. Ministers do not need Parliamentary authority to use these powers but if they are thought by Parliament to have used them improperly, then the Ministers' right to use them can be restricted or removed by Parliament. For example, Tony Blair used royal prerogative powers to authorise Britain's participation in the action in Afghanistan following the events of 11 September 2001, without obtaining the prior approval of Parliament.

The ultimate power of Parliament *vis-à-vis* the Executive is to pass a *Motion of No Confidence* or defeat the government on an issue which the government has identified as an *Issue of Confidence*. If this happens then, by convention, it means the end of the government in office and, if an alternative government cannot be formed, a General Election.

The Sovereignty of Parliament — the people

The previous sections together illustrate the breadth of the Sovereignty of Parliament, but they need to be read in a context. That context is the *political sovereignty* of the people. Parliament is itself a democratically elected body which every five years or so needs to obtain a fresh mandate from the people for whom it acts. Because of this, members of Parliament understand the importance of acting in accordance with the Common Law and with tradition and precedent.

Although the validity, as such, of an Act of Parliament cannot be challenged in a court of law, it is probably true that Parliament would never pass legislation which commanded little or no support from the public who elected it. If, however, a government *did* push through legislation which was not very popular, in the belief that its electoral position was very secure, it might find itself paying the price through the ballot box at the next General Election. The poll tax (community charge) was deeply unpopular and had to be replaced fairly quickly by the council tax.

The political party system itself within Parliament can be argued as reinforcing Parliament's need to legislate always with one eye on the electorate — although the significance of this factor might depend upon the size of a governing or opposition party's majority in Parliament.

The last three paragraphs together argue for the ultimate political sovereignty of the people. The shape of the legislative programme in Parliament will be under the control of the political party forming the government. To arrive at that position that party would have won a General Election. The party will have set out in its election manifesto the kinds of policies it would follow, through legislation if necessary, if elected. The successful party would regard itself as having a mandate from the people for the policies in the manifesto.

Although the manifesto promises/mandate are in no sense a contract between the party/government and the people — the government can, and always will, depart from the manifesto/mandate — nonetheless a large number of significant broken promises or departures may be paid for at the next General Election. The opposition parties will also use the manifesto/mandate as a weapon against a government which is not delivering what it promised the electorate.

Some commentators are now questioning the concept that Parliament derives its democratic legitimacy, in part, from the fact that it is elected by the people. The relatively poor turnout in the 2001 General Election could have been due either to voter apathy or to voter disillusion with politicians. Either way, this gives rise to the idea of a 'democratic deficit' and in turn calls into question whether the people are really that interested in what Parliament does on their behalf.

The Sovereignty of Parliament — the European Union

Finally, the context in which the sovereignty of Parliament needs to be considered is now much broader than the UK. The European Communities Act 1972 declared that European Union law would take precedence over any conflicting Act of Parliament, with the courts, ultimately the EU Court of Justice, as arbiters.

In that sense, the UK's joining the EC in 1973 has not only altered the Constitution, but, some would argue, made Parliament ultimately subordinate to a supra-national court, thus conceding some of its sovereignty. The Human Rights Act 1998, by bringing into play the provisions of the European Convention on Human Rights, has taken the process one step further.

However, it must be remembered that it was Parliament itself which conceded these points. Similarly, it was Parliament itself which approved the arrangements for devolution to Scotland, Wales and Northern Ireland.

2 The Monarchy

The rôle of the Sovereign — the Privy Council — how the Monarchy is funded — the succession and future of the Monarchy

A Constitutional Monarchy

The Monarchy *(www.royal.gov.uk)* is the longest surviving secular institution in the UK; the present Queen can trace her descent directly from King Egbert who united England in 829. The only interruption to the Monarchy, as an *institution,* followed the execution of Charles I, when the Council of State and Oliver Cromwell as Lord Protector ruled from 1649 to 1660. At other times, the *succession* has been interrupted and this has provided Parliament with several opportunities to increase its powers at the expense of the Monarchy.

By a process of evolution, rather than revolution, over a period of a thousand years the Monarchy has changed — from one supported by the doctrine of the 'Divine Right of Kings' to one which, although still nominally governing the country, now does so in reality through others — a *constitutional monarchy.*

The Divine Right of Kings was a doctrine which defended monarchical absolutism, asserting that kings derived their authority from God and could not therefore be held accountable for their actions by any earthly authority such as a Parliament. The doctrine had its origins in Europe and may be traced to the medieval concept of God's award of temporal power to the political ruler, paralleling the award of spiritual power to the Church. Especially during the first half of the 17th century, kings tended to regard Parliament as a necessary evil — to be called to vote for additional taxes but then dissolved soon afterwards. King James I of England (1603-25) was a keen proponent of the doctrine, but it declined as Parliament's power increased and is generally regarded as having been severely damaged with the execution of Charles I in 1649 and abandoned altogether when James II fled in 1688, resulting in the Bill of Rights 1689, establishing that the Sovereign ruled through Parliament.

Originally, all power was exercised by the Sovereign, but not absolutely, since even then, if only for reasons of self-preservation, he was expected to consult the leading men of his realm, lay and clerical. *Magna Carta*, signed by King John in 1215, requiring the Sovereign to consult the barons, is now portrayed as a crucial constitutional document but, in fact, it would have been viewed at the time merely as a written version of the *status quo*.

The process of consultation by the Sovereign was gradually extended. The process of government itself became too complex for the Sovereign to operate himself or herself, so it had to be given to others to carry out on the Sovereign's behalf. These factors eventually resulted in the Parliamentary and Ministerial system which we see today.

Over the same period the real power was transferred from the Sovereign to Parliament so that by the beginning of the 20th century, although government was still in the Sovereign's name, political power lay elsewhere. The Sovereign could no longer control Parliament or exercise real choice of Ministers and Judges — power had finally passed to the people's representatives.

The rôles of the Sovereign — the royal prerogative

The Queen is said to 'personify the State' — the Sovereign stands for the unity of the nation and its standards as a country — she is the Head of the State of the UK. As a matter of strict law, she is an integral part of the Legislature, Head of the Executive, Head of the Judiciary, Commander-in-Chief of all the armed forces and the 'Supreme Governor' of the established Church of England. These powers are derived from the *royal prerogative*. The royal prerogative is, in effect, the legitimate exercise of all of the powers which the Sovereign possesses as Sovereign — in other words, by virtue of the Sovereign's authority. Prerogative powers such as coining money, creating peers, calling and dissolving Parliament, and governing the Church of England still remain with the Sovereign. Other royal prerogative powers such as the power to legislate, raise taxes and deal with emergencies were assumed by Parliament long ago.

However, in practice, the Queen, by convention, now exercises her royal prerogative powers on the advice of her Ministers. Nonetheless, even on that basis the Sovereign still has a significant rôle to play in the process of governing the UK. For example, the Queen:

- summons, prorogues and dissolves Parliament;
- gives the Royal Assent to Bills passed by Parliament;

- formally appoints government Ministers (including the Prime Minister), judges, diplomats, governors, officers in the armed forces and bishops and some senior Church of England clergy;
- keeps track of what the government is doing in her name by: receiving accounts of Cabinet decisions, giving audiences to Ministers (the Prime Minister is usually seen once each week), reading dispatches and signing many State papers;
- holds meetings of the Privy Council;
- issues pardons to people convicted of crime;
- exercises the royal prerogative of mercy in those Commonwealth countries which have retained that final appeal;
- confers peerages, knighthoods and other honours;
- carries out duties which although ceremonial are nonetheless important — such as the State Opening of Parliament and the Trooping of the Colour;
- entertains visiting Heads of State and undertakes formal visits to other countries;
- recognises foreign states and governments (their diplomatic representatives formally present their *credentials* to the Queen before they perform their duties), makes treaties and cedes or annexes territory;
- declares war and makes peace.

However, as explained earlier, most of these rôles are exercised on the advice of other people.

How the Sovereign's rôles are *really* exercised

When the Queen summons Parliament after a General Election or after prorogation, she does so at the *State Opening of Parliament* in the Palace of Westminster. This largely ceremonial but important event takes place in the chamber of the House of Lords, to which the members of the House of Commons are summoned. The *Queen's Speech*, which the Lord Chancellor hands to the Queen, sets out the programme which Her Majesty's government will seek to implement during the next session of Parliament. The speech, *"My government intends…"*, is not written by the Queen but is written for her by the Ministers in the government — she has no say in its content. For example, would the Queen have split an infinitive or written for herself such phrases as *"a dynamic, knowledge-based economy"* or *"providing people with the opportunity to liberate their potential"* as appeared in the 1999 Queen's Speech?

The Queen can prorogue or dissolve Parliament only when formally asked to do so by the Prime Minister. When Parliament is prorogued, another Queen's Speech is given in the House of Lords to which the House of Commons is again summoned by Black Rod. The speech is still written for the Queen by her Ministers but it differs in two respects from that given at the State Opening of Parliament. Firstly, the speech is a retrospective review of what has been done during the session of Parliament which is about to end and, secondly, the speech is delivered by the Lord Chancellor on the Queen's behalf — the last Sovereign to deliver the speech personally at prorogation was Queen Victoria in 1837.

The person appointed by the Queen as Prime Minister is always the Leader of the political party with the largest number of seats or able to command a working majority in the House of Commons. The other important office holders are appointed by the Queen on the advice of the Prime Minister or her Ministers.

The Royal Pardon is exercised only on the advice of the Home Secretary. A recent example (in June 2001) of the use of the Royal prerogative of Pardon was the rare granting of early freedom to two prisoners who had courageously saved the life of a prison warder who had been gored by a boar on a prison farm. The pardon was recommended to the Queen by the Home Secretary.

Honours are conferred by the Queen twice each year — the Honours Lists are published on her official birthday and at New Year — and at the resignation of a government and the dissolution of Parliament for a General Election. These honours are usually conferred on the advice of the Prime Minister. There are exceptions to this: the Order of the Garter, the Order of the Thistle, the Order of Merit and the Royal Victorian Order are the personal gift of the Queen.

A recent development has been the encouragement of more public participation in the honours system; it is now usual for members of the public to submit the names of others whose achievements they think should be recognised through the honours system — although the final decision still rests with the Queen on the advice of the Prime Minister, subject to vetting by a small group of Privy Councillors.

One should not overlook the undoubted contribution which the Queen is in a position to make to the government of the UK. Apart from her important rôle of symbolising the country at home and abroad, the Queen has had 50 years' experience as a constitutional monarch. During that time she has gained a wealth of knowledge about the way successive governments have worked. Walter Bagehot (1826-77), economist, political analyst and editor of *The Economist*, set out a classic definition of the sovereign's power in his *The English Constitution: "the right to be consulted, the right to encourage, the right to warn".*

Although the Queen, constitutionally, has to act on the advice of her Ministers, she has been in a unique position during the weekly audiences to give advice (on a strictly non-partisan basis) to the 10 successive Prime Ministers who have come and gone. The Queen has been known to question the Prime Minister and other Ministers quite closely on proposals set out in the Cabinet or Foreign Office papers which she has read. It is reputed that the Queen caught Harold Wilson out early in his premiership when, during the weekly audience, she expressed interest in a New Town proposal in the Cabinet papers — it was news to him.

Some former Prime Ministers have remarked upon the benefit which they gained from the Queen's advice. Whether other Prime Ministers sought that advice and how much notice they took of it probably depended upon their individual personality and their opinion of their own knowledge and experience.

The Queen's unique experience has also counted for much abroad — especially within the Commonwealth. It is said that the respect which the Queen commands and her calming and unifying influence have helped to repair some of the damage caused to relations between the UK and certain Commonwealth countries by the Thatcher government on the issue of sanctions against South Africa. On that particular issue, some commentators even go so far as to say that without the Queen's influence the Commonwealth might then have disintegrated or the UK been expelled from it.

The Privy Council

Before the 18th century the *Sovereign in Council* or the *Privy Council* was the main source of legislative and executive power — Parliament's rôle was limited to voting funds from time to time. The Cabinet grew out of a committee of the Privy Council and as the system of Cabinet government developed with the transfer of powers to it, so the Privy Council itself became less important as an instrument of government. This explains why Ministers in the Cabinet are also Privy Councillors and meetings of the Cabinet are supposed to be 'privy' or secret. Some modern government departments also started life as committees of the Privy Council.

These days, the principal function of the Privy Council is to advise the Queen on *Orders in Council,* including those granting royal charters of incorporation and setting out the constitutions of dependent territories. Orders in Council are used to enact the various types of delegated legislation and their use can be quite varied — much of the delegated legislation relating to Northern Ireland is made in this way.

The Council also advises the Queen on issuing *Royal Proclamations* — some of which can be quite important, such as those covering the dissolution of Parliament, the coinage and the dates of certain Bank Holidays.

There are now about 400 Privy Councillors and membership, usually for life, is granted by the Queen on the advice of the Prime Minister to people eminent in public, political and judicial life. Members of the Cabinet must be Privy Councillors and, if they are not, they are granted membership of the Privy Council before they take their oath of office as members of the Cabinet. Apart from all members of the Cabinet,

Privy Councillors also include some middle-ranking government Ministers, senior judges and the Leaders of the opposition parties in both Houses of Parliament. Privy Councillors are also appointed from Commonwealth countries.

Although membership is for life, it can be terminated. The last time a Privy Councillor was fired was in 1921 when Sir Edgar Speyer, a philanthropist friend of Prime Minister Herbert Asquith, was convicted of collaboration with the Germans in the First World War. Since then there have been three notable resignations. John Profumo, Secretary of State for War, had to resign when it was discovered that he had lied to the Commons about his adulterous relationship with Christine Keeler, which made him vulnerable to Soviet pressure. John Stonehouse, a former Postmaster General, had to go when he was convicted of theft and false pretences. The most recent example was Jonathan Aitken, who was forced to resign following his perjury at his libel trial (which collapsed) against the *Guardian* and Granada Television. He was subsequently convicted and imprisoned for perverting the course of justice.

Privy Councillors are 'The Right Honourable'; so those MPs who are also Privy Councillors can be identified as such by the use of this title when they are addressed in Parliament and elsewhere. If a Privy Councillor is a lawyer, his or her more formal title is extended to 'My Right Honourable and Learnèd Friend'.

Usually, only a small number (about four) of Privy Councillors is invited to any meeting of the Council — which, by tradition, meets standing up (including the Sovereign), presumably helping to keep the meetings short! The only occasions when the full Privy Council is summoned are when a new Sovereign is crowned or when the existing Sovereign intends to marry. The *Code of Conduct for Ministers* published by the Cabinet Office makes it clear that meetings of the Privy Council are important and have precedence over meetings of the Cabinet. Once a Minister has accepted an invitation to attend a meeting of the Privy Council, he or she is expected to attend — and to be on time, regardless of earlier commitments which might overrun.

The meetings of the Privy Council itself are largely formal. The real work of the Privy Council is done in its different kinds of committee, which the Sovereign does not attend. An example of these committees is the Judicial Committee. The Judicial Committee includes the Lord Chancellor, the Lords of Appeal in Ordinary and other Privy Councillors who hold or have held high judicial office in the UK and in the Commonwealth. The function of the Judicial Committee is to act as the final court of appeal from courts in UK dependencies, the Isle of Man, the Channel Islands and those Commonwealth countries which still recognise this method of appeal.

The administrative work of the Privy Council is done in the Privy Council Office under the supervision of the *Lord President of the Council* who is a Cabinet Minister and who, by modern convention, is also *Leader of the House of Commons*. Following the 1997 General Election this office was held, for the first time, by a woman, who understandably wished to drop 'Lord' from the title and to be known as the *President of the Council* — a practice which has continued since, regardless of the sex of the office-holder.

How the Monarchy is funded

The Sovereign's income is derived from:

- the *Civil List* (to cover official expenses of the Royal Household to enable the Queen to fulfil her rôles as Head of State and Head of the Commonwealth)
- *Grants-in-Aid* from Parliament (to cover upkeep of royal palaces and royal travel)
- the *Privy Purse* (traditional income for the Sovereign's public and private use)
- *personal income* (purely private expenditure).

Civil List

In Anglo-Saxon times the Sovereign's personal lands were distinguished from those held by the Crown, but after the Norman Conquest (1066) they became merged as the Crown Lands. Because the Sovereign was the feudal overlord, his or her land holdings were increased by estates forfeited by convicted rebels or through *escheat* when the existing landholders had no heirs. The Sovereign's personal income was derived from these land holdings and, therefore, progressively increased.

The idea of the *Civil List* dates from 1689, when Parliament, having invited William and Mary to accede to the throne, voted £600,000 specifically for their expenses in 'civil government'. Parliament, by the first Civil List Act in 1697, assigned revenues to the Sovereign to cover both civil and royal expenses. Previously these expenses had been paid entirely from the Sovereign's hereditary revenues and from certain taxes voted to the Sovereign for life by Parliament.

The present Civil List system dates from 1760. In that year, on the accession of George III, the hereditary revenues (the net surplus income from the Crown Lands) were surrendered to Parliament in return for a fixed Civil List, a sum agreed and provided annually by Parliament for meeting the Sovereign's expenses. In recent years, this deal has turned out to be a good one for Parliament. The Crown Lands are now more effectively managed by the Commissioners of Crown Lands and in 1999/2000 contributed £133m to the Treasury; in 1991/92 the contribution was equivalent to £91m at current prices. On the other hand, Head of State expenditure was £35m in 2000/2001; in 1991/92 it was equivalent to £83m at current prices.

Queen Victoria was allowed to grant pensions from the Civil List, on the advice of her Ministers, to people who had achieved distinction in the arts, literature or science, or who had given personal services to the Crown. Later Civil List Acts provided for an annuity to the widow of a Sovereign and introduced the idea that funds could be provided from the Civil List to members of the Royal Family undertaking official duties. At present, about 70% of the Civil List is used to pay the salaries of the 645 employees in the Royal Household. The remainder covers the cost of such events as the Royal Garden Parties (over 48,000 people attend each year) and official hospitality during State Visits.

Other members of the Royal Family receive annual Parliamentary allowances under the Civil List Acts for the performance of their public duties (£2.5m). However, in each year since 1993 the Queen has used her Privy Purse to refund some (£1.5m) of these allowances to Parliament, apart from those for the Queen Mother and the Duke of Edinburgh (£1m). The allowances are reviewed every 10 years and were recently reset to their 1990 levels and will remain at those levels until 2010.

The Prince of Wales (as the 24th Duke of Cornwall) receives nothing from the Civil List because he is entitled to receive, instead, the net income generated by the Estate of the *Duchy of Cornwall*, established by Edward III in 1337 and first made available to the Black Prince, to provide the Heir Apparent and his or her children with an income independent of the Sovereign or the State. The Duchy's landholdings amount to 51,885 hectares, mostly in the south of England (not just Cornwall), and are run on a commercial basis as prescribed by the Parliamentary legislation which relates to it. The Prince of Wales is, in effect, a trustee and must pass on the estate intact for the benefit of future dukes. The net surplus for 1997/98 was £5.9m.

Grants-in-Aid

Grants-in-Aid are provided by Parliament to cover the upkeep of the *Occupied Royal Palaces* and to cover the costs of royal travel.

The property upkeep grant-in-aid (£15.3m in 2000/2001, compared with £16.4m in 1997/98) is provided through the Department for Culture, Media and Sport and is supplied in return for the Sovereign's surrender of hereditary revenues. The *Occupied Royal Palaces* include Buckingham Palace, St James Palace, Kensington Palace and Windsor Castle. The Windsor Castle Fire Restoration project was completed in November 1997 at a cost of £36.6m but with the cost partly offset by income from paying visitors to Buckingham Palace and Windsor Castle. The *Unoccupied* or *Historic Royal Palaces* (such as the Tower of London and Hampton Court Palace) are not part of the Royal Household nor receive government funding, being maintained by the *Historic Royal Palaces Trust* from visitor income and other related income.

The royal transport grant-in-aid (£5.4m in 2000/2001, compared with £19.4m in 1997/98) is now provided through the DTLR (previously through the Ministry of Defence, the Department of Transport and the Foreign and Commonwealth Office) to cover the annual 3,000 official Royal Family engagements in the UK and overseas. Most of the expenditure is on the RAF aircraft of the No. 32 (the Royal) Squadron, the Royal Train (now managed by Railtrack plc) and on chartered commercial aircraft for overseas State Visits. The Royal Yacht Britannia was decommissioned in 1997.

Privy Purse

The *Privy Purse* is derived from the income (but not the capital) of the *Duchy of Lancaster* (£7.3m in 2000/2001), an inheritance composed of 19,268 hectares of land which since 1399 has been available to the reigning Sovereign. The Duchy is separate from the Sovereign's other possessions and is administered by the *Chancellor of the Duchy of Lancaster*, who in recent years has also been a Cabinet Minister. Although the Privy Purse is regarded as the private income of the Sovereign, most of it is used to meet the official expenses of other members of the Royal Family (which would otherwise be entitled to be met from the Civil List), other than the Queen Mother and the Duke of Edinburgh (who receive their own allowances from Parliament).

The Queen's *personal* expenditure as an individual is met from her own personal resources.

Taxation

In the context of *taxation*, the position is as follows. Like everyone else, the Queen has always paid VAT and other indirect taxes. She has paid, on a voluntary basis, local taxes such as the Council Tax. In addition, since 1993 the Queen has paid income tax and capital gains tax on her personal income, again on a voluntary basis. The Privy Purse is taxable, subject to deductions for official expenditure but the Civil List and Grants-in-Aid are not taxable because they are not regarded as remuneration. The Queen's *personal* estate is subject to inheritance tax but transfers from *Sovereign* to *Sovereign* are exempt, because, unlike others, the Sovereign cannot retire and mitigate inheritance tax by passing on property early to the next generation — nor can the Sovereign engage in trade or business to replace resources surrendered through inheritance tax.

The Prince of Wales pays tax on his personal income. As a Crown body, the Duchy of Cornwall is theoretically exempt from tax but the Prince of Wales has since 1969 made voluntary contributions to the Treasury. Like the Queen, since 1993 the net surplus from the Duchy of Cornwall has been subject to income tax, on a voluntary basis.

The Succession and the future of the Monarchy

Succession to the throne was (and still is, at least for now) based on the idea of *male primogeniture* (male first-born) — sons take precedence over daughters and the eldest son succeeds. Prior to the 17th century, this was an almost automatic process. However, when James II fled the country in 1688, this gave Parliament the opportunity to declare that he had thus 'abandoned the government' and that the throne was vacant. Parliament then offered the throne not to James' younger son but to his daughter, Mary, and her husband William of Orange, as joint rulers. This important development emphasised the fact that Parliament now determined who should succeed to the throne, that the Sovereign ruled through Parliament and that the Sovereign could be removed by Parliament if he or she misgoverned the country.

The Act of Settlement 1701 confirmed that it was now Parliament which decided the title to the throne — Queen Anne was childless and Parliament wished to settle the succession and did so through an Act of Parliament. The 1701 Act provided that only Protestant descendants of Princess Sophia, the Electress of Hanover (granddaughter of James I of England/James VI of Scotland) can succeed to the UK throne. The Sovereign must also satisfy specified criteria. Presently, he or she must: not be a Catholic or marry one; be in communion with the Church of England; swear to preserve the Established Church of England and the Established Church of Scotland; and swear to uphold the Protestant Succession. The suggestion that the restriction to Protestants might be removed (on the grounds that in the modern context this restriction could be regarded as discrimination) has become more serious since the implications of the Human Rights Act 1998 are becoming more clearly appreciated. The Commonwealth would need to be consulted, difficulties might arise with the Church of England as the Established Church, and time would need to be found in an overloaded Parliamentary programme for the primary legislation needed to effect the change.

Sons of the Sovereign have precedence over daughters. If the Sovereign has no surviving sons, daughters have precedence over brothers of the Sovereign. If the Sovereign has no surviving children, the eldest brother (and his children) of the Sovereign take precedence (William IV was succeeded by his niece Victoria). If the Sovereign has no children or brothers, succession passes to the Sovereign's sisters in order of their age (Edward VI was succeeded by his half-sisters, firstly by Mary and then by Elizabeth I). Simple, isn't it!

If a son succeeds, he becomes King and his consort becomes Queen. If a daughter succeeds, she becomes Queen Regnant but her husband has no special title. If the new Sovereign is a minor, then a Regency is established for the duration of the minority.

All has not gone well for the Royal Family in recent years — so much so that the Queen described 1992 as her *'Annus Horribilis'* – horrible year; due in part to the disastrous fire at Windsor Castle in November that year and the unsympathetic public response to the implications of that event for the finances of the Royal Family.

The Royal Family has declined in popularity over the last decade as it increasingly presented itself as a dysfunctional family. The matrimonial problems experienced by the Queen's children, while becoming more typical of ordinary people in recent years, have not improved the view taken of the Monarchy by the UK population — people expect the Royal Family to be different. Matters were not improved in 2001 by the business activities of Prince Edward and his wife, the Countess of Wessex. Their experiences highlighted the tensions which are likely to arise when members of the Royal Family are expected to make their own way in the world. Conscious of the decline in public support for the monarchy, the Queen established the 'Way Ahead Group', to produce ideas for making the monarchy more relevant to the 21st century. The problems they face are illustrated by the most recent (April 2001) results of the annual *Guardian*/ICM poll, which showed that 34% of the population felt that the UK would be better off without the Royal Family (compared with 13% in 1987).

Even so, it is likely to be many years, if at all, before the conversion of the UK into a republic becomes more than just a talking point. What is more likely to be considered is changing the rule of male precedence — to enable a daughter to succeed, if more appropriate. The Queen has apparently indicated that she would not have any fundamental objection to this course of action if Parliament and the Commonwealth thought it to be for the best. Indeed, if the Act of Settlement was repealed because of the Human Rights Act, it would be surprising if the rule of *primogeniture* was not removed at the same time.

The Commonwealth

The organisation of the Commonwealth is described in the Chapter on *International and Defence*. The Queen is recognised as Head of the Commonwealth and is Head of State not only in Britain but also in 15 other member countries, where she is represented locally by a Governor-General appointed by her.

The people of Australia, through a referendum in November 1999, decided that they wished to retain the Queen as their Head of State, rejecting the idea of converting from a parliamentary monarchy to a republic. Even though the Queen was reportedly relaxed about whichever choice was made by the people of Australia, the result was nonetheless regarded as something of a boost for the monarchy as an institution. The result may have had something to due with the republican model on offer — a president appointed by politicians rather than elected by the people — which was clearly regarded with suspicion by the voters. Australia may yet become a republic if another referendum offering a more palatable presidential model is offered to the people.

3 Parliament at Westminster

The composition, powers and rôle of the Legislature — the reform of the House of Lords — the conduct of the affairs of Parliament — Parliamentary Standards

Parliament at Westminster

As explained earlier, Parliament *(www.parliament.uk)* consists of three elements — the Sovereign, the House of Commons and the House of Lords; each is separate and constituted on different principles. The chambers in which the two Houses meet are located in the *Palace of Westminster,* which is usually referred to as the *Houses of Parliament.* The three elements meet formally in the same place only on one occasion, the State Opening of Parliament.

There are two Houses of Parliament for historical reasons. In Norman times, the Sovereign was expected to meet all the normal expenses of government from his own resources. If more was needed, for special purposes such as fighting a war, the Sovereign had to call together the barons and high clergy (the 'Magnates' from the *Magnum Concilium* or Great Council — the forerunner of the House of Lords) to authorise extra taxes. As time went on a smaller second body, the *Curia Regis* or King's Council came into existence — semi-professional advisers — a function which much later diverged into the Privy Council. These two bodies were fused during the reign of Edward I (1272-1307).

After a period, even this combined source was not enough, so in the 14th century the Sovereign began to call as well upon the knights and burgesses, representatives of counties, cities and towns for help (the community representatives or 'Commons' — the forerunner to the House of Commons).

These two groups, with the Sovereign, were collectively called 'Parliament', that is a meeting for the purpose of discussion or parley (derived from the Old French *parlement*). At various times during the 14th century the two groups met in separate places and from this developed the bicameral (two chambers) Parliament, the House of Lords and the House of Commons.

As time went on, the Commons came to realise the strength of their position. In the 14th century the Sovereign accepted that taxes should not be levied without the assent of Parliament. During the 15th century the Commons obtained the right to take an active part in converting into law their petitions — their 'Bills'. The position of the Commons was secured in the Glorious Revolution of 1688, when James II fled and the throne was offered by Parliament to William and Mary on condition that henceforth the Sovereign could not legislate or suspend laws without the assent of Parliament.

Parliament still looked to the Executive — originally the Sovereign and later the Sovereign's Ministers in Cabinet — to initiate changes in policy. The Reform Act 1832, by extending the electorate by 49% and abolishing the Rotten Boroughs, started a process of change which steadily reduced what then remained of the Sovereign's influence on the Commons.

Even today, the House of Commons jealously guards its independence from the Sovereign — best illustrated by the ceremonial slamming of the doors of the House of Commons in the face of the *Gentleman Usher of the Black Rod* when he is sent from the House of Lords to summon the Commons to attend the Queen in the House of Lords, for the State Opening of Parliament.

The functions of Parliament

The powers of Parliament have been described in the section in Chapter 1 which discusses the *Sovereignty of Parliament*. The section in the same chapter on the *Separation of Powers* makes the point that Parliament is not, and never has been, part of the Executive — the Sovereign's Ministers.

Although the phrase 'Parliamentary government' is sometimes used to describe the UK's form of government, this can give a misleading impression. The phrase should be read to mean government *through* Parliament, rather than government *by* Parliament. Public policy is formulated by the Executive and put before Parliament for discussion and approval or rejection. The initiative usually lies with the Executive, not Parliament — which is essentially reactive in the business of government.

The functions of Parliament are:
- to make laws;
- to enable government to function by voting for the taxation needed to fund it;

- to examine government policy and the way it is administered; and
- to provide a forum where major issues of the day can be debated.

The House of Commons

As a result of boundary changes introduced on the recommendation of the Parliamentary Boundary Commissions for the 1997 General Election, the House of Commons is now composed of a total of 659 MPs:

England	529
Scotland	72
Wales	40
Northern Ireland	18

The result of the 1997 General Election *(see Appendix A)* was generally regarded by most commentators as historic, given, amongst other things, the size of the Labour party majority (419 seats were won when only 330 were needed for an overall majority).

Why can that result be fairly described as 'historic'? Perhaps it is because:

- the Labour party achieved its largest number of seats since its foundation as a political party at the beginning of the 20th century;
- the Liberal Democrats doubled their number of seats, giving them the largest number of seats held by any third party since 1929;
- the Conservative party's share of the vote (31.4%) was its lowest since 1832, when modern elections were introduced by the Reform Act of that year;
- the Conservative party was wiped out in the larger English cities and in Scotland (for the first time) and in Wales (last time was 1906) — raising interesting questions about which party could now claim to be the official Opposition in those countries;
- the number of women MPs was increased from 62 to 119, the largest ever — of whom 101 were Labour, possibly due in part to the all-women shortlist approach adopted by Labour for a brief period in some parts of the country;
- the number of MPs from ethnic minorities was the largest ever and, later, the first black Minister was appointed; and
- the first ever truly independent MP — Martin Bell, *'the man in the white suit'*— was elected for the Tatton constituency on an anti-sleaze ticket against Neil Hamilton.

A number of by-elections occurred as a consequence of deaths or resignations, but their results had no effect on the overall voting position.

The 2001 General Election *(see Appendix A)* could also be described as 'historic', although for different reasons:
- despite greater availability of postal voting, the turnout (59.3%) was the lowest since the 1918 General Election (57.2%) which took place in the aftermath of the First World War and before women became entitled to the franchise;
- New Labour polled fewer votes than any winning party since the introduction of universal suffrage in 1928;
- the Tories failed to improve their position nationally (they managed to win just one seat back in Scotland but still failed to win any in Wales), resulting in William Hague immediately falling on his sword; and
- the first election as an MP of one of the hereditary peers obliged to leave the House of Lords as a consequence of the 1999 reform — Viscount Thurso.

Martin Bell kept his promise not to stand in Tatton again, standing instead for Brentwood and Ongar at the invitation of disaffected Tories who alleged that their local party had been infiltrated by a Christian fundamentalist group — however, the Essex electors did not give him a second term as an MP. Martin Bell's mantle as an independent MP was taken by Dr Richard Taylor when the electors of Wyre Forest unseated a junior New Labour Minister in a massive protest vote about a single local issue — against the downsizing of Kidderminster Hospital.

The House of Lords before the 1999 reform

The House of Lords consisted of the Lords Spiritual and the Lords Temporal, none of whom was elected — a source of some debate, which is dealt with later.

The *Lords Spiritual* (26) were (and still are):
- the Archbishops of Canterbury and York;
- the Bishops of London, Durham and Winchester; and
- the 21 next most senior diocesan bishops of the Church of England.

The *Lords Temporal* (1,263) were (but no longer are):
- all hereditary peers of England, Scotland, Great Britain and the United Kingdom (but not Ireland) (759);
- Lords of Appeal or 'Law Lords' — life peers (not all of whom are still active) created under the Appellate Jurisdiction Act 1876 to help the House in its judicial rôle as final court of appeal in the UK (27); and
- all other life peers created under the Life Peerages Act 1958 (477, excluding Law Lords).

Prior to the House of Lords Act 1999 reforms, any hereditary peers could sit in the House of Lords, provided they were over 21 and had proved their claim to the title. The number of hereditary peers now able to do this has been limited by the 1999 reforms.

The number of life peers increases steadily as a consequence of the Honours lists. In an article *(New breed of Labour élite riles think tank)* in the *Guardian* on 25 February 2000, Lucy Ward, the political correspondent commented on a report from the Centre for Policy Studies which highlighted *"the rise of a 'new class' of Labour-supporting great and good who, through peerages, taskforce jobs and quango posts, have taken over the reins of power in Tony Blair's Britain"*. The article went on to comment further:

> *"As part of continuing reform of the House of Lords, Mr Blair has created new life peers at an annual rate unprecedented in 50 years. Since May 1997, 176 life peers have been appointed; with around 50 more to come, Mr Blair is on course to become the most prolific creator of life peers of any British prime Minister".*

In fairness, the nature of the Life Peerage system can lead to this kind of criticism against any Prime Minister, because of the way nominations are made to the Queen. It will be interesting to see whether the new independent Appointments Commission promised in the White Paper *A Second Chamber fit for the 21st Century* mentioned later will avoid any further criticism and the continued use of the epithet 'Tony's Cronies'.

It was possible for a peer to disclaim a peerage for his or her lifetime (but it could be reversed), without affecting the rights of their successors. This was usually done by people who preferred to make their contribution to public life in the House of Commons. Examples were Tony Benn (formerly Lord Stansgate), Sir Alec Douglas-Home (Lord Home) and Quintin Hogg (Lord Hailsham). Sir Alec Douglas-Home became Prime Minister — an office which is now held only by a member of the House of Commons. Quintin Hogg changed his mind later after a period in the Commons and became Lord Hailsham again, to be appointed as Lord Chancellor, presiding over the House of Lords. Following the 1999 reforms, it is no longer necessary for an hereditary peer to disclaim his peerage for this objective — hereditary peers have now been given the right to stand as a candidate in a Parliamentary election, to counterbalance the removal of their right to membership of the Lords.

Peerages of both kinds, hereditary and life, are created by the Sovereign on the advice of the Prime Minister — usually to recognise service in politics or public life or because one of the political parties has decided to put the individual in the House of Lords.

Unlike their counterparts in the House of Commons, members of the House of Lords receive no salary, but they can claim expenses, within statutory limits.

The Lord Chancellor presides over meetings of the House of Lords as ex-officio Speaker, sitting on the *Woolsack* — a large cushion-shaped seat. The Woolsack was introduced in the reign of Edward III (1327-77) and was originally stuffed with wool representing the fact that the main source of the country's wealth at that time was derived from the wool trade. In modern times the wool is from several Commonwealth countries, representing the importance of the Commonwealth as an institution.

The Lords must be expected to be a calmer place than the Commons — the words *"Order! Order!..."* will never be heard in the Lords, because it is the House itself, rather than its Speaker, which is responsible for keeping order in its debates!

House of Lords — abolition or reform?

The rôle of the House of Lords is two-fold: firstly, to participate in the legislative process; and secondly, to scrutinise the work of the Commons. The issue of what to do about the House of Lords has been under discussion for many years. Indeed, the preamble to the Parliament Act 1911 envisaged an *elected* upper chamber — an objective which still has to be achieved and probably never will. Nobody can, in truth, convincingly argue that there is no need for a second chamber — the real issue is how the second chamber should be composed.

Those who opposed the existence of the House of Lords and wanted to see its abolition, objected to it for several reasons. Some felt that it was not representative — because many of its members were there by accident of birth rather than by democratic election and additionally they were drawn from an unrepresentative section of society, at that time more likely to have an affinity with the Conservative party. These are not, however, arguments for the abolition of a second chamber. Indeed, there are some who believed that more recent experience in the 1980s and 1990s suggested that the House of Lords was increasingly prepared to demonstrate its willingness to challenge Conservative government legislation — explained as being due to the increasing number of life peers and a general change towards a more questioning and independent attitude of its members, of whatever kind. On the final day before the 1999 reforms came into affect, Lord Strathclyde, who replaced Lord Cranborne as Tory Leader in the Lords, said in his valedictory speech: *"They* [the Lords] *have time and again stood for common sense and the rights of the weak against powerful governments of all colours. History will judge them better than fashion now does"*.

The composition of the House of Lords has been progressively altered since the late 1950s, by the inclusion of appointed Life Peers — moving away from the principle of hereditary membership. The powers of the House of Lords to thwart the legislative will of the Commons have been severely curtailed. Both of these points are discussed in more detail in the next Chapter.

It was said that the limits now placed on the Lords are consistent with the belief that the legislative job of the non-elected House should be one of revision — complementing rather than rivalling the elected House. Certainly, the Lords has provided the government with a useful second sounding board to correct and adjust Bills which might have been poorly drafted. Even the Lords' rejection of a Bill can provide a useful breathing space for further thought.

So, if a second legislative chamber was seen to have a useful function as a check on the work of the first chamber, then perhaps what was needed was reform rather than abolition. Reform could be as simple as removing the voting rights of the hereditary peers — or as complex as reconstituting the Lords (with a change of name — the Senate perhaps?) into a wholly or largely elected second chamber — or anything in between.

House of Lords reform — 1999

Many thought that the reform of the House of Lords would be high on the agenda of the New Labour government following the 1997 General Election. But the first Queen's Speech of the new Parliament contained no reference to it as an issue requiring legislative attention in the first Session. Action was not taken until the beginning of 1999.

The government introduced its five clause House of Lords Bill in the Commons on 19 January 1999, with its White Paper *Modernising Parliament: Reforming the House of Lords* being published on the following day. The Bill did not affect the position of the Lords Spiritual or the Law Lords. Hereditary peers affected by the Bill would keep their titles and would still be able to pass them on to their descendants but would not be able to sit in the House of Lords. They would, however, acquire the right to vote in, and stand as candidates in, elections for Parliament.

The Bill first encountered difficulties in March 1999 when Tony Blair was faced with an all-party motion signed by 131 MPs (including 60 Labour MPs) demanding that the new House of Lords be entirely elected. Having survived that radical challenge, the Bill then encountered further difficulties, as might be expected, when it reached the House of Lords. A compromise on the process of reform had earlier been privately negotiated with Tony Blair by Lord Cranborne (as a consequence of which he was fired by William Hague from his position of the Tory Leader in the Lords).

A key figure in the compromise was a life peer, Lord Wetherill, former Speaker of the House of Commons. A Royal Commission, under the chairmanship of Lord Wakeham, a former Conservative Minister, would undertake a detailed study of the options for the reform of the House of Lords. Until the results of the Wakeham Commission were translated into legislation, there would be a 'transitional' House of Lords in which

92 of the 759 hereditary peers would continue to sit, of whom 90 would be selected through an internal election process. The 'Weatherill amendment' was endorsed (351 votes to 32, with Liberal Democrats abstaining) in the Lords by a cross-party alliance of peers. Lord Strathclyde, the then Tory Leader, supported the Weatherill amendment, describing it as *"making a bad Bill better"* and explaining that *"we welcome it as avoiding the nightmare of a wholly-appointed House"*.

Because of their ceremonial responsibilities, two peers would continue to be members of the Lords without having to stand for the internal election: the Earl Marshal, the Duke of Norfolk; and the Lord Great Chamberlain, the Marquess of Cholmondeley.

Any hereditary peer who registered could take part in the internal elections. The first election covered 15 posts — Deputy Speakers and other office holders. The remaining 75 places were filled by the second elections held on 3 and 4 November 1999, allocated as follows: 42 Conservatives, 28 crossbenchers, three Liberal Democrats and two Labour hereditary peers. The runners in the first election were reportedly characterised by one Lords official as *"the venerable, the pompous and the usual lunatics — the hardworking ones who keep the place running"*.

Prior to the elections, candidates could submit a supporting election statement of theirs of no more than 75 words — they displayed varying degrees of enthusiasm for the process. Lord Morris wrote just: *"It is hardly for me to attempt to proselytise my candidature; it is a matter for my peers"*; he should have tried harder, because he failed to be elected. The Earl of Onslow's flowery prose style, if not his modesty, went down sufficiently well to get him elected: *"It would be as vainglorious to proclaim a personal manifesto as it would be arrogant to list any achievement"*; but Lord Pender's pithy: *"Duty"*, whilst having the obvious merit of brevity, did not convince enough of his fellow peers to vote for him!

There was some controversy over the creation of 10 new life peerages to enable some hereditary peers to remain in the Lords, even though they had not stood for election. The peers involved were 'of first creation' (their hereditary peerages were created in their lifetime and, therefore, in reality they were not that dissimilar from life peers) and the life peerages were intended for those peers who had made a distinguished contribution to the Lords — such as Lord Cranborne, Lord Carrington and the Earl of Longford. The life peerage which caused the most stir (and even astonishment) was that claimed by Lord Snowdon, the ex-husband of Princess Margaret, who had shown little recent interest in the Lords. Although Lord Snowdon was no longer a member of the Royal Family, by convention members of the Royal Family waive their right to sit in Parliament, including other peers 'of first creation' and 'of the Royal blood' such as the Duke of Edinburgh, the Prince of Wales, the Duke of York, the Duke of Kent and the Earl of Wessex.

So, the House of Lords, 734 years after it came into existence, had been reduced in its transitional form, at the 17 November 1999 State Opening of Parliament, from 1,289 to 624 members and was now a largely appointed body:

26	Lords Spiritual
598	Lords Temporal:
27	Law Lords
2	non-elected hereditary peers
92	elected hereditary peers
477	life peers

The partly-reformed House of Lords, even in its 'transitional' form, soon demonstrated its continued resolve to block a Commons Bill, if it felt that the Bill was against the fundamental rights of the citizen. Jack Straw had introduced in the Lords his Bill, the Criminal Justice (Mode of Trial) Bill, removing the right to a jury trial for middle-ranking 'triable-either-way' (triable either by magistrates or by jury) cases. The Lords regarded the retention of trial by one's peers for cases of this type to be so important that, at the end of January 2000, it passed an amendment which effectively killed the Bill. Because the Bill was first introduced in the Lords, rather than the Commons, Jack Straw would have to start again, this time in the Commons.

The total number of the Lords continued to increase after the 1999 reforms, as more life peers were appointed. The political composition (life peers and total) of the Lords, as at December 2001, was:

party	life peers	total
Conservative	173	233
Labour	196	200
Liberal Democrat	60	65
Cross bench	149	181
Lords Spiritual		26
Other	9	9
total	587	714

In the table above, the impact of life peers on the political complexion of the Lords can be seen. The 'Other' category covers peers who are on leave of absence — Lord Archer, whilst he is otherwise distracted, is in this category.

House of Lords reform — post 1999

Until such time as the 'transitional' House of Lords is replaced by a permanent arrangement, there might need to be some process for by-elections for vacancies arising in the elected hereditary peer places — if the 'transitional' arrangement lasts for any length of time.

It was not long before an hereditary peer was elected as an MP — without having to renounce his title first. The Earl of Burford tried, but failed, in the first available by-election, Kensington and Chelsea, but only managed to poll 0.93% of the vote. However, in the 2001 General Election Viscount Thurso succeeded. When will we see the first hereditary peer Prime Minister since Lord Salisbury in 1902?

The transitional House of Lords has tried to soften the blow for the 'rejected' hereditary peers. The longstanding tradition that the eldest sons of peers may sit on the steps by the Woolsack to listen to House of Lords debates has been extended to hereditary peers themselves — and in anticipation of an enthusiastic response, additional room has been found for the overflow in a balcony overlooking the chamber!

The background issues against which the Wakeham Commission did its work included:

- what is to be the rôle of the second chamber?
- how is the second chamber to be composed — appointed or elected or both?
- is an entirely appointed chamber the best option? Appointment through political patronage may be just as unsatisfactory as by accident of birth — 'Tony's Cronies' is one epithet which has been used since Tony Blair declared his intention to create sufficient additional life peers to give Labour parity with the other parties in the Lords.
- is an entirely elected chamber the best option? Avoiding the second chamber becoming a clone of Parliament could be achieved through different constituencies, periods of office, election dates and voting systems.

House of Lords reform — Wakeham Royal Commission

The Wakeham Commission presented its report, *A House for the Future* (Cmnd 4534), at the end of January 2000. The Commission's report required consideration by a Joint Committee of both Houses of Parliament and there was some suggestion that the New Labour government would be in no hurry to take action and that the 'transitional' arrangements might continue for some time.

The recommendations of Wakeham were as follows:

- A new (unnamed by Wakeham — left 'to evolve') chamber would consist of about 550 members.
- All members would have a renewable 15-year period of office.
- The minority (65, 87 or 195 (Wakeham couldn't decide)) would be elected on a regional basis at the same time as the EP elections (one-third of the regions being elected every five years); the elections for 87 or 195 places would be direct through the regional list system of PR; the minimalist 65 would be

chosen by a proportional 'reading off' of votes at the previous General Election.

- The remaining majority would be nominated by a new independent Appointments Commission, independent of the Prime Minister of the day and avoiding party patronage.
- Hereditary peers would not be entitled to membership.
- Existing life peers created prior to the publication of the report could opt to continue membership for life; any life peers created after the publication of the report and prior to the implementation of the proposals would be deemed to have been appointed for a 15 year period of office; thereafter, there would be no connection between a life peerage and membership of the second chamber — new members, appointed or elected, would not be offered a life peerage.
- The 26 Lords Spiritual would be replaced by 16 Church of England bishops, five members representing other Christian denominations and at least five representing non-Christian faiths.
- The 27 Law Lords would remain.
- The Appointments Commission would make appointments reflecting the balance of political opinion across the UK, with no single political party having an overall majority and with about 20% of the appointees being cross-benchers. The Commission would be obliged to appoint at least 30% women, working towards eventual gender balance. Ethnic minorities would be represented at least in proportion to their level in the population as a whole.

The rôle of the second chamber would be fourfold:

- bringing different perspectives to bear on the development of public policy;
- giving a voice in Parliament for all parts of British Society;
- continuing to play a rôle as one of the checks and balances within the Constitution; and
- providing a voice for the nations and regions of the UK at the centre of public affairs.

The relationship with the Commons would be largely unaltered, with the second chamber retaining the Lords' 'suspensory veto', as provided for by the Parliament Acts — delaying, but not stopping, a Bill supported by the Commons in two successive sessions. The second chamber would also be expected to respect, in its dealings, the governing party's General Election manifesto and be circumspect about challenging the clear views of MPs on public policy. The second chamber would, however, have increased powers to delay and report its concerns on subordinate legislation (statutory instruments) and would set up committees specifically to consider the constitutional and human rights aspects of Commons activities. Senior Commons Ministers might be encouraged to make statements and answer questions in appropriate committees of the second chamber.

House of Lords reform — the 2001 White Paper

In November 2001, the government published its proposals in a White Paper: *A Second Chamber fit for the 21st Century:*

- the 92 elected heredity peers would lose their seats;
- the existing Life Peers would retain their seats, but as a transitional measure;
- the link between peerage and membership of the Lords would disappear;
- the size of the second chamber would be capped at 600, after a transition period of 10 years;
- the majority of members of the second chamber would be nominees of the major political parties;
- about 120 members would be independent of party politics appointed by a new statutory Appointments Commission;
- about 120 members would be elected to represent the regions and nations; and
- there would be a continuing (but unspecified) rôle for Church of England Bishops and Law Lords.

The White Paper invited views on the overall balance of the second chamber, the period of office for appointed and elected members, and what actions should result in a member's disqualification.

The government's proposals largely follow those of the Wakeham Commission, but emphasise their preference for limiting the ability of the second chamber to enforce any disagreement with the Commons. At some stage, the government will publish the Bill required to give effect to these proposals and it will be interesting to see its progress through Parliament.

The value of a second chamber with sufficient courage and independence to challenge what the government was doing with its massive majority in the Commons became evident when David Blunkett tried to push through his Anti-terrorism, Crime and Security Bill in December 2001, in response to the events of 11 September 2001. The point at issue was that David Blunkett was trying to create a completely new offence of 'incitement to religious hatred' on the back of his Bill. The Lords took the view, not unreasonably, that the issue of religious hatred was too important to be tacked on to a Bill which was being promoted as emergency legislation about other matters. The Lords believed that the issues surrounding incitement to religious hatred required proper and widespread consultation, before soundly-based legislation could sensibly be enacted. The government had to back down when it realised that, apart from the merit of the Lords' arguments, there was no prospect of the Lords conceding that point. Of some concern was the apparent view within the government that the Lords should not interfere with the government's policies within the elected Commons — missing the point of the basic importance of the separation of powers between the Executive (even though most, but not all, of the individual members of the Executive might have been elected) and the Legislature. The government could hardly argue that the Lords lacked political legitimacy, since its composition was as a result of the House of Lords Act 1999, promoted by the same government.

In some ways, this episode could not have come at a worse time for the government's White Paper proposals. On 31 December 2001, the *Times* reported that the political website *(www.yougov.com)* showed that amongst the respondents to that site there was little support for the White Paper. About 81% agreed that the Lords should be reformed, but a small percentage (2%) agreed with the government that only 20% of the Lords should be elected. Instead, 67% believed that at least half of the Lords should be elected, whereas 31% believed that the whole of the Lords should be elected. Within a short space of time, it became clear that the New Labour government would have difficulty with its proposals, not least in Parliament — there was little or no support for them and anything other than at least 50% of elected members would have a hard time making it through the legislative process. How this is resolved remains to be seen.

The meeting of Parliament at Westminster

The life of a Parliament is up to five years, divided into 'Sessions', each normally lasting about a year — usually beginning and ending in October/November.

Parliament does not sit for the whole year. During periods called 'Recesses', MPs are able to deal with their other duties or take a holiday. Both of the Houses have Recesses of two or three weeks at Christmas/New Year, and about a week at Easter and at the end of May. There is also a long Summer Recess through August, September and early October. Recess dates vary each year and are usually slightly different for the two Houses. At the suggestion of the Modernisation Committee, in 1999 the House of Commons had a short additional Recess for three days during the February half-term.

Parliament can be 'recalled' during a Recess if the circumstances demand it. For example, the Commons was recalled during the Gulf War, after the Northern Ireland agreement in 1998 and after the events of 11 September 2001.

Each Session begins with the 'State Opening of Parliament', with the 'Queen's Speech' outlining the government's legislative plans for that Session. A Session comes to an end by Parliament being 'Prorogued' and Parliament is said to 'stand prorogued' until the next Session begins, usually after about a week. Public Bills which have not been passed by the time Parliament is prorogued are lost — so there tends to be an acceleration of the legislative process towards the end of the Session after the Summer Recess.

The Sessions are 'adjourned': on each sitting day; over the weekend; and for the Recesses. The average annual number of sitting days is about 159 for the Commons and 140 for the Lords.

The life of a Parliament comes to an end at its 'Dissolution' by the Queen, these days at the request of the incumbent Prime Minister to enable a General Election to take place.

Both Houses of Parliament hold their meetings in public and their deliberations are now accessible to many more people since they are covered by radio and television. As far as the Commons is concerned, the Speaker's cry: *"Order! Order!"* should now be well-known!

The proceedings (verbatim) of both Houses are published in the Official Report, otherwise known as *'Hansard'*. Hansard is published daily and weekly when Parliament is sitting and is now available on the Parliament website (*www.parliament.uk [sic]*). The name 'Hansard' was officially adopted in 1943 after Luke Hansard (1752-1828), the printer of the *House of Commons Journal* from 1774. The first, more detailed, official reports were published in 1803 by the political journalist, William Cobbett, in his *Political Register*. This was the first time that the Press were allocated seats in the Public Galleries of the House. Cobbett sold his business to Luke Hansard's son, who was printing the *Political Register* at the time, and it remained with the Hansard family until 1889. It is now published by HMSO. The Hansard Reporters in the Commons sit in a gallery above the Speaker and take down every word verbatim. In the Lords, the Reporters sit in a special box in the gallery, facing the Lord Chancellor.

The records of the Lords from 1497 and the Commons from 1547 are available to the public through the House of Lords Record Office.

Parliamentary Privilege

One particular aspect of this was discussed in the first chapter in the context of *Conventions*. Each House of Parliament has rights, privileges and immunities to protect it from unwarranted interference in carrying on its work — these are enjoyed by each House collectively and by each member individually.

These rights include freedom of speech (actions for defamation cannot be brought for what is said in Parliament); freedom from arrest in civil actions; exemption from serving on a jury; the collective right of access to the Monarch; the right of each House to control its own proceedings (including excluding the public, *'strangers'*, if it wishes) and to punish any person for breach of any of its privileges or for contempt.

Members of Parliament

Members of Parliament are elected to the House of Commons through universal suffrage — all people over the age of 18 and eligible to vote having a say in who should be their representative. The ballot is secret and unlike some countries, such as Australia, voting is not compulsory. This was amply demonstrated by the poor turnout for the 2001 General Election.

Once elected, an MP has responsibilities to his or her constituents and to his or her party, both locally and at Westminster.

An MP is expected to represent the interests of all his or her constituents regardless of how they voted. Any constituent who feels aggrieved about an issue will almost certainly write to their MP to enlist his or her help in trying to resolve the problem — the MP will then write to the relevant Minister, government department or local authority, intervening on the constituent's behalf. MPs can also represent their constituents within Parliament by asking Questions, both Written and Oral, submitting Early Day Motions and requesting an Adjournment Debate — all about local issues. MPs receive an allowance to help them deal with this correspondence, often enabling them to employ a secretary or researcher. Space was so limited at Westminster that not every MP could be given office space, even on a shared basis. The position has changed since the opening of Portcullis House, the purpose-built building across the road from Westminster Palace.

As far as their political party is concerned, most MPs will have been adopted as the official candidate of their party, through a formal selection process. As a result of that they will receive financial and other practical support for fighting their election campaign — from their party at national and local level and from organisations having some sort of affinity with the aims of their party (for example, many Labour MPs are sponsored by a trade union). MPs will, therefore, be subject to their party's whip as soon as they take their places in Parliament. The need for this financial and other support to succeed in being elected also explains why the election of truly independent MPs, like Martin Bell and Dr Richard Taylor, is exceptionally rare.

MPs will spend a large part of their time at Westminster, but, if they are sensible, they will return to their constituencies quite frequently to meet the officers of their local party or association to keep them informed and to meet, face-to-face, with their constituents at advertised 'surgeries' in the constituency. Keeping the local party or association informed is important, even if the seat is a safe one, because there is always the risk of deselection — even local Conservatives are prepared to ditch a sitting MP if he or she is believed to have become an electoral liability.

As far as Westminster is concerned, MPs will have campaigned on some local issues but largely on the basis of the policies set out in their party's Election Manifesto. Consequently, when the time comes to implement that Manifesto, the MPs will be expected by their party hierarchy to vote according to their party line on any issues coming before the House of Commons.

Occasionally, if the issue is recognised as one which should be decided according to individual conscience (for example, the reintroduction of capital punishment), the MPs will be allowed to vote as they wish — a 'free vote'. Adherence to the party line — party discipline — is maintained through the whip system.

As a matter of last resort, an MP whose political behaviour displeases the Chief Whip can have the 'whip withdrawn' from them, usually until they see the error of their ways — this excludes them from the party's meetings and information systems within the House, but they still remain MPs. An recent example of this was the withdrawal of the whip from a group of Eurosceptic Conservative MPs for a time in the final year of the Parliament before the 1997 General Election.

Whips and votes in Parliament

Government business is steered through Parliament by the *Government Chief Whip* in each House, under the direction of the Prime Minister and the Leaders of the two Houses, and in consultation with the *Opposition Chief Whip*. Each House refers to the other as *'another place'*.

The *Leader of the House of Commons* is a Minister of the Crown and a member of the Cabinet, now usually also holding the office of *[Lord] President of the Council*. The Leader has prime responsibility for organising the business of the House and responding to the wishes of the House for opportunities to debate matters of concern to it.

The Government Chief Whip in the House of Commons is formally known as the *Parliamentary Secretary to the Treasury*. The Government Chief Whip has a Deputy and a number of Assistants to help him or her. Their job is to implement the decisions of the Leader of the House.

Some Chief Whips are more subtle than others in the methods by which they try to keep the foot-soldiers (the backbench MPs) 'on message'. The New Labour government, rightly or wrongly, has gained a reputation for being preoccupied with 'control-freakery'. At the beginning of November 2001, an internal paper was leaked in which a group including the Chief Whip (Hilary Armstrong) and the Leader of the House (Robin Cook) proposed that about 100 backbench Labour MPs would be regarded as 'sponsors'. The activities of these 'sponsors' would be co-ordinated by Parliamentary Private Secretaries and those chosen as 'sponsors' *"would have to accept that they would [work] under general Ministerial direction and in accordance with departmental policy"*. Although this proposal was presented as a move to involve backbenchers in government policy-making and give them a clearer rôle and career ladder, others were less sure, describing it as *"a crude and patronising attempt to extend the whips' control across the Parliamentary Labour Party"*. The MPs were, however, given assurances by the government which persuaded enough of them to support the initiative — it remains to be seen how it all turns out. Apart from conflicting with the time-honoured backbench rôle of monitoring the activities of the Executive, the use of the word 'sponsor' in this context turned on its head the usual meaning of the word (in terms of the direction of the patronage involved).

Sometimes the phrases *'usual channels'* or *'behind the Speaker's Chair'* are used in Parliament, particularly when an issue has arisen and someone has to find time for it in the programme of business. This phrase refers to the Whips as a group who meet, often with the party leaders, to reach agreement on the changes to the programme needed to accommodate the new issue.

The Whips keep their respective members informed of forthcoming parliamentary business through issuing their *Weekly Whip* — often with the aim of ensuring that their voting strength is maintained. The relative importance of an item is indicated by the number of times it is underlined — once, twice or three times. If an issue is especially important to their party, the item will be underlined three times in the list from the Whip — *a three-line whip* — and the MP or Peer will be expected to attend to vote, with no excuses (even illness) being accepted! Failure to attend a three-line whip may result in the MP or Peer 'having the whip withdrawn' or even being expelled from the Parliamentary party.

However, individual MPs can avoid having to attend to vote and yet maintain their party's voting strength by *pairing* with an Opposition MP — both agreeing not to attend to vote and, in effect, cancelling each other's votes. These arrangements, which have to be approved by the Whips, are frequently used by MPs who would find it difficult to attend to vote. Pairing can be short-term or long-term, lasting for months or years. Since pairing is an informal arrangement, it does not feature in the rules of the House.

The pairing system is a sensible and convenient one, but it is based on custom and practice and can be unilaterally withdrawn by any party at any time. This was done by the Labour Party in the last few months prior to the 1997 General Election, because of perceived abuse of the pairing system by the Conservatives — with the consequence that MPs on both sides, some of whom were quite ill, had to make the journey to Westminster to vote, especially since the Conservative government's majority was by then in single figures.

Often the Speaker first tries to declare the result of a vote on the basis of the volume of support for or against the proposition when it is put to the vote. If that approach is challenged, the Speaker calls for a vote by announcing 'Clear the Lobbies'. This results in the House being 'Divided' and a 'Division' is held. The police order all 'Strangers' (non-MPs) to leave the Members' Lobby, and they also go through the other public rooms of the House shouting 'Division'. Division Bells ring throughout the Palace of Westminster and in specific restaurants, pubs and private houses nearby, where MPs may usually be found. MPs do not have to attend a debate in order to vote, so they have to be warned that voting is in progress when they are not in the Chamber.

It is then a race against time (usually eight minutes) for any MP hearing the bells to reach (often running on foot!) the relevant Lobby alongside the Chamber, before the Lobby doors are closed. MPs make their way to the Chamber, where the Whips will remind them which way, if any, their party is voting. To vote, the MPs enter the relevant Lobby — Ayes (to the right of the Speaker) or Noes (to the left). The official Clerks of the House record the names of the MPs voting and the Tellers count heads. There are four Tellers, two from each side of the House (usually the Whips) and two in each Lobby. When the counting has finished, the Tellers hand the result to the Speaker who announces the result formally to the House; "The Ayes/Noes have it". Divisions rarely take less than 10 minutes to complete and those where most MPs decide to vote can take as long as 15 minutes.

In the House of Lords, the process is broadly similar except that, being an apparently more civilised place, the supporters enter the Contents Lobby and the opponents the Not Contents Lobby!

Unusually in this modern age, neither the Commons nor the Lords has adopted a mechanical or electronic voting system. This was considered in 1998 but rejected.

Lobbies and Lobby Correspondents

There are several Lobbies in the Palace of Westminster and they are used for different purposes and by different people. In the context of Parliament, a Lobby is a room which serves as a meeting place.

The Lobbies in which voting takes place were mentioned in the previous section.

The octagonal Central Lobby is, as its name suggests, in the middle of the Palace and separates the Commons (to the north) from the Lords (to the south) and is where members of the public come to ask to meet their MP.

The Members' Lobby is next to the Commons Chamber and is where MPs collect their messages and where the Chief Whips' Offices are located. It is decorated with statues of former Prime Ministers.

The Peers Lobby is next to the Lords Chamber and is where members of the Lords can meet and discuss forthcoming business.

'Lobby Correspondents' are journalists who have special access to Parliament and are allowed into the Members' Lobby, from which they get their name. They are able to talk to MPs, Ministers and the Prime Minister's Press Officer. They can also go into one of the bars in the House of Commons — 'Annie's Bar' — which is reserved for MPs and Lobby Correspondents. This special access enables Lobby Correspondents to be very well informed about what is really happening in Parliament but they usually do not disclose their sources of information.

Front, Back and Cross Benches

In the House of Commons there are two rows of benches down either side of the Chamber. The Speaker sits at one end, between the two rows of benches, behind a large Table on which, amongst other things, sits the Mace (which is a symbol of power) and two Despatch Boxes. In spite of their name, the Despatch Boxes contain bibles rather than documents or despatches.

The members of Her Majesty's government, by tradition, sit on the 'front bench' on the Speaker's right hand. The members of the Official Opposition (in effect the Shadow Cabinet) sit on the opposite front bench. Government Ministers or Shadow Ministers will rise and go to, and lean upon, the relevant Despatch Box to speak.

MPs who are not members of the government or the Opposition will sit on the other benches on the relevant side of the chamber — the *backbenches*. Such MPs are known as backbench MPs and the way in which they can participate in the business of the House is dealt with later.

Much the same arrangement is adopted in the House of Lords (where, incidentally, the seats are red, rather than green!), but with some important differences. The meetings there are presided over by the Lord Chancellor sitting on the Woolsack and there is an extra set of benches, directly facing the Lord Chancellor, for those peers (Bishops, Law Lords and others) who do not espouse any political party — the *cross benches*.

MPs never resign!

MPs usually hold office until the dissolution of Parliament just before the next General Election. A casual vacancy can be caused by death, elevation to the House of Lords or by 'resignation'. Strictly speaking, an MP cannot resign in the ordinary sense of the word and, if that is the result they wish to achieve, then they must disqualify themselves by applying to the Chancellor of The Exchequer for appointment either as *Steward* or *Bailiff of the Chiltern Hundreds* or *Steward of the Manor of Northstead*. These are recognised technically as 'offices of profit under the Crown', even though they are unpaid, and lead to automatic disqualification from holding office as an MP.

The two main political parties in Parliament

Although the Liberal Democrats would like to think otherwise (at least for recent years), there is a predominantly two party system in the UK — it has been so for the last 150 years. Since 1945 those two parties have been the Conservative and Labour parties. The Conservative and Labour parties organise themselves differently in Parliament.

The Conservative and Unionist Members' Committee (the 1922 Committee) consists of all Conservative backbench MPs in the Commons and usually meets weekly (traditionally early on Thursday evenings).

The 1922 Committee is reputedly named after the year in which a group of Conservative backbenchers decided to end the coalition between their party and the Liberal Party which had subsisted for the purposes of the First World War and had carried on after the end of the War. At a meeting in the Carlton Club on 19 October 1922, Conservative MPs defeated Chamberlain as Party Leader and, consequently, Lloyd George as Prime Minister. The 1922 Committee was, however, established the following year, 1923.

The basis upon which the Conservative front bench can attend meetings of the 1922 Committee depends upon whether the party forms the government or the Opposition. If there is a Conservative government, then Ministers can attend meetings of the 1922 Committee only by invitation; if in Opposition, all Conservative MPs, including those in the Shadow Cabinet, have the right to attend.

The Parliamentary Labour Party consists of all members of the party in both the House of Commons and the House of Lords and usually meets at Wednesday lunchtime. Again, how matters are arranged depends upon whether there is a Labour government. If there is a Labour government, then communications between the government and its backbenchers in both Houses are handled by a parliamentary committee — half are elected by the backbenchers themselves and half are representatives appointed by the government. If the party is in Opposition, the affairs of the Parliamentary Labour Party are organised by a parliamentary committee — this time entirely elected — which also acts as the Labour Shadow Cabinet.

The organisation of these parties, and the Liberal Democrat party, outside Parliament is described in a later Chapter.

The Speaker

The Speaker is the most important officer of the House of Commons — and is often regarded as the First Commoner in the Land. The office is an ancient one: it started with Peter de Montfort being appointed the first 'Parlour' of the Commons in 1258. The title of 'Speaker' was first used by Sir Thomas Hungerford in 1377. The rôle of the Speaker as the champion of Parliament's freedoms dates from 1642 when William Lenthall courageously stood up to Charles I in his arguments with Parliament. The practice of the Speaker being neutral and above party politics developed during Arthur Onslow's tenure from 1728-61. 1992 saw the first woman Speaker, Betty Boothroyd, a Labour MP and former Tiller Girl. Her successor,

Michael Martin, another Labour MP, elected in 2000, was the first Roman Catholic Speaker since the Protestant Reformation of Henry VIII. His election was also unusual for another reason — it ran against the modern convention that the office of Speaker rotated between the political parties and it should have been the turn of the Tories.

One of the rôles of the Speaker is, literally, to speak for the Commons in its dealings with the Sovereign and the Lords. More recently, the Speaker's rôle has developed further — into protecting the interests of the Commons *vis-à-vis* the government of the day, especially where the government has a large majority which it takes for granted in its dealings with the Commons. This explains why the office of Speaker is held by a serving MP who is not a Minister of the Crown and why the MPs have tended to react adversely to any attempt by the government of the day to influence their choice of Speaker.

When first taking office, the Speaker sometimes appears to be reluctant and needs to be dragged to the chair by his or her sponsors — this is one of the many odd customs of the House of Commons and may be due to natural modesty; but it may have something to do with the fact that in previous centuries the job of Speaker could be risky if the Sovereign was not favourably disposed towards the Commons. In fact, nine Speakers met violent deaths — but not in recent centuries!

The Speaker is chosen by all the other MPs following an election which, by convention, is run by the Father of the House, the longest serving MP. The Speaker is elected at the beginning of each new Parliament and when a vacancy occurs. By convention, the Speaker continues to hold office until he or she decides to retire and until that time is re-elected unopposed.

When Betty Boothroyd announced her retirement from October 2000, the procedure for the election of her successor (the 152nd Speaker) was in the hands of 84 year old Sir Edward Heath, as the Father of the House. On this occasion, the number of candidates was so large (12) that attempts were made to persuade Sir Edward to modernise the previous, rather arcane, process which involved a series of motions, addresses and amendments — in which everything would depend on the order in which the candidates were put to the vote. In its place, Sir Edward was urged to use a single election to reduce the candidates to the two favourites who would then be the subject of a second election. He decided to stick with tradition and used his 'discretion' about the candidate batting order, with the result that it took over six hours to select the Speaker.

The MPs were not impressed by the New Labour government's lobbying for a Tory Speaker (it was the Tories' turn next, according to a convention dating back 30 years) and demonstrated their independence from the Executive by voting in a Labour Speaker, Michael Martin, a former shop steward, in preference to Sir George Young, an Old-Etonian former Tory Cabinet Minister. However, when the time came to re-elect Speaker Martin for the new Parliament following the 2001 General Election, the new Father of the House (Sir Edward Heath having retired as an MP), Tam Dalyell, was faced with the prospect of a contest. The threat of a contest arose because Speaker Martin was thought by some to have been less than robust in defending the rights of Parliament against the government; and to have shown bias against the Tories in his conduct of debates. In the event, the convention was honoured and Speaker Martin was re-elected unopposed.

The Commons' choice of Speaker has to be approved by the Sovereign and this is done in a formal ceremony in the House of Lords, before the Lord Chancellor and the Lords Commissioners. The Commons' choice is always approved and the Speaker goes on, in the name and on behalf of the Commons of the United Kingdom, to claim: *"their ancient and undoubted rights and privileges, and especially to freedom from arrest, to freedom of speech in debate, and to free access to Her Majesty whenever occasion may require it, and to the most favourable construction of all their proceedings"* — which he or she always receives.

On taking office the Speaker discards any previous party allegiance. The Speaker and the three Deputy Speakers do not normally vote and do not speak except to fulfil their office. If there is a tied vote, the Speaker has to cast a vote, one way or the other, to break the deadlock but will not comment on the merits of the issue; the vote will usually be cast in favour of the government, as a matter of convention.

The Speaker lives in an apartment in the Palace of Westminster (Speaker's House) and will spend most of his or her working life in the Palace. The apolitical nature of the Speaker's office means that special arrangements are made, by tradition, to protect the interests of the Speaker as a sitting MP and the interests of the Speaker's own constituents. Being Speaker is a full-time job, so the normal constituency work of an MP is undertaken for the Speaker by MPs in adjoining constituencies. When the time comes for the Speaker to seek re-election as an MP at a General Election, the other main parties will not, by tradition, field candidates to oppose the Speaker.

The Speaker's most public rôle is presiding over meetings in the House, trying to maintain order and apply the Standing Orders (rules of debate) of the House in some-times heated debates. MPs may contribute to a particular debate only if called upon to do so by the Speaker. To achieve this, MPs must 'catch the Speaker's eye' by standing or half standing in their place. MPs can also write or talk to the Speaker in advance to indicate their interest in taking part in the debate. In the end, it is still up to the Speaker to decide which MPs have caught his or her eye and they are then invited by name to speak. MPs must sit down and stop speaking if the Speaker stands to call for order (*"Order! Order!"*) or to interrupt the debate. Generally speaking, an MP can speak only once on an issue, unless the House has decided to sit 'in committee' — when the rules of debate are more relaxed.

Parliamentary procedure is based on custom and precedent, which are only partly covered by its Standing Orders. The Speaker has to enforce the rules of the House, ensuring that the proper procedure is followed and minority rights protected. If a particular point of difficulty is not covered by the Standing Orders, the Speaker will then have to fall back on previous practice to find the answer and will often consult and quote from a famous treatise on Parliamentary procedure, *Parliamentary Practice,* originally written by Sir Thomas Erskine May, who was Clerk of the House from 1871-86. The treatise, referred to as *Erskine May,* has since been regularly updated by successive Clerks of the House.

Sometimes, even custom and precedent fails the Speaker, as happened in May 1997 when Betty Boothroyd decided that the two Sinn Féin MPs Martin McGuinness and Gerry Adams should not be permitted the normal facilities enjoyed by MPs in Parliament because they refused to swear the MPs' oath of allegiance to the Crown. The circumstances were unprecedented but that did not prevent Betty Boothroyd from making a decision which she thought to be right and which would be supported by most, if not all, of the other MPs. It was not until January 2002 that Martin McGuinness and Gerry Adams were finally given access to office facilities (and allowances) at Westminster, but they were still prohibited from taking their places in the Commons, because of their continued refusal to swear the Oath of Allegiance to the Crown.

The powers of the Speaker are considerable:

- controlling the debates, including deciding when the debate on an issue should end and be voted upon and adjourning or suspending a sitting if matters get out of hand;
- certifying some Bills as 'Money Bills', which affects the way they are handled and effectively prevents the House of Lords from delaying their passage;
- ordering an MP who has broken the rules to leave the chamber or starting the process of suspending an MP for a period;
- signing various warrants, including committal to prison for contempt of the House;
- administering the House through chairmanship of the House of Commons Commission; and
- notionally chairing the Boundary Commissions (under the Political Parties, Elections and Referendums Act 2000, the new Speaker's Committee will supervise the new Electoral Commission to which the Boundary Commissions' responsibilities will eventually be transferred).

Parliamentary Committees

There are four kinds of parliamentary committee: Committee of the Whole House, Standing Committee, Select Committee and Joint Committee.

Committee of the Whole House

Either House can turn itself into a *Committee of the Whole House* to debate Bills in detail after their Second Reading — the Committee Stage (see the section *Stages of a Bill* in the next Chapter). This arrangement enables unrestricted discussion, by the House itself, suspending the usual rule of only one speech per member. The very important Bills, having constitutional implications or which are emergency measures, are dealt with in this way — such as the Accession to the European Communities Bill in 1972 and the Maastricht Treaty Bill in 1992.

Standing Committees

House of Commons *Standing Committees* are set up to consider Public Bills (other than Money Bills), clause by clause, at the Committee Stage and then report their findings to the House. Standing Committees do not have names, but are referred to by letters of the alphabet — Standing Committee A to H (there can be up to eight at any one time).

Although the name 'Standing Committee' implies that the committee is permanent, in fact it is not — each only exists while it is considering that particular Bill. A new committee is set up for each Bill, of between 16 and 50 MPs, reflecting the political balance in the House — containing the government Minister responsible for the Bill, Opposition spokespeople, a Government Whip and an Opposition Whip.

There are Scottish, Welsh and Northern Ireland 'Grand Committees' to consider the principles of Bills specifically relating to those countries.

The House of Lords has a similar kind of arrangement, although the standing committees there are differently named and constituted.

Select Committees

Select Committees are set up by the House of Commons for a specific job, usually involving some sort of investigation and scrutiny or to deal with 'housekeeping' issues. A select committee can be established for a Parliament, for a session, or for as long as necessary. There is a range of Select Committees which are more or less permanent and spend their time examining the work of specific government departments and related agencies and they can build up an expertise on the particular government department they cover.

A 'joint committee' consists of a select committee of the Commons and a select committee of the Lords appointed to meet as a single committee under one chairman.

Select committees fall into groups. The committees in the first group are known as 'domestic committees', which advise the House of Commons Commission and the Speaker on services to the House. The committees concerned are: Accommodation and Works; Administration; Catering; and Finance and Services. The committees in the second group are about the House and its administration: Broadcasting; Liaison; Standards and Privileges; Procedure; Selection; Standing Orders; and Modernisation of the House of Commons. The third group of committees are connected with the scrutiny of proposed legislation: Deregulation; European Legislation; Statutory Instruments (Joint Committee); and Consolidation etc. Bills (Joint Committee). Committees in the fourth group are concerned with issues external to the House: Committee of Public Accounts; Committee on Public Administration; and Environmental Audit.

The final group of committees are the 'departmental select committees'. At present, following the changes in Whitehall departments after the 2001 General Election, there are 16 departmental committees: Culture, Media and Sport; Defence; Education and Skills; Environment, Food and Rural Affairs; Foreign Affairs; Health; Home Affairs; International Development; Northern Ireland Affairs; Science and Technology; Scottish Affairs; Trade and Industry; Transport, Local Government and the Regions; Treasury; Welsh Affairs; and Work and Pensions.

Most of the departmental select committees consist of 11 members, although some are larger and all of them, like Standing Committees, reflect the political balance in the House.

The committees work in different ways: carrying out a full inquiry which takes written and oral evidence, which then results in a published report; holding a single session to scrutinise a particular issue; arranging informal seminars with experts in a particular field; making visits in the UK and elsewhere to see how things are done in practice; looking at departmental spending plans; or examining the text of draft legislation. A committee normally has several subjects under consideration at any one time.

The committees usually meet at least once each week while Parliament is in session and meet in private or public as they see fit. Such select committees are powerful and can require Ministers, civil servants and, indeed, any person or body, to attend for questioning. The results of these investigations by the select committees are an important check on the Executive, can be debated in the House (there are 30 opportunities for this each year) and are published (since 1997/98, also on *www.parliament.uk*).

Formal reports go through various drafts and the final version is usually approved by consensus within the committee. Where there are differences of opinion they are resolved by voting on formal amendments which are recorded in the minutes of the committee. The relevant government department is expected to reply to a formal report within 60 days. The reply is either a 'memorandum' to the committee (which is then published by the committee as a special report) or a White Paper published by the government.

There are fewer select committees in the House of Lords (because scrutiny of the Executive is not practised there), covering the judicial activities of the House, the European Union and Science and Technology.

Joint Committees

Joint Committees, having members drawn from both Houses, are appointed for each session to deal with *Consolidation Bills* (a Consolidation Bill is one which does not involve new law, but merely brings together existing statutes to simplify matters — and therefore is taken through an expedited procedure because detailed scrutiny is not required) and to deal with delegated legislation (Statutory Instruments). These are the Joint Committees mentioned in the section on select committees.

Backbenchers

The backbenchers have an important rôle in checking on the intentions and actions of the Executive and are able to do so in a variety of ways. This is despite the efforts of the Whips to exert control over the backbenchers — see the earlier section on *Whips and votes in Parliament* for an example of attempts to do this.

Although what follows relates to the House of Commons, broadly similar opportunities exist for backbench members of the House of Lords.

One of the most serious Parliamentary 'crimes' which can be committed by a Minister is deliberately 'misleading' the House when explaining his or her actions to the House — this is usually regarded as sufficient to mean that the Minister should do the decent thing and resign as a Minister.

The term 'mislead' is used because, by custom, the word 'lie' cannot be used by one MP of another in the Commons. An example can be found in the speech made by former Home Office Minister Ann Widdicombe about the former Home Secretary Michael Howard, in the Commons in May 1997, during the law and order debate on the Queen's Speech. This was an attempt to stymie his chances of winning the Tory Party leadership after John Major lost the 1997 General Election. She described Michael Howard as having *"an exquisite way with words"* and she accused him of misleading the House by *"denial and refuge in semantic prestidigitation"* in giving his version of the circumstances surrounding the dismissal of the Governor of Parkhurst Prison after the mass breakout of IRA prisoners from there.

Backbenchers can ask questions, take part in debates, and propose motions. Individual MPs can also gain the opportunity to introduce their own Bills into Parliament, although their chances of success in having their proposals turned into law are not very great. This is described in the section on *Primary legislation* in the next Chapter.

Backbench MPs can also use the opportunities for debate provided by the Queen's Speech, by any motions for the *censure of the government* (which come out of the government's time), and during the consideration of legislation.

Membership of the Standing and Select Committees mentioned earlier also provides backbench MPs with the opportunity to put the Executive to the test.

Questions can be raised in a variety of ways; the questions (of whatever kind) and their answers are recorded in *Hansard*. Questions are just answered — there is no immediate debate on their subject matter — but one might be promised for later.

Oral Questions

'Question Time' lasts for one hour on Monday, Tuesday, Wednesday and Thursday, immediately after Prayers. Even though the questions are written down and included in the Order Paper, they are referred to as 'Oral Questions', because they are answered orally. Questions may not be asked about issues which have been devolved to Scotland or Wales and each MP is limited to two questions per day. Government Ministers answer MPs' questions on a rota basis, dealing only with those questions which relate to their Ministerial responsibilities. Since Oral Questions are printed in the Order Paper, they are not read out when the MP is called upon by the Speaker to ask the Question, but just referred to by their number on the Order Paper. Supplementary questions are allowed from that MP and other MPs. When the Speaker has decided that enough supplementary questions have been asked, the next Oral Question is called. Questions and answers are reported in *Hansard*. Any Oral Questions on the Order Paper which are not answered by the close of Question Time receive a written answer later which then appears in *Hansard*. Oral Questions which do not make the 'Five O'Clock Shuffle' receive no answer at all.

There is usually only time for about 15 to 20 questions to be asked (about 70 are usually submitted), so a ballot has to be held to determine the order in which they are asked. This is called the 'Five O'Clock Shuffle' after the time of day at which the ballot is conducted. Those questions higher up the order stand a better chance of being asked (if not necessarily answered to the satisfaction of the MP concerned!).

In the House of Lords, the arrangements are different — up to four questions may be asked at the beginning of each day's session and answered by the relevant government representative in the Lords.

Sometimes Oral Questions may be answered by the Minister saying *"I will write to the Hon Member ..."* — such a reply is referred to as a 'Will Write' reply. Replies given in this way are not published in *Hansard*, but are placed in the House of Commons Library for MPs' reference. Where the question relates to the activities of an executive agency established under the Next Steps Initiative, the reply is given by the agency's chief executive, rather than the Minister.

Prime Minister's Questions

There is a separate 'Prime Minister's Question Time' during which the Prime Minister answers questions (referred to as PMQs). PMQs must be in written form for inclusion in the Order Paper. Because of this, most will ask the Prime Minister a formulaic question about his diary commitments in the forthcoming week. The real question for the Prime Minister to answer emerges during the supplementary question which follows. Backbenchers are allowed one supplementary question; the Leader of the Opposition is allowed up to three or four; while the Leader of the next largest opposition party is allowed up to two supplementary questions. The Prime Minister may not be aware of the content of the supplementary questions, although it would be surprising if he was unaware of supplementary questions to be asked by loyal New Labour backbenchers.

PMQs have changed since the advent of New Labour. The time allowed used to be 15 minutes on Tuesday and Thursday, but is now 30 minutes on Wednesday afternoons. The reason given by Tony Blair for this change was that he believed that answers to PMQs under John Major had become increasingly argumentative, superficial and largely a waste of time. The new arrangement does not seem to be any better at producing a more worthwhile exercise in holding the Prime Minister to account — some of the PMQs have the appearance of being 'planted', since they are hardly robust, and provide Tony Blair with an opportunity to blow the government's trumpet.

Private Notice Questions

Unlike Oral Questions, a Private Notice Question (PNQ) can be given without the usual three days notice, although the relevant Minister must be notified before the question is asked. To be allowed at all, a PNQ must be genuinely urgent and about a matter of public importance. The use of PNQs is strictly controlled by the Speaker and on average, only two or three are permitted each month. A PNQ is usually taken at the end of Question Time and this can give it a degree of prominence.

Written Answer Questions

In terms of volume, most questions are tabled for a 'written answer' since there is no limit to the number of such questions which an MP may table — sometimes up to 250 written answer questions can be tabled in one day. In an average session there can be a total of up to 40,000 questions, of which about 2,500 are answered orally. If the cost of answering a written question is likely to exceed £550, the government department can refuse to answer it.

Adjournment Debates

Adjournment Debates are a useful tool for MPs to raise, for debate, issues of concern to their constituents. The formal motion is "That this House do now adjourn". There are three types. Just before the House adjourns for the night at the end of each business day there is a 30 minute period in which such issues can be raised and debated. A similar, but longer (three hours), opportunity exists before the House adjourns for each Recess. As an experiment, as part of the Jopling Reforms, some adjournment debates (for which a ballot takes place) are held on Tuesday and Wednesday mornings, freeing up some Fridays for MPs to deal with constituency business (thus called 'non-sitting Fridays'). The 'Jopling Reforms' were a package of measures recommended in 1991/92 by the *Select Committee on Sittings in the House* chaired by Michael (now Lord) Jopling MP. Some (but not all) of those recommendations were introduced as an experiment in January 1995 either through temporary standing orders or through agreement between the political parties.

Emergency Debate

Finally, at the end of Question Time, MPs can seek to move the adjournment of the House, in order to provide an opportunity to debate a *"specific and important matter that should have urgent consideration"*. To do this, an MP has to apply first to the Speaker for permission and, like the Private Notice Questions mentioned earlier, the Speaker exercises very tight control. The MP rarely succeeds in his or her request — only one or two are allowed each year and then only on issues of national importance. When permission is given, the issue is debated for three hours, usually on the following day, in an 'Emergency Debate'.

Early Day Motions

Issues can also be raised in a way which provides MPs with a means of gauging the support of other MPs for their concerns. Each day, *Early Day Motions* (EDMs) can be tabled for subsequent debate, although no date is fixed for that debate. EDMs are seldom debated but their real purpose is for MPs to put on record their opinion on a subject and canvass support for it from the other MPs. The EDM can be signed by more MPs later. Only about six or seven EDMs attract over 200 signatures; 70 or 80 manage to achieve over 100 signatures; many will attract only one or two signatures. The amount of support for an EDM can be of real help to an MP seeking to persuade the government to address the concerns in other ways. Ministers and Whips do not usually sign EDMs, and Parliamentary Private Secretaries are not encouraged to do so. The Speaker and Deputy Speakers never sign EDMs.

EDMs remain in existence for the rest of the Session in which they were tabled. At the end of the Session all EDMs fall, but they can be resurrected in the next Session. However, the signatures have to be collected again from scratch. Some EDMs reappear in successive Sessions.

There are several kinds of EDM. The Opposition may put down an EDM in the name of the Leader of the Opposition and this is how the Opposition gives warning that it may seek a formal debate on the issue covered by the EDM. An Opposition EDM is probably the kind most likely to be debated. A group of MPs within a political party can put down an EDM, to air a view which is different from that previously expressed by the party. EDMs tabled by government backbenchers may be aimed at altering government action. An EDM can be tabled by one of the smaller parties to highlight their policy on an issue. An all-party EDM can put forward a view which transcends political parties, especially about social issues, and it is this type which attracts the larger numbers of signatures. Sometimes, pressure groups might lobby MPs to table and support an all-party EDM. At the other end of the spectrum, some EDMs may offer congratulations to a particular football or cricket club or raise an issue of local concern. Finally, individual MPs may decide to table an EDM if they have been prevented by the Rules of the House from asking Questions on a specific issue.

Opposition Days

There are 20 *Opposition* Days in each session, when the Opposition is able to choose the subject for debate. The 20 days are shared — 17 are used by the Leader of the Opposition and three by the Leader of the third largest party.

Parliamentary Standards

MPs, because of their representative rôle, come under a great deal of pressure. There are organisations whose sole purpose is to lobby Ministers and MPs on behalf of their paying clients — to seek to influence government and legislation in Parliament. Some MPs will be sponsored or may be retained as Parliamentary advisers by particular organisations — often involving payment to the MP.

There are obvious difficulties in this, because conflicts of interest can exist which are not readily apparent. So, over the last few years, Parliament has introduced a range of procedures aimed at preventing such conflicts of interest or at least bringing them out into the open. Some, it has to be said, have achieved only mixed success.

The Commons maintains a public *Register of MPs Interests* — financial and some non-financial. The register is updated annually and MPs are expected to keep their entry in the register up-to-date and accurate. An MP with a relevant interest must declare that interest when speaking in the House or committee and must disclose it when giving notice of a question or motion. Similar disclosures must be made during any other proceedings in the House and in any dealings with Ministers, civil servants or other MPs.

Failure by particular MPs to do this was one of the features of the notorious *'cash for questions'* affair, in which allegations were made that certain MPs had received undisclosed cash and other benefits in return for asking specific questions in Parliament. Somewhat surprisingly, failures by MPs to make a full and accurate declaration in the register are still occurring in 2002, even though the rules must, by now, be fairly clear.

In November 1995, the Lords agreed to set up a similar *Register of Interests* for its members. Also in 1995, the Commons went further and banned MPs from acting as advocates for any issue which was related to the source of any of their financial interests. However, the Committee on Standards in Public Life now has an important rôle in respect of both Houses of Parliament, with the Parliamentary Commissioner for Standards having responsibilities in respect of conduct in the House of Commons.

Committee on Standards in Public Life

In October 1994, John Major invited Lord Nolan to become the first Chairman of the Committee on Standards in Public Life *(www.public-standards.gov.uk)*. The Committee was then known as the 'Nolan Committee'. The short-hand reference to the Committee usually takes the name of its current chairman, so the 'Nolan Committee' later became the 'Neill Committee' (Lord Neill), and then the 'Wicks Committee' (Sir Nigel Wicks).

The Committee's terms of reference were:

> *"To examine current concerns about standards of conduct of all holders of public office, including arrangements relating to financial and commercial activities, and make recommendations as to any changes in present arrangements which might be required to ensure the highest standards of propriety in public life. For these purposes, public life should include: Ministers, civil servants and advisers; Members of Parliament and UK Members of the European Parliament; members and senior officers of all non-departmental public bodies and of national health service bodies; non-Ministerial office holders; members and other senior officers of other bodies discharging publicly funded functions; and elected members and senior officers of local authorities".*

At an early stage, the Committee produced its *'Seven Principles of Public Life'*, which applied to all aspects of public life:

- *Selflessness:* Holders of public office should act solely in terms of the public interest. They should not do so in order to gain financial or other benefits for themselves, their family or their friends.
- *Integrity:* Holders of public office should not place themselves under any financial or other obligation to outside individuals or organisations that might seek to influence them in the performance of their official duties.

- *Objectivity:* In carrying out public business, including making public appointments, awarding contracts, or recommending individuals for rewards and benefits, holders of public office should make choices on merit.
- *Accountability:* Holders of public office are accountable for their decisions and actions to the public and must submit themselves to whatever scrutiny is appropriate to their office.
- *Openness:* Holders of public office should be as open as possible about all the decisions and actions that they take. They should give reasons for their decisions and restrict information only when the wider public interest clearly demands.
- *Honesty:* Holders of public office have a duty to declare any private interests relating to their public duties and to take steps to resolve any conflicts arising in a way that protects the public interest.
- *Leadership:* Holders of public office should promote and support these principles by leadership and example.

The Committee produces occasional reports on the issues covered by its terms of reference and by the end of 2001 had produced seven such reports. The Seventh Report, published in 2000, covered Standards of Conduct in the House of Lords. The Committee's First Report, published in 1995, covered MPs, Ministers, civil servants, quangos and NHS bodies. That Report included recommendations to Parliament that there should be a Parliamentary Commissioner for Standards, who should be *"significantly independent"* with *"fixed and fair arrangements"*, which should be *"routinely and firmly enforced"*.

Parliamentary Commissioner for Standards

As a consequence of the Nolan Committee's First Report, the first *Parliamentary Commissioner for Standards*, Sir Gordon Downey, was appointed in 1995. He was replaced by Elizabeth Filkin; however, her contract was not renewed (about which, more later).

The Commissioner's rôle is to advise MPs on issues to do with standards and to undertake a preliminary investigation into complaints of alleged breaches of rules by MPs. The Commissioner's report on the outcome of the investigation is presented to the House of Commons Select Committee on Standards and Privileges. The Commissioner has no responsibilities in respect of the House of Lords.

Sir Gordon's first big test was the *'cash for questions'* affair involving Neil Hamilton MP and although his report was complete, it remained unpublished because he could not present it to the Select Committee due to the dissolution of Parliament for the 1997 General Election, which some people suggested was unusually early. However, *'sleaze'* continued to be a General Election issue. Sir Gordon's report was published later and his conclusions in respect of Mr Hamilton were not favourable — he believed that he had found 'compelling evidence' of wrongdoing by Mr Hamilton. The voters at Tatton had, by then, already decided that they preferred the BBC war correspondent and the 'Man in the White Suit', Martin Bell, to their sitting MP, Mr Hamilton. Although Mr Hamilton later sought to challenge and discredit Sir Gordon's conclusions before the Select Committee and elsewhere, he finally came unstuck on 21 December 1999 when the jury (in the libel proceedings he had brought against Mohamed Al Fayed) unanimously declared him to have been corrupt in the 'cash for questions' affair. Whatever else the jury's verdict meant, they had vindicated Sir Gordon Downey's judgment.

The Parliamentary Commissioner for Standards is appointed by the *House of Commons Commission,* under the chairmanship of the Speaker. When Elizabeth Filkin was appointed to replace Sir Gordon Downey, she assumed that her first term of office would be renewed. That was not to be, because the Commission had decided to advertise her job (reducing its hours and pay at the same time) and require her to reapply for it, along with any other applicants. The writing was clearly on the wall, in spite of assurances from Robin Cook, as Leader of the House, that she had been *"neither sacked nor dismissed"*. So, in late November 2001, she wrote a rather forthright letter to the Speaker explaining why she would not be reapplying — alleging *"unchecked whispering campaigns and hostile press briefings"* against her and the placing of *"insuperable obstacles"* to her independence. In spite of off-the-record briefing against her, many commentators speculated that her meticulous investigations in respect of prominent New Labour MPs John Prescott, John Reid, Peter Mandelson, Keith Vaz and Geoffrey Robinson had touched a raw nerve and proved to be rather uncomfortable for those involved and their friends and supporters. Others suggested that she had investigated some complaints which were either trivial, unfounded, or tit-for-tat between political adversaries.

Whatever the rights or wrongs, the issue was who her replacement would be. The problem for New Labour was that it had promised in 1997 that it was 'anti-sleaze', and yet it was then seen in December 2001 as sacking and downgrading the 'sleaze buster'. The handling of the affair prompted doubt about the real willingness of MPs to be subject to independent and rigorous scrutiny, regardless of the rhetoric they might use. The public reputation of MPs and Parliament was not improved by their appearing to require standards elsewhere in public life which they were obviously not prepared to accept for themselves.

Martin Bell, the 'Man in the White Suit' and, by then, a former MP, was apparently headhunted but was reported as saying that *"no one with any honour would take Filkin's job"*. The Editor of the *Guardian*, Peter Preston, applied for the job on the basis that, if appointed, he would be even more frightening to MPs that Elizabeth Filkin — although he was not holding his breath that he would be shortlisted! At the beginning of December 2001, Tony Wright, the Labour Chairman of the Commons Public Administration Committee, questioned Tony Blair in Parliament: *"Do you know of any public institution apart from this one, where the people who are regulated have the ability to choose and dismiss the person who regulates them?"*. The Prime Minister was lost for a reply.

The episode, apart from any doubts about the commitment of MPs to independent regulation of their conduct, made almost inevitable the fairly rapid announcement by the Wicks Committee that it would now examine the whole issue.

Standards in the House of Lords

The Seventh Report of the Committee on Standards in Public Life, published in 2000, covered conduct in the House of Lords. Unlike the First Report concerning the House of Commons, this Report was not prompted by any scandal or crisis. Rather, the Seventh Report was seen as being relevant to the changes in the membership of the House of Lords (see earlier in this Chapter) and the possibility that it would have a higher public profile following those changes.

The Seven Principles mentioned earlier also provided the basis for this Report which also paid regard to the concept of 'proportionality' — that a course of action should be proportionate to the problem or deficiency which it seeks to remedy. The Report recommended:

- the adoption of a short Code of Conduct;
- the mandatory registration of all peers' relevant interests;
- the tightening up of the present guidance on lobbying to ensure public confidence in its propriety;
- a review of the House of Lords' induction arrangements with a view to providing more detailed guidance about the operation and scope of the conduct rules;
- the appointment, where appropriate, of an *ad hoc* independent investigator to assist the *Sub-Committee on Lords' Interests* in cases involving a serious allegation of misconduct (this is the Lords' equivalent of the Parliamentary Commissioner for Standards).

The House of Lords, in July 2001, accepted the report's recommendations and adopted a new Code of Conduct, to come into force after 31 March 2002.

4 The Legislative Process at Westminster

The process of making legislation

Types of legislation

There two main types of legislation — primary legislation and secondary (or subordinate or delegated) legislation. *Primary legislation* comprises the Bills passed by Parliament. *Secondary legislation* comprises Orders in Council, Statutory Instruments and local bylaws.

The trend over the past 20 years has been for the principles, only, of the more complex legislation to be covered by primary legislation (Enabling Acts), with the detail being filled in later (occasionally, never) by statutory instrument. Often, at the time of the passage of the Enabling Act, the government does not yet know how the principles enshrined in the Act will be translated into detail later through statutory instruments.

White and Green Papers

The government can consult people and bodies on its legislation through White and Green Papers — but does not always do so. Where the government has a clear idea of what it wants to do and how that is to be done, it can issue a *White Paper* for consultation, inviting comments on the detail of its proposals. The White Paper itself can be debated in Parliament and the outcome of the White Paper process normally forms the basis of a Bill in the next session.

However, the government's thinking on an issue may not yet have crystallised and it can invite more fundamental comments on how the issue might be dealt with — through a *Green Paper*.

Primary legislation

There a four types of primary legislation: Public Bills, Private Members' Bills, Private Bills and Hybrid Bills.

A *Public Bill* is one introduced by the government to alter the general law of the land, usually to give effect to the proposals set out in the Queen's Speech. They are intended to be of general application throughout the UK or in any of its constituent countries. Such Bills can be introduced either in the House of Commons or in the House of Lords.

A *Private Members' Bill* can arise in one of two ways. Firstly, early in each Session, MPs can take part in a *ballot* for the opportunity to introduce their own Bill on one of 20 Fridays (Private Members' Bills Fridays) in the Session when Private Members' Bills take precedence over government business. The first 20 names drawn in the ballot are the winners.

The second method involves the use of the *'Ten Minute Rule'*. On most Tuesdays and Wednesdays, for a short period at the beginning of public business, individual MPs can seek leave to introduce their Bill — if the motion is opposed, the MP can make a short speech for 10 minutes in support and the opposing member a short speech against. It is highly unlikely that 10 minute rule Bills will go very far and their primary purpose is to enable a backbench MP to raise an important issue in Parliament.

A good example of a 'Ten Minute Rule' Bill occurred in December 2001, when Kevin McNamara MP introduced his Bill to repeal the Act of Settlement 1701 (to remove the bar on Catholics from succeeding to the British Monarchy) and to repeal the Treason Felony Act 1848 (to end the criminal offence of advocating the abolition of the Monarchy, even by peaceful means, for which the maximum penalty would be life imprisonment). The Bill also provided for the rewording of the Oath of Allegiance to the Crown, which each MP was expected to swear; the wording of the Oath posed difficulties for some MPs, in addition to the Sinn Féin MPs. The Bill got nowhere, but it refreshed a continuing campaign by the *Guardian* to obtain a High Court declaration that the 1848 Act was incompatible with Article 10 of the Human Rights Act 1998 (freedom of speech) — so that the newspaper could campaign for the abolition of the Monarchy without the *Guardian's* editor being in jeopardy of prosecution (the last time this happened was in 1883).

Private Members' Bills which involve the expenditure of public money cannot go to the Committee Stage unless the government agrees to finance the Bill's proposals. Private Members' Bills seldom make much progress, but some do — for example: the Marriage Act 1994 and the Building Societies (Joint Account Holders) Act 1995. Quite often Private Members' Bills gain the support of the government and are then effectively taken over by it.

A *Private Bill* is one which is promoted by local authorities or other bodies or individuals to extend their powers or to authorise them to carry out local projects such as railways, roads and harbours, often affecting the rights of specific individuals. Examples are those promoted to authorise Grand Prix road racing on the streets of Birmingham in the mid 1980s and local authority Bills to authorise more permanent new tramways, such as in Manchester and Sheffield. The Proposers of these Bills have to follow a stringent special process to persuade Parliament to give them powers which go beyond, or are in conflict with, the general law. This involves the Proposers having to give evidence and answer questions from the Parliamentary committee and from any objectors — and the objectors themselves can appear and put their case. The process starts with a Petition by the person or body which wants a change in the law. These Petitions have to be presented to Parliament on or before 27 November each year. The Chairman of the Ways and Means Committee in the Commons and the Lord Chairman of Committees in the Lords, determine in which House consideration of the Private Bill should start. As a rule, substantial local authority legislation and other complex Bills start in the Lords, but Bills which are politically contentious start in the Commons.

A *Hybrid Bill* is one which is introduced as a Public Bill but which is found to affect private interests. Such a Bill follows a special procedure which uses parts of the Public and Private Bills processes, giving the private interests affected by the Bill a chance to put their case.

Subordinate legislation

Secondary, Subordinate, or Delegated legislation can be made by a Minister of the Crown or by statutory corporations or local authorities, provided they follow the specific procedure laid down by Parliament when it delegated the power to legislate. There are three main groups: Orders in Council, Statutory Instruments and local bylaws.

Orders in Council are submitted by Ministers, for approval by the Sovereign at a meeting of the Privy Council. Parliament usually, but not always, agrees the draft Order in Council before it is submitted by the Minister. Much of the delegated legislation relating to Northern Ireland is made in this way.

Statutory Instruments are made by Ministers (often to flesh out the detail in a new Enabling Act or update the detail in an old one) but require the agreement of Parliament. The Enabling Act will usually specify which procedure is to be followed — affirmative or negative — in seeking Parliament's agreement.

The *affirmative procedure* means that the Statutory Instrument will not come into existence unless positively approved by resolution of Parliament. The *negative procedure* means that the Statutory Instrument will come into effect automatically if, after 40 days, no resolution has been passed objecting to it.

Most statutory instruments (there are about 2,000 each year) are scrutinised by the Select Committee on Statutory Instruments, rather than by the main body of MPs.

Local Authority *Bylaws* require the approval of a Minister but are not, themselves, considered by Parliament itself.

The stages of a Bill

A Bill can start in the House of Commons or the House of Lords. A simplified description of the process which a Bill follows in the House of Commons is:

- *First Reading:* when the Bill is first presented, there is no debate and only its title (not its contents) is read out. The Bill will be printed (but not Private Members' Bills) and will then await its Second Reading, which may be on the next day or several weeks later.

- *Second Reading:* this is the first time that the proposals in the Bill are debated and voted on — but just the general principles at this stage. This normally takes place during an afternoon (in Parliamentary terms, the period between 4pm and 10pm) although if the Bill has major implications, this stage can run over several days. If the Bill obtains its Second Reading it goes on to its Committee Stage.

- *Committee Stage:* the Bill is usually referred to a standing committee for detailed consideration and amendment, clause by clause. However, the Committee Stage can be carried out by the House itself — a Committee of the Whole House. This happens where the Bill needs to be passed urgently or where the Bill contains proposals of significance for the Constitution. In some cases, a combination of a standing committee and a Committee of the Whole House is used — this process is nearly always used for the annual Finance Bill.

- *Report Stage:* the results of the Committee Stage are reported on the floor of the House and further amendments can be made before the Bill goes on to its Third Reading, which is usually straight away. The Report Stage itself can be very time consuming and may involve late night sittings, with the usual 10pm finish being suspended for that purpose.

- *Third Reading:* at this point the Bill is reviewed and debated in its final form — in the Commons, detailed amendment is not allowed, but in the Lords the Bill can be amended even at this stage. Once a Bill has been read a third time, it is passed to the House of Lords.

- *The House of Lords:* always referred to as *'another place'*. The Bill goes through much the same process again, but the Committee Stage in the House of Lords is usually taken on the floor of the House — a Committee of the Whole House.
- *Lords Report to the Commons:* amendments made by the second House must be agreed by the first House before the Bill can receive the Royal Assent. If there are significant differences, then a Joint Committee is set up to try to resolve them. If agreement cannot be reached on a Bill which started in the Lords, it is unlikely to become law, because no time will be allocated for its further debate in the Commons. Under the Parliament Acts, the Lords cannot delay a money Bill started in the Commons and can only delay any other kind of Commons Bill by up to 13 months — after which time the Bill is presented to the Sovereign for the Royal Assent, regardless of the views of the Lords.
- *Royal Assent:* this is given (not personally since the reign of Queen Victoria in 1854) by the Sovereign in Norman French, *'La Reine le Veult'*, and has not been refused since 1707. The Bill is now an Act and part of the law of the land, as reflected in the sentence which precedes every Act: *"Be it enacted by the Queen's Most Excellent Majesty, by and with the advice and consent of the Lords Spiritual and Temporal, and Commons, in this Parliament assembled, and by authority of the same, as follows:"*

Speeding up the process

The passage of a Bill through its various stages can be delayed, deliberately, by excessively long speeches by the Opposition or the submission of hundreds of amendments — with the aim of preventing it ever reaching the end of the legislative process and becoming law. 'Filibustering' is what happens when an MP makes a very long speech; this delaying tactic was used by Irish MPs in the 19th century, who wanted independence for Ireland and held up legislation to cause problems for the government of the day.

For those with an etymological bent, 'Filibuster' is one of those curious words whose current usage has little to do with its original meaning. The origin of the word is the Spanish 'filibustero', a piratical adventurer or freebooter who pillaged the Spanish colonies in the 17th century. The word was then used to describe anyone who engaged in unauthorised activities against a foreign government. This, in turn, led to its present-day use to describe anyone adopting obstructionist tactics to oppose government legislative activity

This can be prevented by the government having Parliament pass an *Allocation of Time Motion,* usually referred to as a *'Guillotine',* which limits the time to be taken by the various stages of a specific Bill. This guarantees that the Bill will be passed by any deadline (by a specific date or in a fixed number of sittings) which the government may have in mind and tends to concentrate the Opposition's mind on what clauses in the Bill are really important!

The Guillotine was first used in 1887 on the Criminal Law Amendment (Ireland) Bill following a marathon debate in the Commons lasting some 35 days — and some all-night sittings. The most recent example of such a motion was that in June 1997 for the Referendums [sic] (Scotland and Wales) Bill, when 250 amendments had been put down for debate, threatening to stall the whole devolution process. Although some Conservatives described New Labour's actions as *"the most drastic way of silencing debate known to Parliament"* — *"Stalinist Dictatorship"* — their own government had regularly used the device — a record 10 times in the 1988/89 session.

Another way of bringing a debate to a conclusion, so that a vote can be taken before the Bill is talked out, is a *Motion of Closure.* This, however, requires a petition to be submitted to the Speaker by not less than 100 MPs. Even if 100 sympathetic MPs sign up to the petition, the final decision still rests with the Speaker.

If there are many amendments to a Bill which are substantially similar, then these can be grouped together by the Speaker and the House business managers, so that they are effectively debated as a group and only once — thus saving Parliamentary time. This process is sometimes referred to as a *Kangaroo.*

The Opposition

In any healthy democracy, the Opposition has an important rôle to play. In the UK, the Opposition is regarded as the party having the highest number of seats in the Commons after the party which has formed the government. The Opposition party is known as *Her Majesty's Loyal Opposition.*

This recognition is taken one stage further by the Leader of the Opposition, the Opposition Chief Whip and the Opposition Deputy Chief Whip receiving additional allowances to enable them to carry out their responsibilities in Opposition.

The Opposition can contribute positively to the legislative process by proposing amendments to Bills — amendments which, although they might reflect Opposition policies, are nevertheless an improvement which finds majority support in Parliament.

Parliament, as a forum for debate, will be used by the Opposition to set out their views and policies so that the public, who will be asked to elect them at the next General Election, know what they are. The Opposition can do this by using one of the Opposition Days at its disposal, as described in the section on *Backbenchers* in the previous Chapter.

The Opposition also scrutinises the Executive and to enable it to do that effectively, it will appoint its own Shadow Cabinet of specialist spokesmen who will shadow the Ministers to whom they have been assigned. By these means, the Shadow Cabinet will build up experience and knowledge of some (but not all) of the important issues of government. In this way they can be thought of as almost a 'government in waiting', ready to take over at a moment's notice (that is all that they will have) if they are successful at the next General Election.

5   Devolution

The historical background to devolution — the Scottish Parliament — the National Assembly for Wales — the Northern Ireland Assembly — the English Regions

Before looking at the present arrangements for devolution it may be useful to consider how the various countries involved came to be associated with one another in the first place.

Historical background — Wales

Wales has the longest formal association with England, in terms of integration with English government. Following the departure of the Romans in the 5th century and the subsequent advance of the Anglo-Saxons from the east, a number of kingdoms in Wales, including Gwynedd, Powys, Dyfed and Gwent, tried to unite, but never completed the process. The Norman Conquest reached southern Wales by 1093 and by the late 13th century the rest of Wales had come under English sovereignty.

By Acts of 1536 and 1543, Wales was incorporated within the Realm of England and English became the official language of the country. Over the next few centuries the Welsh people did their best to preserve their Celtic cultural heritage and this is reflected in their traditions of non-conformist religion and in the relative popularity of the Liberal, and then the Labour, parties. The Welsh Nationalist Party *(Plaid Cymru)* was founded in 1925 but its influence was not reflected in Parliamentary election successes until the 1960s.

Historical background — Scotland

Before Roman times the inhabitants of Scotland consisted of many tribes and despite several attempts the Romans were never able to establish an effective presence north of Hadrian's Wall. By the middle of the 9th century the separate kingdoms of the region united into a largely Celtic monarchy which lasted for several hundred years. When Edward I of England attempted to impose direct English rule over Scotland in 1296, the Scots revolted until, in 1328, Edward III recognised Robert Bruce, as Robert I of Scotland. The later Stuart monarchs maintained close ties with France but the Scottish Reformation led by John Knox caused the influence of France and of the Catholic Church to wane. In 1567 the Catholic monarch, Mary, Queen of Scots, was forced to give up the Scottish throne in favour of her infant son, James VI. It was at this stage that the Presbyterian Church became the Established Church in Scotland.

When Elizabeth I of England died childless in 1603, James VI of Scotland (a relative of hers) succeeded her on the English throne as James I. Scotland and England still remained separate kingdoms albeit under a single monarch. However, in 1707 the Parliaments of both countries passed the *Act of Union*, by which England, Scotland and Wales came together to form the *Kingdom of Great Britain*. In accordance with the 1707 Act, Scotland dissolved its own Parliament and sent MPs to the Westminster Parliament. Guarantees were given to protect the Scottish laws and courts and the Presbyterian Established Church. The union with England and Wales survived the unsuccessful Jacobite rebellions of 1715 and 1745.

Historical background — Northern Ireland

The historical connection between Northern Ireland and England is altogether more complex, as might be imagined from the recent attempts at a settlement.

Until the 20th century the history of Northern Ireland formed part of Irish history as a whole. By the 8th century, Ireland's clans had grouped themselves into five provinces, the northern one of which was Ulster. The independence of Celtic Ireland survived until 1171, when Henry II of England, after Papal encouragement, invaded and proclaimed himself overlord of the entire island.

The English Reformation brought new pressures upon a Catholic Ireland and during the 16th and 17th centuries Catholics fled from Ireland, leaving their land to be occupied by Protestant Scottish and English migrants — especially in Ulster. By 1692 Protestants controlled Ireland, encouraged by the victory of William III (William of Orange — hence Orangemen) over the deposed James II at the Battle of the Boyne in 1691. Anglicans effectively controlled the land and political offices, even though they only accounted for about 10% of the population. They denied access to basic civil rights not only for Catholics but also for Presbyterians and Nonconformists.

During the next century, Irish Protestants began to agitate for less control from England. However, following an attempted revolt in Ireland, the Act of Union 1801 created the _United Kingdom of Great Britain and Ireland_. The union was not popular in Ireland and the differences between Catholics and Protestants increased. The position was not helped by the Great Famine of 1846-51, when over 2 million Irish people had to emigrate, many to the USA.

As explained in the previous Chapter, in the 19th century Irish MPs used the tactic of filibustering to hold up legislation to demonstrate their wish for independence for Ireland. Home Rule Bills were introduced in 1886, 1893 and in 1912-14. The outbreak of World War I postponed their implementation. The Easter Rising of 1916 involved Ireland being declared a republic at Dublin's General Post Office but, after five days fighting by the Irish Volunteers (later renamed as the Irish Republican Army (IRA)), the rebels had to surrender. The consequent reprisals from Westminster only served to alienate even those people prepared to give Home Rule a chance. In the 1918 General Election, Sinn Féin won 73 of the Irish seats, more than twice as many as the Unionist parties. By that time southern Ireland was in a state of civil disobedience and, by 1920, large areas were under the _de facto_ control of the IRA.

Westminster passed the Government of Ireland Act 1920, which provided for the establishment of two 'Home Rule' Parliaments, one in Belfast covering six (which now form Northern Ireland) of Ulster's nine counties, with the other in Dublin covering the 23 counties of southern Ireland along with the remaining three counties of Ulster (which together now comprise the Republic of Ireland).

However, the Roman Catholic majority in southern Ireland, stirred by the Easter Rising of 1916, preferred total independence to the Home Rule on offer, while the Protestant majority in the six Ulster counties preferred union with Great Britain but were prepared to accept Home Rule. After a truce with the IRA and then the _Anglo-Irish Treaty_ signed in December 1921, southern Ireland became first the Irish Free State with Dominion status within the British Empire and later a republic named Éire, eventually leaving the Commonwealth in 1949.

As far as Northern Ireland was concerned, from 1921 it was a sectarian state, controlled and ruled by the Protestant majority. The Northern Ireland Parliament met at Stormont in Belfast, with chambers for its House of Commons and Senate. The Civil Rights Movement started in Ulster in 1968 leading to street riots and increasing violence between Catholics and Protestants. British troops were called in to assist the Royal Ulster Constabulary (RUC) to keep the peace. In response, the IRA mounted a prolonged terrorist campaign in an effort to force the withdrawal of British troops as a precursor to Northern Ireland's unification with the Irish Republic. Protestant terrorist organisations responded in kind.

By 1972, sectarian violence became so bad that the Northern Ireland Constitution, Prime Minister and Parliament were suspended, initially for just one year. A power-sharing experiment (the _Sunningdale Agreement_) was then tried but had to be abandoned after five months in the face of a Loyalist workers strike. Northern Ireland was thereafter ruled directly from Westminster with the Cabinet post of Secretary of State for Northern Ireland being viewed as the most difficult and dangerous job in the UK government.

Devolution from Westminster

Having set the historical background, the recent (and varied) devolution processes in Scotland, Wales and Northern Ireland will be described. The section on Northern Ireland consists of a sketch of the process which led to the new Northern Ireland Executive, rather than a description of how it works in practice, since its brief and fragile existence has been periodically suspended from February 2000.

The nature of devolution differs between one country and another, and, therefore, anomalies are bound to emerge as the devolved institutions develop their own identities and policies. The greatest extent of devolution is to Scotland, where not only the power to legislate is devolved but also a limited power to vary taxation to pay for activities special to Scotland — the so-called 'Tartan Tax'. At the time of writing (February 2002), this power to vary taxation had not yet been used.

However, it did not take long before anomalous consequences within the UK caused by devolution in Scotland started to appear. Means-tested maintenance grants for students had been phased out in the UK in favour of student loans — which, coupled with the requirement to pay tuition fees, had caused financial difficulties for most students. The Scottish Executive announced its intention to reintroduce student maintenance grants for Scottish students to help them meet their tuition fees — much to the chagrin of Westminster! The move may have been designed to head off an even more embarrassing policy defeat in the Scottish Parliament — the removal of tuition fees in Scottish Universities by an alliance of SNP, Scottish Conservative and Scottish Liberal Democrat MSPs.

Scotland — the referenda

The Royal Commission on the Constitution recommended in 1973 a form of legislative devolution for Scotland and this resulted, after a difficult time through Parliament, in the Scotland Act 1978. The 1978 Act required there to be a referendum which needed to be supported by 40% of the Scottish electorate (not just those voting); in the event, although 52% of those voting in the March 1979 referendum supported the idea of a Scottish Assembly (as it was then to be called), this only amounted to 33% of the total electorate and the proposal failed.

In the succeeding period from 1979-97, although they allowed the special treatment of Scottish business in Parliament, the Conservative governments were unenthusiastic about devolution and the idea had to wait for the return of a Labour government for its resurrection. The *Scottish Constitutional Convention* (SCC) produced a series of reports and the final one, *Scotland's Parliament, Scotland's Right,* formed the basis of the devolution policy in New Labour's manifesto for the 1997 General Election. The New Labour government produced a White Paper in July 1997, *Scotland's Parliament,* and this led to a referendum on 11 September 1997. The main difference from 1979 was that the referendum was held before the legislation, rather than after it and it covered two aspects — not only devolution of legislative powers but also the power to vary taxes in Scotland. The turnout was 60% and the successful outcome of the referendum (74% voted for the Parliament and 64% voted for tax varying powers) led to the Scotland Act 1998.

The spadework in setting up the Scottish Parliament was undertaken by a Consultative Steering Group (CSG) set up by the Secretary of State and including all the relevant political parties and civic groups and interests. The CSG report, *Shaping Scotland's Parliament,* formed the basis of the new Parliament's Standing Orders when it was opened for the first time by the Queen on 12 May 1999. To mark the occasion, Dr Winifred Ewing MSP, Mother of the Scottish Parliament, announced: *"The Scottish Parliament, adjourned on the 25th day of March in the year 1707, is hereby reconvened".*

The *Separation of Powers* was one of the objectives highlighted in *Shaping Scotland's Parliament.* The separation is as important in Scotland as in any other democracy and is achieved by a system of checks and balances between the *Legislature* (the Scottish Parliament), the *Executive* (the Scottish Executive) and the *Judiciary* (the Scottish Court of Session).

Scottish Parliament — MSPs

The Parliament *(www.scottish.parliament.uk)* is elected for a four year period of office and consists of 129 *Members of the Scottish Parliament* (MSPs). There is no reason why an individual cannot be both an MP and an MSP and, if they are, the letters MP MSP appear after their name. However, it is expected that such joint membership will not exist for long — MSPs will quickly be expected to concentrate their activities in Edinburgh rather than Westminster.

Seventy-three MSPs were elected in the constituencies by the first past the post system and the remaining 56 were elected from regional lists. Each elector had two votes — one for one of the named candidates for the constituency and the second for a political party in the regional lists. The regional electoral areas were based on the European Parliamentary constituencies and their purpose was to ensure that the overall number of seats occupied by each political party reflected, as nearly as practicable, their share of the overall vote. The 1999 results *(in Appendix A)* show how the Additional Member system of proportional representation works in practice, in the scale of the adjustment through the regional allocations needed to redress the lack of proportionality produced by the first past the post system used in the constituencies.

Scottish Parliament in action

The Scottish Parliament meets in its temporary home at the Church of Scotland Assembly Hall, The Mound, Edinburgh — known as the 'Debating Chamber' or the 'Chamber'. This arrangement will continue until the new Scottish Parliament buildings, at Holyrood at the foot of the Royal Mile in Edinburgh, are ready — planned for 2003.

One of the MSPs is elected to be the Presiding Officer (equivalent to the Speaker at Westminster) who is supported by two Deputy Presiding Officers. Their rôle is: to chair meetings of the Parliament; convene and chair meetings of the *Parliamentary Bureau* (which organises the parliamentary business programme); interpret the Parliamentary Rules during meetings; and represent the Scottish Parliament in discussions with other parliamentary or government bodies.

A full session of the Scottish Parliament normally lasts for four years from the date of a general election. Each session is divided into 12-month Parliamentary Years, which in turn are divided into 'sitting days' or 'recess' periods. On 'sitting days', the full Parliament tries to complete its business by 5.30pm, except on Fridays when the target finishing time is 12.30pm. However, matters are arranged so that the full Parliament does not clash with the meetings of its Committees (usually all day Tuesday and Wednesday afternoon). The business programme as agreed by the Parliamentary Bureau is administered by the *Clerk of the Parliament* and appears in the *Business Bulletin*. The proceedings of the Parliament and its committees are published in the *Official Reports*.

Issues are raised at meetings of the Parliament by MSPs in several ways: by asking oral questions; by submitting written questions; and by giving notice of or moving a Motion.

Scottish Parliamentary Committees

Much of the Scottish Parliament's work is done through its 18 Committees, as suggested in *Shaping Scotland's Parliament*. This method is intended to achieve greater public involvement in the work of Parliament, to provide MSPs with a worthwhile rôle and to facilitate holding the Scottish Executive to account.

The Standing Orders envisage two types of committee: 'mandatory committees' which are required to be established (such as the Standards Committee, the Public Petitions Committee and the Equal Opportunities Committee) and 'subject committees' to examine a particular subject or area of public policy. Each committee consists of between five and 15 MSPs and is chaired by a *Convener*. Meetings are held in public and can take place anywhere in Scotland. A committee will usually appoint one of its members as its *Reporter* on a specific matter. MSPs can take part in the meetings of a committee of which they are not a member but cannot vote. Committees can appoint advisers and can require the attendance of witnesses and the production of documents.

The business of the committees is taken up with examining: the policy, administration and financial arrangements of the Scottish Executive; proposed legislation in the Parliament and in the Westminster Parliament; and the application of EU and international laws and conventions in Scotland.

The Scottish Parliament, unlike Westminster, is *unicameral* (it only has a single chamber as a legislature). The rôle of a second legislative chamber is undertaken by the committees.

Scottish Parliament — legislative competence

The Scotland Act 1998 set the devolution framework, including the limits within which the Scottish Parliament can legislate — its *legislative competence*. The Scottish Parliament is responsible for most 'domestic' Scottish matters while international matters remain at Westminster. The key areas of responsibility devolved to the Scottish Parliament and the Scottish Executive appear in slightly more detail in *Appendix B*.

Areas of responsibility which have been retained (or 'reserved') by Westminster are: constitutional issues; foreign and defence policy; most economic policy; social security; and medical ethics.

Scottish Parliament — the legislative process

There are four types of Bill which can be introduced into the Parliament: *Executive* (by a Minister); *Committee* (by the Convener of the Committee); *Members'* (by an MSP, with the support of another 11 MSPs); and *Private* (by a Promoter). A Minister will sensibly consult the relevant committee(s) before introducing an Executive Bill.

However it is introduced, each Bill must be accompanied by three documents:
- a *Written Statement* by the Presiding Officer that the provisions of the Bill are within the legislative competence of the Scottish Parliament, highlighting any provisions thought to be outside its devolved powers;
- a *Financial Memorandum* setting out an estimate of the administrative, compliance and other costs of the Scottish Executive, local authorities, other bodies and businesses and individuals in meeting the Bill's obligations; and
- an *Auditor General's Report* if the Bill intends to charge expenditure to the Scottish Consolidated Fund — confirming or otherwise the appropriateness of such a charge.

If the Bill is an Executive Bill, more has to be supplied:

- a *Written Statement* by the relevant Minister that the Bill is within the legislative competence of the Scottish Parliament;
- *Explanatory Notes*, containing an objective summary of the Bill's provisions; and
- a *Policy Memorandum,* setting out the Bill's policy objectives, any alternative approaches considered, consultation exercises and their outcome and the impact of the Bill on a variety of issues such as equal opportunities, human rights, sustainable development and island communities.

Once introduced, a Bill will have to pass through three stages before it can receive the approval of the Scottish Parliament and the Royal Assent:

- *Stage One* involves an examination of the Bill's general principles and is normally handled by a Subject Committee, usually referred to as the *Lead Committee*. If the Bill envisages the use of delegated legislation, then it is also referred to the *Subordinate Legislation Committee*. The full Parliament considers the report of the Lead Committee and decides whether or not to allow the Bill to proceed to Stage Two.
- *Stage Two* now involves a more detailed, line by line, examination of the Bill either by the Lead Committee or by another Committee or by the full Parliament or by any combination of these, depending on the nature of the Bill. At this stage, amendments can be made and debated; and if those amendments affect any proposed delegated legislation, the Subordinate Legislation Committee joins in by producing its own report.
- *Stage Three* involves the final consideration of the Bill by the full Parliament. Again, at this stage amendments can be made and debated. Parliament now decides whether the Bill, in its present form, should be *passed* and at least 25% of all MSPs must vote on this issue (whether 'for', 'against' or 'abstain'). After it has been passed, up to half of the sections of the Bill can be referred back for further Stage Two consideration, but when the Bill later returns to the full Parliament, further amendments are only allowed on the referred-back sections. At this final point Parliament decides whether or not to *approve* the Bill. Once a Bill has been passed and approved, it is submitted by the Presiding Officer to the Sovereign for the Royal Assent, whereupon it becomes an *Act of the Scottish Parliament.*

The Scottish Executive

The political party or parties with a working majority in the Scottish Parliament form the Scottish government (the *Scottish Executive*) in relation to all devolved matters. The MSPs select their nominee for the Queen to appoint as the *First Minister* (equivalent to the Prime Minister). The First Minister has responsibility for making recommendations to the Queen for the appointment of the *Scottish Ministers* and the two *Scottish Law Officers* (the Lord Advocate and Solicitor-General for Scotland). A more detailed description of the Scottish Executive *(www.scotland.gov.uk)* appears in *Appendix B.*

The powers and duties previously exercised by UK Ministers in Scotland in relation to devolved matters have been transferred to the Scottish Ministers. Given the existence of the matters reserved to Westminster, there are still three UK Ministers with specific Scottish responsibilities: the Secretary of State for Scotland, the Minister of State for Scotland and the Advocate General for Scotland.

Wales — the referenda

The arrangements for devolution in Wales are significantly different from (and less extensive than) those in Scotland. There is no devolved power to legislate or vary taxation. Instead, the devolution derives from a delegation of the Welsh Secretary's own administrative powers and duties.

Following its General Election manifesto commitment, the New Labour government published, in July 1997, a White Paper *A Voice for Wales* describing its proposals for devolution in Wales. There followed a referendum on 18 September 1997 and the people of Wales supported the proposals, although the result was hardly a resounding endorsement: turnout 50%, with just 50.3% voting in favour. Parliament then passed the Government of Wales Act 1998 which, coupled with the National Assembly for Wales (Transfer of Functions) Order 1999, provided the legal and constitutional basis for The *National Assembly for Wales* (Cynulliad Cenedlaethol Cymru), which met for the first time on 12 May 1999.

National Assembly for Wales — AMs

The Assembly *(www.wales.gov.uk)* is elected every four years and the first election took place on 6 May 1999. There are 60 *Assembly Members* (AMs) — 40 are elected for constituencies and 20 are elected on the basis of four for each of five regions. An individual AM can also, at the same time, be an MP, in which case the letters AM MP appear after their name — but as already suggested in the Scottish context, joint membership will soon cease to be a feature. As for the Scottish Parliament, each elector has two votes — one is used for electing a constituency member and the other is used for a regional list. The 1999 election results appear in *Appendix A* and, as for Scotland, illustrate the impact of the Additional Member system of proportional representation.

Welsh Assembly and Welsh Secretary

The *Secretary of State for Wales* (the Welsh Secretary) and the Welsh MPs still have seats at Westminster. Laws passed in Parliament still apply to Wales. What is different is that the powers and responsibilities of the Welsh Secretary were devolved by the 1999 Order to the National Assembly from 1 July 1999.

The rôle of the Welsh Secretary has changed somewhat as a consequence of the devolution process. The Welsh Secretary still looks after the interests of Wales within the UK Cabinet, steers legislation relating to Wales through Parliament, and has responsibility for making sure that devolution in Wales is working effectively by membership of a joint Ministerial Committee between the UK government and the devolved administrations.

In the context of Wales itself, the Welsh Secretary has the power to transfer the Welsh budget from the Treasury to the National Assembly, which can then determine its own spending priorities for that budget provision. The Welsh Secretary consults the Assembly on the UK government's legislative programme so far as it affects Wales and he can take part in the plenary sessions of the Assembly but he cannot vote.

Apart from determining budget priorities, the Assembly has power to develop and implement policies relevant to Wales in a wide range of policy subjects, in much the same way as Parliament and the Cabinet does for England. For example, the Assembly can fund, direct and make appointments to NHS bodies in Wales; administer EU Structural Funds made available for Wales; and can determine the content of the National Curriculum to be taught in Welsh schools.

Welsh Assembly in action

The *Presiding Officer*, elected by the members of the Assembly, chairs the Assembly and performs a politically neutral rôle analogous to that of the Speaker of the House of Commons. There is a Deputy Presiding Officer chosen in the same way.

The *executive* functions of the Assembly are carried out through the *First Minister* and a number of *Assembly Ministers* elected by the Assembly. The name 'Minister' superseded 'Secretary', which was used when the Assembly first came into existence. The Assembly delegates its responsibilities to the First Minister (usually drawn from the largest political party) and the First Minister, in turn, delegates those responsibilities to the Assembly Ministers.

The First Minister and the Assembly Ministers collectively form the *Assembly Cabinet* which takes the day-to-day decisions. The First Minister is responsible for ensuring that the Assembly Cabinet works effectively as a team and for maintaining collective responsibility. In addition, he has specific responsibility for constitutional matters, Europe and cross-cutting issues. The current (2002) portfolios of the Assembly Ministers are listed in *Appendix B*.

78

The Assembly meets in public in plenary sessions in Cardiff and the Presiding Officer arranges the conduct of the business through the *Business Secretary* and *Business Committee*. In each week in which the Assembly meets in plenary session, at least 15 minutes are set aside for oral questions of the First Minister. Within every four week period of plenary sessions, similar periods are set aside for oral questions of each Assembly Minister.

Once a week, before the conclusion of a plenary session, any member (but not an Assembly Minister) can propose a motion or topic for a short debate. Urgent matters of public importance can be raised if the Presiding Officer agrees.

Underpinning the Assembly in plenary session is a series of committees — *Subject Committees*, used for policy development and scrutiny, having a membership which reflects the overall political complexion of the Assembly; and *Regional Committees*, looking at local issues within each of the regions, having a membership drawn from the relevant electoral region and constituencies.

Northern Ireland — from the Anglo-Irish Agreement to the Framework Document

The search for a peaceful solution in Northern Ireland has been extremely complex and sensitive (the present fragile progress, while momentous, has yet to be consolidated) and what follows is the very briefest of summaries which includes only a selection of the major events. In the Northern Ireland context, every stage of the peace process, no matter how small or informal, is crucially important.

In November 1985 the UK and Irish governments signed the *Anglo-Irish Agreement* (the Hillsborough Agreement). Both governments recognised that any change in the status of Northern Ireland could come about only with the consent of the majority of the people there. The Agreement also endorsed the Westminster policy of seeking devolution in Northern Ireland on a basis that would secure widespread acceptance within the community.

The Anglo-Irish Agreement led to a series of talks between the two governments which eventually closed in November 1992 without formal agreement, but the talks themselves had provided a valuable foundation for what was to follow.

In December 1993 the UK Prime Minister, John Major, and the Éire Taoiseach, Albert Reynolds, issued a *Joint Declaration* from 10 Downing Street (the *Downing Street Declaration*) which set out the constitutional principles and the political realities which safeguarded the interests of both sides of the community in Northern Ireland. One of the key features of the Joint Declaration was that participation in future discussions about the way ahead would only be open to democratically mandated political parties which had established a commitment to exclusively peaceful methods.

On 31 August 1994 the IRA announced their "complete cessation of military operations" and on 13 October 1994, the Combined Loyalist Military Command announced their own ceasefire. Sporadic violent events have still occurred, but these ceasefires led to a variety of initiatives, including a marked reduction in the security arrangements in Northern Ireland. The ceasefires also enabled the Prime Minister and the Taoiseach to launch, in February 1995 in Belfast, *A New Framework Agreement,* a joint British and Irish government consultative document. Shortly afterwards, the UK government published *A Framework for Accountable Government in Northern Ireland* setting out its own consultative proposals for possible new democratic institutions in Northern Ireland.

Northern Ireland — from the Framework Document to the Good Friday Agreement
The IRA ceasefire effectively came to an end with the London Docklands bomb in February 1996 but even so some momentum for progress was maintained. Former US Senator George Mitchell was sent by President Clinton, at the invitation of the British and Irish governments, to assist in further negotiations and this resulted in the six 'Mitchell Principles'. The Northern Ireland Forum met for the first time in June 1996 but Sinn Féin were excluded until they agreed to be bound by the Mitchell Principles and restored their ceasefire. Even the explosion of an IRA bomb in Manchester city centre in June 1996 and a later IRA bomb at British Army Headquarters in Co Antrim did not completely derail the peace process, but Sinn Féin continued to be excluded from formal talks.

In July 1997, following the 1997 General Election, when Gerry Adams and Martin McGuinness, President and Vice-President of Sinn Féin, were elected as Westminster MPs, the IRA announced the renewal of its ceasefire and an international commission on decommissioning of arms was established under the chairmanship of a retired Canadian General, John de Chastelain. In September 1997 Sinn Féin signed up to the Mitchell Principles and multi-party talks started in earnest at Stormont. However, those talks made little progress and their venue was switched to Lancaster House in London to give them some impetus, but they later returned to Stormont. Senator George Mitchell, as independent chairman of the multi-party talks, then decided to issue his deadline for an agreement — 9 April 1998. A form of agreement was finally reached the day following the deadline after working through the night — on Good Friday 1998.

Northern Ireland — from the Good Friday Agreement to the Assembly
The production of the Good Friday Agreement was just the start — it still had to be signed. Whether the Agreement would become a reality depended on the outcome of two referenda — one in the Irish Republic, the other in Northern Ireland — and a 'yes' vote was by no means certain even though the two governments, British and Irish, were pushing hard for it.

Various building blocks were put in place in anticipation of a 'yes' vote — Westminster enacted the Northern Ireland (Elections) Act 1998 to provide for elections to an Assembly at Stormont; the Irish Parliament passed the 19th Amendment to the Irish Constitution, to enable the Irish claims to Northern Ireland to be formally abandoned at the appropriate time; and Sinn Féin changed its constitution to allow participation in the Northern Ireland Assembly elections.

In the final days before the referenda on 22 May 1998, Tony Blair produced his handwritten pledges to the people of Northern Ireland, and President Clinton sent a personal message to the people of Northern Ireland calling on them to vote 'yes'. There was a huge turnout on 22 May (Éire 81%; Northern Ireland 56%) — it was the first all-Ireland poll since the 1918 General Election. The result was a decisive 'yes': Éire 94%; Northern Ireland 71%. There could be no doubt about the wishes of the ordinary people of Ireland, north and south.

However, all was not yet plain sailing — the issue of decommissioning of terrorist arms threatened to stall the process at that stage (and in February 2000 resulted in the suspension of devolution). On 25 June 1998 the first elections for the Northern Ireland Assembly were held. The elections for the 108 seats were held using the Single Transferable Vote system of proportional representation, with six seats in each of the 18 Westminster constituencies. The results appear in *Appendix A*; the Ulster Unionist Party (UUP) gained the most seats (28), with the Social Democratic and Labour Party coming second (24). The notes on subsequent adjustments in *Appendix A* illustrate the fractured nature of Northern Ireland politics.

The new Northern Ireland Assembly met for the first time on 1 July 1998 — including representatives of those parties who had been opposed to the Good Friday Agreement. The Secretary of State for Northern Ireland, Mo Mowlam, appointed Lord Alderdice as the initial Presiding Officer of the Assembly. The Assembly elected David Trimble MP (then UUP Leader) as 'First Minister Designate' and Seamus Mallon MP (then Deputy Leader of the SDLP) as 'Deputy First Minister Designate'. The word 'Designate' indicated that more had yet to be done before a fully working power-sharing Executive could come into existence. The attempt at the next Assembly meeting to run the *d'Hondt* procedure (see the next section for an explanation of what this means) for the appointment of Ministers failed when the criteria were not met: the Ministers could only hold office if they included at least three designated Nationalists and three designated Unionists. The fundamental significance of this condition came to the fore again in February 2000, when the devolution arrangements were suspended.

Northern Ireland — from Assembly to Executive
Progress again began to stall but a single horrendous event probably proved to be a turning point, producing consequences not intended by the bombers — the Omagh

Bomb. On 15 August 1998, 29 people died as a result of a bomb exploded in Omagh by the 'Real IRA' (rIRA), a dissident splinter group who disagreed with the political direction of the Sinn Féin leadership. There was such shock and outrage at the Omagh Bomb that a number of paramilitary organisations felt obliged to declare ceasefires, including, eventually, the rIRA.

Both Westminster and, very significantly, the Irish Parliament passed emergency legislation to deal with terrorism. On 3 September 1998, President Clinton visited Northern Ireland to deliver his keynote address in Belfast, followed by speeches by Tony Blair, David Trimble and Seamus Mallon. Intense diplomatic activity, both formal and informal, continued over many months, with further interventions by Tony Blair, Taoiseach Bertie Ahern, and President Clinton.

During October and November 1999, Senator Mitchell returned from the US to chair negotiations to 'review' the Good Friday Agreement. Eventually, although it was 'touch and go' until the last minute, progress was made by pressing ahead with the new Executive in advance of actual arms decommissioning and by placing trust in good faith.

Once the breakthrough had been made, events moved very rapidly at the end of November 1999: on 29 November the Northern Ireland Assembly, under the chairmanship of Lord Alderdice as Presiding Officer, again triggered the d'Hondt procedure for the appointment of Ministers in the new power-sharing Executive (the first for 25 years) and, this time, 10 Ministers were successfully appointed, 601 days after the Good Friday Agreement.

The d'Hondt procedure (named after its inventor, the Belgian Victor d'Hondt) is an arithmetical 'largest average' formula used (for example in Austria, Belgium, Finland, and Switzerland) as a means of allocating places proportionately between parties. In the Northern Ireland context, the order of nominations was derived from applying divisors of 1, 2 and 3 to the number of seats held by each party and then ranking the results of the calculations in descending order. The party with the largest d'Hondt result made the first nomination (and choice of portfolio), followed by the party with the next highest result, and so on until all 10 seats had been filled. The Alliance Party with only six seats did not produce a sufficiently high d'Hondt result (even using a divisor of 1) to feature in the nomination process at all (try it for yourself!):

Party	Assembly	Executive	d'H order
Ulster Unionist Party (UUP)	28	3	1,5,8
Social Democratic and Labour Party (SDLP)	24	3	2,6,10
Democratic Unionist Party (DUP)	20	2	3,7
Sinn Féin (SF)	18	2	4,9

The 10 Ministers and their portfolios are listed in *Appendix B*. The first appointments process was interesting in several ways. The Republicans ended up with the portfolios

connected with education and health. In accepting Ian Paisley's DUP nomination for Minister of Regional Development, Peter Robinson (Deputy Leader of DUP), while expressing his opposition to the Agreement and a united Ireland, nonetheless added: *"The religious conviction or political opinion of any person or group will form no part of the judgment I will make on any matter. I shall work for everyone in the community, seeking for them a better deal. I consider myself to be the servant of all and the master of none".*

On 1 December 1999 Direct Rule came to an end when the House of Lords and the House of Commons approved, for the Queen's signature, the devolution order under the Northern Ireland Act 1998, transferring power from Westminster to the Assembly at Stormont. Peter Mandelson, the new Secretary of State, commented that he was pleased to be losing most of his powers so soon after coming into office.

On 2 December 1999:

- At 9.00am in Dublin, the Anglo-Irish Agreement was replaced by the *British-Irish Agreement*, bringing into formal existence the *North-South Ministerial Council* and the *British-Irish Ministerial Council* as envisaged in the Good Friday Agreement.
- At 9.20am the Irish Parliament replaced Articles 2 and 3 of the Irish Constitution, thus abandoning the Republic's claims to Northern Ireland.
- At 3.00pm the new Executive of the Northern Ireland Assembly met for the first time, although representatives of the DUP refused to attend.
- At 8.30pm the IRA declared that it would be appointing an anonymous 'interlocutor' to meet with General de Chastelain and the international decommissioning body.

Northern Ireland Assembly (MLAs) and Executive

Following the devolution of power to the New Northern Ireland Executive on 2 December 1999 under the terms of the British-Irish Agreement, the Secretary of State for Northern Ireland still retained responsibility for constitutional, financial and security issues relating to Northern Ireland — including international relations, defence, taxation, law and order, police and criminal justice policy. There was also a number of agencies retained within the Northern Ireland Office at Whitehall, including the Northern Ireland Prison Service, the Compensation Agency and the Forensic Agency of Northern Ireland. Apart from the reserved matters, full legislative and executive power was transferred to the Assembly.

Taxation was not devolved, so the Executive's Minister of Finance and Personnel would produce a budget for running Northern Ireland for approval by the Assembly, and the Secretary of State would then negotiate with the Treasury. The likely first budget for the Executive would have been in the region of £8.3bn, out of a total Northern Ireland budget of £9.9bn (including reserved matters).

Even these momentous events were just the beginning of the next stage. Much depended on what happened in the first few months of 2000. The issue of decommissioning still had the potential to derail the whole process. The price which David Trimble had to pay for the grudging endorsement of his party for the creation of the Executive was to hand over his postdated resignation, which would be used if there was no actual IRA progress to decommissioning by February 2000. However, its potential for disrupting the progress which had been made might have been sufficiently diminished if the mutual leap of faith taken in setting up the Executive could be shown to have been justified in other directions. As Pat Doherty (Vice-President of Sinn Féin) was reported to have said to the *Boston Herald: "Do you think that it is conceivable that, if the institutions are working and if the ceasefire is holding and that arms are not being used, that the whole thing would be collapsed? That would be just lunacy"*.

Northern Ireland — back and forth between Executive and Direct Rule

As it turned out, Pat Doherty's version of lunacy prevailed. By the Unionist deadline of February 2000, General de Chastelain was unable, initially, to report any convincing progress towards the physical decommissioning of illegally-held weapons and explosives by any of the terrorist organisations, although the main focus was on the IRA. Diplomatic activity to save the situation was, again, intense. Senator Mitchell expressed his reluctance to be called back, yet again, to 'review' the Good Friday Agreement. Sinn Féin stuck to a semantic view of the wording of the Good Friday Agreement and maintained that all that had been required of them was to use what influence they had over the IRA to start decommissioning arms; they also considered that the fact that the weapons were not being used ought to be enough, disregarding the widely-held view that illegally-held arms had no place in a free democracy.

Sinn Féin may have been strictly correct in maintaining their view of the precise wording of the Agreement but they misread the situation. Most of the ordinary people of Ireland and the UK had been expecting rather more — an actual start by the IRA in decommissioning its arms, once the devolved arrangements were in place and were working. The understandable mistake seems to have been that most people believed that Sinn Féin was the political arm of the IRA (and could speak for it) when, in fact, Sinn Féin demonstrably had insufficient influence over the terrorists when it really counted — Gerry Adams could not deliver. The Unionists felt that their 'leap of faith' had been betrayed — and it seemed inevitable that David Trimble would be expected by his party to implement his postdated resignation.

Meetings between the Irish Taoiseach, Bertie Ahern, and Sinn Féin, and between Bertie Ahern and Tony Blair failed to produce the required 'clarification', and the UK

Parliament passed the legislation required to suspend the devolution arrangements, as being the least harmful course of action. Despite last-minute statements by the IRA about their future intentions as reported by General de Chastelain, these were judged by the UK government as being too vague and too late. Suspension took place on 11 February 2000. 'Suspension' by the UK government was chosen to avoid the resignation of David Trimble as First Minister which would have had the effect of destroying the devolution arrangements altogether, because of the voting arrangements within the Assembly. The thinking was that at least something suspended could be brought out of suspension at some time in the future when circumstances had sufficiently improved.

So, the second attempt at power-sharing in Northern Ireland failed after just two months, in spite of the best endeavours of the UK and Irish governments and in the face of the clearly expressed democratic wish of the majority of the people of Ireland, both north and south of the border.

The suspension of the Assembly and the Executive, and the resumption of Direct Rule from Whitehall, lasted until 30 May 2000. What brought the suspension to an end was some movement on decommissioning and the willingness of the Ulster Unionist Party to allow David Trimble to re-enter the power-sharing Executive with Sinn Féin. In spite of this, the violence in Northern Ireland continued and during the first half of 2001, there was a series of bomb explosions in London.

Progress on decommissioning was too slow for the Unionists. To keep the peace process alive, there were political discussions involving Tony Blair and Bertie Ahern, both before and following the UK 2001 General Election. Bill Clinton also paid another visit, to reconfirm his faith in the peace process. All of this diplomatic effort failed to dissuade David Trimble from resigning as First Minister. His resignation had the effect of collapsing the power-sharing arrangement. At this point, there were two courses of action open to the UK government. One was to suspend the arrangements altogether and return to Direct Rule, as had happened in the previous year. The other was to take a chance and use the Assembly Rules to give a breathing space — these Rules allowed a six-week period in which a new First Minister and Deputy First Minister could be elected; otherwise new elections for the Assembly would have to be held. The problem with new elections was that the hard-line Unionists might do rather better than they had in the 1998 Assembly elections, so the second option was chosen and intensive diplomatic talks resumed at Weston Park in July.

It was time for the Good Friday Agreement to be reviewed anyway and the Western Park talks resulted in the UK and Irish governments publishing their joint Implementation Plan for the Good Friday Agreement. The governments gave the political parties the deadline of 6 August to respond to the Implementation Plan. At the deadline date, General de Chastelain announced that the International Commission on Decommissioning was satisfied by new methods proposed by the IRA, although the IRA changed its mind shortly afterwards. There were still some last-minute problems, so on 10 August the Northern Ireland Secretary suspended the Assembly for one day, which effectively started the six-week period running again.

In the event, the Assembly was restored on 11 August 2001 and the deadline for the election of the First Minister and Deputy First Minister became 22 September. The political parties were unable to agree, so it was necessary for the Northern Ireland Secretary to suspend the Assembly, yet again, for one day, to start the six week period again. The new deadline was 3 November 2001. At long last, at a rather difficult meeting of the Assembly on 6 November, David Trimble was re-elected as First Minister and Mark Durkan as Deputy First Minister, by a narrow majority amongst the Unionist members but with a unanimous vote from the Nationalists.

The stimulus for this might have been the events of 11 September 2001. In the context of those events, it was difficult to see any real distinction between the paramilitary organisations in Ireland (including the IRA) and the other terrorist organisations which were being vilified and pursued elsewhere in the world. On 22 October 2001, Gerry Adams asked the IRA to begin decommissioning and decommissioning started the following day.

At the time of writing (February 2002), the Northern Ireland Assembly and Executive are still working. Whether that remains the case can never be certain in the fragile political situation in Northern Ireland. The next Assembly elections will be a critical factor in determining the direction in which the power-sharing arrangements will move. To establish the current position, the websites of the Northern Ireland Office *(www.nio.gov.uk)*, the Northern Ireland Assembly *(www.ni-assembly.gov.uk)* and the Northern Ireland Executive *(www.nics.gov.uk)* should provide information. If the previous sections of this Chapter have not satisfied the quest for information about the political history of Northern Ireland, the website *www.cain.ulst.ac.uk* provides an up-to-date and exceptionally detailed chronology, year by year.

The English Regions

The extent of devolution in the other countries does not really justify the idea of similar arrangements in England — especially since all countries, even those with a measure of legislative devolution, remain part of the UK. Even so, the New Labour 1997 General Election Manifesto suggested that there would be legislation to allow referenda on elected regional government, but this has yet to happen. The government has since indicated that any referenda would be regional, rather than national and would only take place if there was sufficient interest within a particular region.

Equally, the enthusiasm within English local government (a very interested group) for some form of regional arrangement is mixed. The greatest interest appears to be in those regions where there is a significant presence of all-purpose unitary authorities. Those regions where there are few unitary authorities appear to be less interested in regional government.

What the ultimate form of English regional government will be remains unclear — is it true devolution down from central government or does it involve the removal of powers from the upper tier of local government? The developments to be considered are: the creation of Government Offices for the Regions; Regional Development Agencies; and Regional Chambers. The next logical progression is some form of directly elected forum in each Region — a White Paper is promised for mid 2002.

Government Offices for the Regions

There are nine Regional Offices, first established in 1994: North West; North East; Yorkshire and the Humber; West Midlands; East Midlands; East of England; South West; South East; London.

The Regional Offices provide a base for the regional activities of the: Home Office; Department for Culture, Media and Sport; Department for Environment, Food and Rural Affairs; Department for Education and Skills; Department of Trade and Industry; Department of Transport, Local Government and the Regions; and Department for Work and Pensions. Their activities are now co-ordinated by the Regional Co-ordination Unit within the Cabinet Office.

Regional Development Agencies

Regional Development Agencies (RDAs) were created in eight English regions on 1 April 1999 following a White Paper *Building Partnerships for Prosperity* and the Regional Development Agencies Act 1998. London's RDA was created on 1 April 2000. Each RDA has a Board of 13 members of whom four are drawn from relevant local authorities determined by the Secretary of State.

The RDAs are statutory organisations with responsibilities for promoting economic development and regeneration, business efficiency, employment, and development, especially sustainable development.

These purposes are achieved through a Regional Strategy (the first job of each RDA was to produce this) which would cover issues such as: regeneration; inward investment; matching skills with market needs (by means of a *Skills Action Plan*); and EU funding. The RDA is expected to cooperate closely with the relevant Government Office for the Region and the relevant local authorities, and to account for its actions through its regional *Chamber*. The RDA also had responsibility for the Single Regeneration Budget (SRB) from 1999-2001.

The RDAs outside London have adopted a variety of names: One NorthEast [sic];

North West Development Agency; Yorkshire Forward; Advantage West Midlands; east midlands development agency [sic]; East of England Development Agency; South West of England Regional Development Agency; and South East England Development Agency.

Regional Chambers

Regional Chambers are bodies which have been established in each of the eight regions outside London, building on any existing arrangements at regional level developed by local authorities for partnership working. They are recognised by the government as appropriate representatives to be consulted by the RDAs when drafting their Regional Strategy. The Chambers are not directly elected but are, instead, appointed by the Secretary of State, with 70% local authority representation and 30% representation of a variety of bodies such as the CBI, TUC and the Learning and Skills Councils.

The Chambers have, like the RDAs, adopted a variety of names, most of which include the rather grandiose word 'Assembly': North West Regional Assembly; North East Regional Assembly; Regional Chamber for Yorkshire and the Humber; West Midlands Regional Chamber; East Midlands Regional Assembly; East of England Regional Assembly; South East of England Regional Assembly; and South West Regional Assembly.

6   The UK Government

The Prime Minister — the Cabinet — Ministers — government departments — the Civil Service

The UK government

Her Majesty's government *(www.ukonline.gov.uk)* is the Prime Minister and a group of Ministers who are collectively responsible for managing the national affairs of the UK in the name of the Sovereign. Devolved governmental arrangements in Scotland, Wales and Northern Ireland are described in the previous Chapter.

The composition of the government will vary from time to time, in terms of the number of Ministers and their titles. New Ministerial offices can come into existence and existing ones disappear; and functions can be shuffled around between Ministers by the Prime Minister. The latest example of this happened immediately after the 2001 General Election *(see Appendix B)*.

Ministers may have responsibilities for a particular government department or may hold one of the more formal non-departmental offices with few responsibilities, so that they can then concentrate on other specific areas of activity in support of the government.

Ministers have been appointed from amongst the people sitting in Parliament for some time. It suited the Sovereign for his or her Ministers to be in Parliament so that they could exert influence for him or her over Parliament. The arrangement also suited Parliament because the Ministers could more easily be held to account for their actions if they were sitting in Parliament.

This practice has now become a convention and, furthermore, the convention has evolved so that it is generally the case that Ministers are drawn from the Commons. This makes the Commons more powerful, in that it is the main route to Ministerial office. The fact that Ministers remain MPs means that they are readily accessible to and can be waylaid by the backbench MPs in the Commons, and they retain an affinity with backbenchers since, even as Ministers, they still retain their constituency responsibilities.

The convention is also that Ministers will remain in post only if they remain in Parliament. If a Minister ceases to be an MP, they will usually lose office, unless special arrangements are made to preserve their position — either by elevation to the House of Lords or arranging for the vacation of a safe seat to which they can be quickly re-elected.

Not more than 95 holders of Ministerial office are entitled to sit and vote in the Commons at any one time, presumably as a safeguard to preserve a sensible balance between the Executive and backbench MPs.

There will usually be several Ministers drawn from members of the Lords, even though its legislative powers have been reduced. The reason for this is that it suits the government to have someone in that House able to muster support for it when it matters and to answer questions on its behalf there.

Some of the Ministers will be members of the Cabinet. However, it is sometimes the case that there is a small group of advisers around the Prime Minister who are not always members of the Cabinet and may not even be Ministers. Such a group can have a significant influence on the development of government policy. These people are often referred to as the *'Kitchen Cabinet'* — a term first used in America during President Andrew Jackson's administration in 1830 to describe that kind of arrangement — and used in the UK context of Harold Wilson's premiership.

The Prime Minister

The Cabinet was originally chaired by the Sovereign. However, that changed when the Elector of Hanover came to Britain, to become George I. He could speak little or no English and was not particularly interested in politics. So, the job of chairing the Cabinet was given to the *First Lord of the Treasury*, Sir Robert Walpole. Walpole took advantage of this to become the most important of the Sovereign's Ministers — the prime or first Minister — during the 1721-24 government. The office of Prime Minister is generally regarded as starting at that period.

These days, the Sovereign appoints as Prime Minister the MP sitting in the Commons who leads the party with a majority of seats there. It is this political support in the Commons, together with the power to recommend the Sovereign to appoint and dismiss Ministers, which provides the basis of the Prime Minister's own authority.

The Prime Minister is, by tradition, *First Lord of the Treasury* and *Minister for the Civil Service*. The formal office of Prime Minister is unpaid; it is the other offices which produce the Prime Minister's salary. The Prime Minister is able to wield significant power and influence through chairing and controlling the meetings of the Cabinet and setting the agenda for meetings of the Cabinet and its committees.

The phrase *'primus inter pares'* (first amongst equals) is used in some textbooks to describe the nature of the Prime Minister's relationship with the other Ministers. In practice, that theoretical definition has to be considered in the light of the personal character and determination of the particular occupant of the office — which can result in various styles of leadership, ranging from a consensus style to one which is more directive or even 'Presidential', which is discussed later.

The Prime Minister's Office is at 10 Downing Street which is also usually his or her official residence in London and the base for the Cabinet Office. In Tony Blair's case, because of the size of his young family, 11 Downing Street is used as the domestic residence — with the agreement of the Chancellor of the Exchequer. There is a house in the country — Chequers — which is also available to the Prime Minister.

In addition to the Cabinet Office, the Prime Minister also has a Private Office in which is based the Prime Minister's Principal Private Secretary and a group of civil servants. Depending upon the character of the individual concerned, some members of the Private Office can become prominent in the public eye — for example, Sir Bernard Ingham, Margaret Thatcher's Press Secretary and Tony Blair's Press Secretary, Alistair Campbell.

The rôle of the Prime Minister

The most important functions of the Prime Minister *(www.number-10.gov.uk)* are to: chair meetings of the Cabinet; appoint and allocate work to Cabinet committees; oversee the work of the government; and allocate functions to Ministers. He or she also keeps the Sovereign informed of government business conducted in the Sovereign's name, during a weekly audience with the Sovereign. The Prime Minister is also Minister for the Civil Service.

There are other responsibilities of the Prime Minister in relation to appointments — including recommending whom the Sovereign should appoint as: Church of England archbishops, bishops and deans; senior judges, including the Lord Chief Justice; Privy Councillors; lords-lieutenant; and Poet Laureate and Constable of the Tower. There are also appointments to many public corporations (such as the BBC) which are made on the recommendation of the Prime Minister.

As explained in previous chapters, the Prime Minister also makes recommendations to the Sovereign for the conferment of most honours and peerages.

Constraints on the Prime Minister

The sources of the Prime Minister's authority mentioned above are also the sources of the constraints upon him or her. Even if the Prime Minister appears to be a strong personality, he or she is still not necessarily able to follow personal whim in a way which does not command support — or not for very long.

One of the bases of the Prime Minister's position is as the Leader of the party which has a majority of members in the House of Commons — members who can be expected to vote for the government's proposals. It follows that the individual can no longer continue as Prime Minister if the Parliamentary party decides that it would like a new Leader or if the backbench members are not prepared to vote consistently in support of the government in the Commons.

The Prime Minister needs to pay continual attention to maintaining a proper dialogue with the backbenchers in order to be confident of their continued support — even if the Parliamentary majority is significant. It becomes even more crucial if that majority is slim. So, a sensible Prime Minister will take pains to keep the 1922 Committee or the Parliamentary Labour Party (as the case may be) fully informed and will be prepared to take into account their views. *Prime Minister's Question Time* is, perhaps, a more tangible example of a constraint upon the Prime Minister by back-benchers in the Commons itself.

The other basis of the Prime Minister's authority is the ability to recommend the appointment and require the resignation of Ministers. The government will work effectively only if the Ministers maintain their collective responsibility and pull in the same direction. The breadth of modern government is too great for the Prime Minister to do it all, so he or she has to rely upon the contributions from Ministers.

Any group of Ministers will contain a range of personalities, some strong, who will have their own responsibilities to protect and may have their own personal agenda. It makes sense for a Prime Minister to have a Cabinet which reflects the range of ideological ideas amongst the senior MPs. Apart from improving the quality of the decision-making at Cabinet level (and improving the chances of backbench support for Cabinet decisions), this also can have the advantage of stifling dissent by fixing the people concerned with the convention of collective responsibility, although this does not always work in practice!

If the support of Ministers for the Prime Minister starts to weaken, then that will soon become evident (they may leak it themselves) and raise question marks about the future of the Prime Minister. In other words, there will come a point when the maxim *primus inter pares* really does count for something after all, regardless of the Prime Minister's own strength of character. Once uncertainties about continued support for the Prime Minister arise amongst the Ministers, those uncertainties can rapidly be brought to the notice of the backbenchers and will tend to accelerate the momentum for change.

The fate of Margaret Thatcher is a case in point which illustrates both of these constraints in action. It became widely known that she had begun to ride roughshod over Cabinet decisions, making up her own policy as she went along, and this was not liked. This aspect of her leadership style came in for particular criticism from Sir Geoffrey Howe in his resignation speech to the Commons in November 1990 (see the later section on *Cabinet government — modern political reality*), which is generally regarded as dealing a fatal blow to Margaret Thatcher as Prime Minister.

In the subsequent fight for the leadership of the Conservative Party — which she lost — many of her Cabinet colleagues had told her privately that they thought that she would lose the second ballot — an indication of their loss of confidence in her. In addition, many in the Parliamentary party believed that they would lose the next General Election if she remained the party Leader. She was forced to vacate 10 Downing Street, clearly bitterly disappointed, in favour of her successor John Major.

A later section, *Cabinet government — modern political reality*, discusses how the modern style of Premiership can sit rather uneasily with the concepts of *primus inter pares* and *Collective Responsibility*.

Secretaries and Ministers

There are various kinds of Minister in the government. After the Prime Minister, the most senior are the *Secretaries of State* — or to give them their proper title, Her Majesty's *Principal Secretaries of State*. Constitutionally, Secretaries of State are regarded as the channel of communication between the Sovereign and the people and, by convention, the more important of them are appointed at a meeting of the Privy Council, where they signify their acceptance of office by kissing the Sovereign's hand.

Secretaries of State have responsibility for the major government departments and are always members of the Cabinet. Secretaries of State are usually called *'Secretary of State'*, or *'Secretary'*, but some have other titles — *The Chancellor of the Exchequer* or *President of the Board of Trade* (aka Secretary of State for Trade and Industry), for example.

The next most senior type of Minister is *Minister of State*. A Minister of State is a Minister who does not have responsibility for a government department. However, such a Minister is often found in the larger departments, supporting the relevant Secretary of State and even taking responsibility for supervising a part of the department's work.

A Minister of State is not usually (but can be) a member of the Cabinet. Again, some Ministers of State have special titles — *[Lord] President of the Council, the Chancellor of the Duchy of Lancaster, the Lord Privy Seal* and *the Paymaster General* are the usual examples. Occasionally, there will be a Minister of State called *Minister without Portfolio* — in other words, a Minister who, unlike the others, has been given no portfolio of responsibilities.

The purpose of those Ministers of State who are not based in a government department is to undertake other work for the government given to them by the Prime

Minister. They can sometimes be much more influential than their title suggests. For example, Peter Mandelson (then popularly referred to as the Labour Party's 'Spin Doctor') was appointed by Tony Blair as Minister without Portfolio *"to assist in the strategic implementation of government policies and their effective presentation to the public"*. Although he was not a member of the Cabinet, he sat on all of its committees and was attached to the Cabinet Office liaising with the Downing Street Policy Unit. That is, until he was forced to resign and enter (temporarily) the political wilderness following the disclosure of his unorthodox £375,000 home loan from Geoffrey Robinson.

The lowest level of Minister is usually referred to as a *Junior Minister*, although they can still often have the title of 'Minister', with or without a further description in brackets to explain their responsibilities — all very confusing! Such Ministers are appointed to assist the more senior Ministers in their departmental work and are not members of the Cabinet. Their proper title depends upon the status of the departmental Minister whose work they support. If the senior Minister in the department is a Secretary of State, then the Junior Minister will be a *Parliamentary Under-Secretary of State*. If, however, the senior Minister they assist is not a Secretary of State, then the junior Minister is called *Parliamentary Secretary* and is likely to have a mix of Parliamentary and departmental duties. The description of Ministers and departments (of different sizes and importance) in *Appendix B* explains how all of this works in practice. Ministers of all kinds are expected to comply with the Ministerial Code.

To complete the picture, mention should be made here of *Parliamentary Private Secretaries* — even though they are not Secretaries or Ministers in any of the senses used so far in this section. These are MPs who are appointed, with no additional salary, to support the political work of a Minister in his or her Parliamentary liaison with other backbench MPs. Presumably the people concerned are prepared to take on these responsibilities as the first rung on the ladder to Ministerial office. They should not be confused with the Minister's *Private Secretary,* who is a civil servant provided to support the work of the Minister as a Minister of the Crown.

Deputy Prime Minister

The title *First Secretary and Deputy Prime Minister* is a fairly recent one (created July 1995) and, in a way, is slightly at odds with the concept of *primus inter pares*. What was novel was the 'First Secretary' part of the title — there had been 'Deputy Prime Ministers' before — George Brown was one notable example. What was intended by having a 'First Secretary' in relation to a Prime Minister was never clearly understood and the title is hardly ever referred to. The title was abandoned when New Labour came to power in 1997, but it has since been resurrected to describe John Prescott's title after the 2001 reshuffle — 'Deputy Prime Minister and First Secretary of State'.

As far as a 'Deputy Prime Minister' is concerned, the relationship between that office and the other Ministers is also difficult to describe. Commentators often speculate upon the reason why the Prime Minister felt it necessary to concede that kind of power to the individual — consolation prize in a party leadership election, perhaps?

The Deputy Prime Minister is likely to have wide-ranging responsibilities simply because the job is ill-defined, but the precise rôle will probably depend upon the interests of the person concerned and their inclination to involve themselves in the work of the other Ministers.

The first occupant of the office of First Secretary and Deputy Prime Minister was Michael Heseltine and some commentators suggested that the creation of the post had a lot to do with the fight for the leadership of the Conservative Party and with the need to keep that party together thereafter. Apart from any general responsibilities (similar to those allocated by Tony Blair to Peter Mandelson, during his time as Minister without Portfolio), Michael Heseltine's interests lay in Trade and Industry — reflecting his former position as *President of the Board of Trade* — a title which he had revived for the office which had in recent years been called the *Secretary of State for Trade and Industry.*

The office of Deputy Prime Minister survived the 1997 General Election, occupied by John Prescott (described by the *Guardian* as the *'Minister for Everything'*). However, the rôle of the office then seems to have changed, since it was combined with Environmental issues — John Prescott's formal title was *Deputy Prime Minister and Secretary of State for the Environment, Transport and the Regions.* This creation of a 'Superministry' under the Deputy Prime Minister did not turn out as well as expected. At the end of 1999, there seems to have been widespread speculation about the effectiveness of John Prescott's personal performance, especially in relation to solving the nation's transport problems. The public's perception of John Prescott's commitment to promoting public transport could not have been improved when he acquired the soubriquet 'Two Jags'. The then DETR Minister of State, Lord (Gus) MacDonald, was given prime responsibility for transport, a development widely interpreted by commentators as a signal that John Prescott's job would not survive the next General Election and might even have ended before then.

The commentators were, however, confounded. John Prescott survived the 2001 reshuffle, to be brought within the 'Prime Minister's Department' *(see Appendix B)*, to oversee the work of the Regional Co-ordination Unit, the Government Offices for the Regions and the Social Exclusion Unit.

Cabinet government — political theory

The Cabinet, on average, comprises about 20 Ministers selected by the Prime Minister and occupies a central position in the political system. The size of peacetime

Cabinets in the 20th century has ranged from 16 (Bonar Law 1922) to 24 (Wilson 1964). The Blair 1999 Cabinet consisted of 22 people; the Blair 2001 Cabinet, 23 people.

In theory, the rôle of the Cabinet is to:

- initiate and decide upon the government's policy;
- control the government; and
- co-ordinate the government departments.

In other words, the Cabinet is the place where major decisions on policy are to be made or, more likely, proposals from its committees are to be ratified and where conflicts between government departments are to be resolved. Whether, in the most recent years of Tony Blair's Premiership, this can still be said to be the case, is discussed in the section *Cabinet government — modern political reality*.

The Cabinet meets on Thursday each week while Parliament is in session and at other times if the Prime Minister so wishes.

Votes have rarely been taken in the Cabinet — to preserve the concept of Cabinet collective responsibility, the Prime Minister sums up his or her view of the conclusion of a discussion and this then becomes the view of the Cabinet, recorded as such in the minutes. Just as the Cabinet meetings are secret, so are the minutes, although they may become eligible for later publication as public records under the 30 year rule. In spite of that, insights into the processes within the Cabinet, sometimes quite detailed, can often be gained from the published diaries of ex-Cabinet Ministers.

Cabinet government does have its critics: Ministers are often generalists, or are appointed to offices for which they have little previous experience (Jack Cunningham's appointment as Minister for Agriculture, Fisheries and Food by Tony Blair is a recent example).

Shuffling Ministers between jobs is also viewed as a mixed blessing. Some people believe that it can take a Minister about two years to understand their job fully; on the other hand, others argue that moving Ministers around stops them from 'going native'.

Finally, Ministers are often so overloaded with their departmental responsibilities that they cannot afford the time to consider, properly, any of the wider topics which come up from the Cabinet committees for Cabinet approval.

Strictly speaking, the Cabinet, in its executive rôle, is deciding what advice to give the Sovereign in the government of the country. The convention is that the advice is *always unanimous* — in other words, every member of the Cabinet is expected to support a collective Cabinet decision even if he or she disagrees with it. Any differences of opinion are to be kept secret within the Cabinet itself. If the Minister refuses to accept or later opposes the Cabinet decision, he or she is expected to resign. An example of this occurred in 1985 when Michael Heseltine resigned from Margaret Thatcher's Cabinet because he disagreed with the decision to back the sale of the Westland Helicopters company to the US Sikorski company — Michael Heseltine favoured an Italian consortium as the means of helping Westland out of its difficulties, but he was not supported by his Cabinet colleagues.

In recent years the convention has been extended to all Junior Ministers, and even to the unpaid and unofficial Parliamentary Private Secretaries, even though none of them is a member of the Cabinet. That is the theoretical position on what is termed *Collective Responsibility*.

Cabinet government — modern political reality

In reality, the modern implementation of collegiate Cabinet government is somewhat different. It is worth considering how Cabinet government has developed during the latter part of the 20th century, and especially since the arrival of a New Labour government. It may well be that the changes are inevitable in a modern world where Her Majesty's government is expected to respond promptly and appropriately to the external pressures imposed on it. The changes do, however, enable some commentators to raise the issue of whether Tony Blair's style of Premiership is becoming ever more 'Presidential'.

Before considering the present-day approach of Tony Blair, it is worth looking briefly at how his predecessors worked with their Cabinets.

In whatever light the Prime Minister might regard his or her Cabinet, he or she should take care to keep them informed of what he or she is doing. Anthony Eden made that mistake in 1956 when he made a secret alliance with France and Israel to invade Egypt to regain possession of the Suez Canal, when it had been nationalised by President Nasser. He did not inform his Cabinet about this beforehand and later paid the price for that omission when he had to resign on being forced to withdraw from Suez.

Harold Wilson was a flexible and very shrewd operator. He has been described as the 'player manager' of his Cabinet. In pre-New Labour days, the Labour Party had significantly opposing points of view within it, and Harold Wilson took care that those opposites were represented in his Cabinet. Cabinet meetings saw wide-ranging discussions. In 1975, one of the critical issues facing the Cabinet was the referendum on the UK remaining in the European Community. The Cabinet was split down the middle and Harold Wilson allowed members of his Cabinet to break the *Collective Responsibility* approach and campaign on opposing sides. This was unprecedented, but it meant that there was no need to sack dissenting Ministers and that the issue of Europe would not break up the UK government.

James Callaghan's big problem was the UK economic crisis (inflation hit an annual rate of 28%) and it was necessary for the International Monetary Fund (IMF) to give a loan to save the UK economy. As before, the Labour Cabinet was deeply divided. Callaghan's approach was to hold a series of Cabinet meetings over a two-week period.

Ministers were encouraged to make their own written submissions which were then subjected to questions and debate within the Cabinet. The result was that the IMF loan was approved and no Ministers felt it necessary to resign — a good example of the benefits of a true collegiate approach.

Margaret Thatcher's approach has already been touched upon in the earlier section on *Constraints on the Prime Minister*. She preferred the Cabinet to follow her lead and did not encourage dissenting views; she tended to pre-empt discussions by making her own statement first, taking the view that the Prime Minister should lead. During the Falklands War, the style of the War Cabinet appeared to be more collegiate. However, Margaret Thatcher's style then reverted to being dominant and this led to increasing disenchantment within her Cabinet. Michael Heseltine resigned as a Minister — the resignation was remarkable because it was the first time in over 100 years that a Minister had resigned while the Cabinet meeting was in progress. Other resignations followed later.

Margaret Thatcher had a tendency to depart from Cabinet decisions, especially on Europe, as explained by Sir Geoffrey Howe in his resignation speech: *"The task has become futile... of trying to pretend there was a common policy when every step forward risked being subverted by some casual comment or impulsive answer* [by Mrs Thatcher]".

In reaction to the authoritarian Thatcher style, John Major went in the opposite direction. As it happened, John Major's Cabinet was all male and was known as the 'Cabinet of Chums'. Cabinet meetings were longer, as all views were canvassed in the new consensual approach. However, this approach started to break down when some Eurosceptics joined the Cabinet. The meetings became more divisive, as became widely known due to the 'leaking' which took place, and John Major became increasingly beleaguered. Although one Minister was sacked, the leaking continued and John Major issued his 'put up or shut up' ultimatum. He resigned as Leader and although he narrowly survived John Redwood's challenge to his continued leadership, his days were numbered.

Tony Blair's approach, under New Labour, is different again. Of the present (post 2001 General Election) Cabinet, nearly one-third are women. The Prime Minister's approach is that a Cabinet of 23 members is too large to function effectively — there is some merit in that point. Instead, the more sensitive issues tend to be dealt with outside Cabinet meetings — in Cabinet committees or in small groups, often on a bilateral basis between Tony Blair and the relevant Minister. There is nothing especially new in this, since all of his predecessors worked in this way to some extent — the difference is that Tony Blair has gone much further down this road.

Despite speculation about their personal working relationship, one group is the Prime Minister and the Chancellor of the Exchequer. The best example of this occurred on the day following New Labour's 1997 General Election victory. Gordon

Brown announced that, in future, interest rates would not be a political decision but would, instead, be decided by the Monetary Policy Committee of the Bank of England. There had been no prior discussion of this in the Cabinet; they were told about it after the media.

The nature of Blair Cabinet meetings is different. They are much shorter (often only about 30 minutes) because they are more in the way of briefing meetings, a reporting exercise the purpose of which is to bring the Cabinet 'up-to-speed' on what has happened and what is planned to happen in the following week. There are no problems about the leaking of Cabinet discussions, because the Prime Minister' Press Secretary (who attends Cabinet meetings) briefs the media almost immediately on what took place at the meeting. No votes are taken at Cabinet meetings — again, nothing necessarily new in that. Instead, the approach seems to be that Tony Blair uses the Cabinet meeting to hear what his colleagues have to say and then he makes up his own mind, which may or may not be consistent which the majority view of the Cabinet. An example of this was whether or not New Labour should proceed with the Dome project; the majority of the Cabinet was reportedly unhappy about this, but Tony Blair was at the Dome site a few hours later, expressing the government's support for the project. Collective discussion and debate about political strategy is more likely to occur at occasional 'Away Days' held at Chequers.

Tony Blair's view of the rôle of the Prime Minister is to deliver the government — in much the same way as he delivered New Labour. As *Appendix B* shows, there has been a steady accretion of power by the centre, especially at Number 10. The Prime Minister's closest advisers are not elected and there are more of them — with White House style titles such as 'Chief of Staff', 'Head of Government Relations', and 'Director of Communications'. In some ways, these can be regarded as the modern version of Harold Wilson's 'Kitchen Cabinet' mentioned earlier.

The New Labour government appears to be more concerned than its predecessors on central control and ensuring that, even with a large majority in Parliament, MPs and others stay 'on message'. A good illustration of this is the apparent involvement of Tony Blair and his office in changing the arrangements for selecting the Labour candidate for Mayor of London, with the clear intention of favouring Frank Dobson over Ken Livingstone — in this respect, he failed. Two other illustrations occurred within a few days of each other in January 2000: the announcement by Tony Blair of extra resources for the NHS during the flu epidemic, without any apparent prior discussion with Cabinet colleagues; and his decision to authorise the export of spares for Hawk jet fighters to Zimbabwe for use in a war in a neighbouring state, the Congo — effectively driving a coach and horses through Robin Cooke's ethical foreign policy.

This new style of Premiership may be the right one to adopt in today's age, where the media seems to be just as much interested in personalities as they are in policies.

Media preoccupation with personality is, again, not entirely new. The policies of the Conservative government under Mrs Thatcher were called 'Thatcherite'; supporters of New Labour, for whom conservatism (with a small 'c') was anathema, were called 'Blairites'; the term 'Majorite' never seems to have been used of anything!

The label increasingly applied to this style is 'Presidential'. This view may be over-simplistic in the UK context, but it is not discouraged by Tony Blair's increasing personal profile, especially on the international scene after the events of 11 September 2001. Number 10 also developed its own website *(www.number-10.gov.uk)*, not to be confused with the Cabinet Office website *(www.cabinet-office.gov.uk)*. Tony Blair indicated his intention to 'broadcast' to the Nation once each week via the Number 10 website; Bill Clinton only thought it necessary to contact the people of the US about once a month.

The amount of media attention enjoyed by Tony Blair is greater than that experienced by his predecessors in office, by other members of his own government and by the prominent members of both Opposition parties. Although the content of much of that media attention is influenced by briefing by special advisers, occasionally things do not turn out as Tony Blair would wish. He had a very uncomfortable (and well publicised) experience at the 2000 WI Annual Conference at Wembley when he gave what was regarded by his audience as a party political speech — those advising him in preparing for the event had missed the fact that one of the main tenets of the WI is that it is non-party political. He was more than a little embarrassed when he was heckled and given a slow handclap.

Perhaps the preoccupation with personality started in earnest during Margaret Thatcher's term, derived from her strength of character — *"This lady's not for turning"* — but her particular style was ultimately her undoing. Tony Blair's style is certainly less authoritarian than Margaret Thatcher's and the remainder of his Cabinet colleagues appear to be prepared to go along with it. In that sense, it would be interesting to speculate on whether *primus inter pares* still holds good.

Cabinet Office

The Cabinet Office *(www.cabinet-office.gov.uk)* consists of the Cabinet Secretariat and the Office of Public Service. The practice of keeping minutes of Cabinet decisions was introduced in 1916 by Lloyd George — and this led to the system which exists today — the Cabinet Secretariat. The Cabinet Secretary is also the Head of the Home Civil Service (reflecting one of Prime Minister's paid offices: Minister for the Civil Service). There was speculation that the two rôles might be split when Sir Robin Butler retired. However, the present Cabinet Secretary, Sir Richard Wilson, has retained the dual responsibilities.

The importance of the Cabinet Office has grown considerably since the New Labour government came into office and driven largely by proposals in the recent White

Paper on *Modernising Government*. The Cabinet Secretariat is made up of six individual secretariats: the Economic and Domestic Affairs Secretariat; the Defence and Overseas Affairs Secretariat; the European Secretariat; the Constitution Secretariat; the Central Secretariat; and Intelligence Support Secretariat.

Cabinet committees

The complexity of modern government has led, inevitably, to overload on members of the Cabinet or to issues requiring more detailed consideration than can be accommodated at Cabinet meetings. A partial solution to the problem is the Cabinet committees, which are also bound by secrecy and are supported by the Cabinet Secretariat. There are three general types: standing, ad hoc or Ministerial.

Standing committees are permanent and appointed for the duration of the Premiership; *ad hoc committees* exist to look at specific issues and are disbanded when their job is done; and *Ministerial committees*, rather confusingly, consist only of civil servants.

Cabinet committees can be a particularly effective tool by which the Prime Minister is able to control how an issue reaches the full Cabinet — and any recommendations attached to it. The people appointed to the committees are carefully chosen

Ministerial Responsibility

As already explained, Ministers can have departmental responsibilities. There is a convention, known as *Ministerial Responsibility,* which requires a Minister to accept responsibility to Parliament for his or her own personal conduct; the general conduct of the department for which he or she has responsibility; and the policy-related actions or omissions of his or her civil servants. The theory is that if a serious event of that kind occurs, then the expectation is that the Minister concerned will resign.

Again, in reality, matters can be different. More often than not, the decision on whether or not a particular Minister has to go will be taken by the Prime Minister. The Prime Minister may decide that the interests of the Party require the Minister to brazen it out, at least for a time — although in recent years with the increasing sensitivity to 'sleaze', the interests of the Party now dictate a rapid departure. The best recent example of a Minister doing the 'decent thing' was Lord Carrington when he resigned (together with two other Ministers) as Foreign Secretary when Argentina invaded the Falklands — some might argue that the event was so serious that the Prime Minister herself should have resigned.

However, there have been other examples where a Minister has not resigned when most people considered that resignation was amply justified — instead, pragmatism had become the more important consideration. The best example of this was Norman Lamont who defended the UK's membership of the Exchange Rate Mechanism (ERM), only for the UK to be forced to withdraw in September 1992 after a disastrous run on the Pound, on 'Black Wednesday', which threatened a melt-down in the UK economy. By any objective standard, Mr Lamont should have resigned immediately from the Treasury — but he didn't, presumably because this would have reflected badly on the quality of Mrs Thatcher's government. He was, however, fired some time later and, like Sir Geoffery Howe, used his 'resignation' speech to criticise Mrs Thatcher's style of leadership.

The advent of the semi-independent (but still departmental) Agencies within government departments has muddied the waters even more. Some cynics would say that the Agencies now provide a Minister with the ideal situation: the Minister can still play an influential part, unofficially, in the direction of the Agency and yet avoid responsibility when things go wrong, by claiming that the fault was an administrative or 'operational' one by the Agency, rather than a policy fault for which he or she should take responsibility.

Some would say that such a distinction is not envisaged by the convention of Ministerial Responsibility; others would argue that it is now unrealistic to expect a Minister to take responsibility for literally everything which happens in the department or any of its executive agencies. An example of this is the catalogue of serious shortcomings in the Prison Service which resulted in the eventual dismissal of Derek Lewis as the Director-General of the Prison Service (for which he won £220,000 damages for wrongful dismissal in the settlement of his High Court action against the Home Secretary). Many people felt at the time that Michael Howard should have resigned as Home Secretary under the convention of Ministerial Responsibility — but he didn't, arguing that he did not interfere in the running of the Prison Service and that the faults were 'operational' and not his responsibility.

Ann Widdicombe's May 1997 speech to the Commons about Michael Howard has already been mentioned (see the section on *Backbenchers* in a previous Chapter). Her comments included: *"We demean our high office if we mistreat our public servants. We demean ourselves if we come to this House and indulge in a play of words which... may be unsustainable"*.

Some commentators would now argue, with some justification, that resignation in accordance with the convention of Ministerial Responsibility has to all intents and purposes disappeared — or will only be honoured if the shortcoming can be shown to have been the direct personal responsibility of the Minister concerned.

Government departments

The day-to-day work of government is done not by Ministers but by government departments, staffed by civil servants, under Ministerial supervision. In other words, government is actually delivered by civil servants (as permanent managers of their departments) rather than by Ministers (temporary politicians in titular charge of a department). Government departments are accountable to Parliament through their supervising Secretary of State or Minister.

One of the most striking features of UK government is that although a complete change of government is more or less instantaneous after a General Election, the actual day-to-day work of government seems to go on without much interruption. This can be due to the Shadow Cabinet arrangement in which the members of the new government are able to gain experience of the work of government and build up links with the senior staff of the Civil Service.

However, the ease with which the transition from one government to another takes place is largely due to the existence of the Civil Service, the staff of which are unaffected by a change in government in managing the delivery of government services. The similar transition of power in the USA is altogether more lengthy and traumatic. However, there may be straws in the wind suggesting a change in approach here — see the later section *Civil servants — non-political?*

'Whitehall' is the term usually applied to the government departments as a whole, but it is more properly applied to the central departments, the Great Offices of State: the Foreign and Commonwealth Office; the Home Office; and Her Majesty's Treasury.

There are others which still retain the word 'Office' in their title: the Northern Ireland, Scotland and Wales Offices. Others still preserve the word 'Ministry' in their titles: the Ministry of Defence.

The remainder usually have the word 'department' in their title: Department of Health, for example. Over time, the name of a department can change as its functions change: for example the Department of Education and Science (DES) became the Department for Education (DfE) then the Department for Education and Employment (DfEE), and is now the Department for Education and Skills (DfES).

Some departments, like the Ministry of Defence, cover the whole of the UK. Others, such as the Department for Work and Pensions, cover the UK, with the exception of Northern Ireland. The Department for Environment, Food and Rural Affairs is primarily concerned with England. These specific examples are still true following devolution — Scotland, Wales and Northern Ireland have devolved responsibilities for government which affect the other departments.

In England, many departments have some sort of regional presence. The *Government Offices for the Regions* look after the regional programmes of the Home Office; Department for Culture, Media and Sport; Department for Environment, Food and Rural Affairs; Department for Education and Skills; Department of Trade and Industry; Department of Transport, Local Government and the Regions; and Department for Work and Pensions.

Departments are usually headed by Ministers, but some can be headed by civil servants who are accountable to Parliament through a designated Minister — for example, the Ministers in the Treasury are responsible for the Inland Revenue, HM Customs and Excise and a number of other departments and agencies.

A list of current (2002) government departments and the more significant of their related agencies is set out in *Appendix B*.

Charter Mark and 'joined-up' government

The start in improving the delivery and responsiveness of public services was made by John Major when he introduced his *Citizen's Charter* in 1991. The purpose of this initiative was to produce 'a revolution in public services' by raising and emphasising the quality of service delivery. It covered all government departments and agencies, the National Health Service, nationalised industries (since largely disappeared), privatised utilities, local government and the universities. A set of public service principles was set out in the Citizen's Charter — under headings such as: standards; information and openness; choice and consultation; courtesy and helpfulness; putting things right; and value for money. The Prime Minister's Citizen's Charter Advisory Panel judged the winners, whose achievement was rewarded by the *Charter Mark of Excellence*.

The programme is now run by a section within the Cabinet Office, dealing with the Charter Mark *(www.chartermark.gov.uk)* and the new Central Government Beacon Scheme. The Charter Mark criteria have been changed to emphasise factors such as: promoting access and choice; encouraging innovation and partnerships to improve service delivery; and involving users and consulting front-line staff. To widen the appeal of the Charter Mark scheme, a new system of self-assessment and increased assessor feedback have been introduced. From January 2002, the Charter Mark scheme has been extended to internal support services which do not have direct contact with the public.

The Central Government Beacon Scheme is similar to that operated for local government. The idea of 'beacons' is that they share their innovative ideas and experience with other organisations who might benefit — *"Organisations with high-quality performance in public service should illuminate other areas of government"* as Cabinet Office Gus MacDonald explained.

The word 'joined-up' started to be used with a variety of words ('thinking', 'government' and 'working') by the New Labour government. The Effective Performance Division within the Cabinet Office was also involved in a series of initiatives aimed at improving joint working and partnerships between government departments, executive agencies and quangos. The mechanisms used by the Division included Integrated Service Teams and People's Panels to establish where the problems were and what could be done to solve them through Service Action Teams.

The Civil Service

The Civil Service is the ultimate responsibility of the Prime Minister in his capacity as Minister for the Civil Service and is the ultimate management responsibility of the Cabinet Secretary, as Head of the Home Civil Service. The Minister for the Civil Service is authorised by the Civil Service Order in Council 1995 (as amended) to make regulations and give instructions about the management of the Civil Service. The Civil Service Code is an example of the use of this power.

There are more than 60 departments and 100 executive agencies, which collectively employ about 480,000 people. Over two-thirds of civil servants now work in executive agencies. The Civil Service staff are divided between the Senior Civil Service and the other grades. The various grades of the Senior Civil Service and examples of the kind of work that they do are described in *Appendix B*. The Senior Civil Service consists of those staff in grades 1 to 5.

Civil servants are servants of the Crown — or, more realistically, they owe allegiance to the government of the day. The Civil Service Code, last revised in 1999 to take account of devolution, defined the rôle of the Civil Service *(www.civilservice.gov.uk)* as:

> *"The constitutional and practical rôle of the Civil Service is, with integrity, honesty, impartiality and objectivity, to assist the duly constituted government of the United Kingdom, the Scottish Executive or the National Assembly for Wales ... whatever their political complexion, in formulating their policies, carrying out decisions and in administering public services for which they are responsible.*
>
> *...*
>
> *Civil servants should conduct themselves with integrity, impartiality and honesty and should give honest and impartial advice to the Minister ... without fear or favour, and make all information relevant to the decisions available to them. They should not deceive or knowingly mislead Ministers, Parliament ... or the public.*
>
> *...*
>
> *Civil servants should conduct themselves in such a way as to deserve and retain the confidence of Ministers ... and to be able to establish the same relationship with those whom they may be required to serve in some future Administration. They should comply with restrictions on their political activities".*

These principles can be contrasted with those applied to special advisers, as described in the later section on *Special advisers, spin doctors and consultants*.

The modern Civil Service has a long history and is still changing to reflect modern conditions. The principles underlying it have their origin in the Northcote-Trevelyan Report of 1854 which aimed to put the civil service on a more professional and neutral footing, after years of corruption and nepotism.

All appointments are made on merit by fair and open competition — one of the objectives of the Northcote-Trevelyan Report, which took some time to achieve after 1854. The independent Civil Service Commissioners are responsible for selecting people for the Senior Civil Service via the Civil Service Selection Board. The responsibility for recruiting all other staff rests with the department or agency itself — this can be done within the department/agency or using private consultants or using the government's Recruitment and Assessment Services Agency. Since 1995, departments and agencies have been obliged to publish their recruitment arrangements.

There is a *Fast Stream Development Programme,* through which graduates with exceptional ability are recruited — about 300 graduates are recruited through this programme each year — including specialists such as economists and statisticians. There is also an increasing emphasis on Europe and there is a European Division which recruits people with the necessary interest and skills for relations with the EU. Senior civil servants are encouraged to gain experience of industry and other areas of activity in order to broaden their personal skills. Similarly, exchanges of senior staff between central and local government also take place. The emphasis on good management and performance was confirmed by the requirement that all departments should have achieved *Investors in People* certification by 2000.

Civil servants — non-political?

There can be interesting arguments surrounding the interaction between Ministers and their senior civil servants — about the extent to which each can be drawn into the other's theoretical area of responsibility. The dividing line between policy (the Minister's preserve) and execution of that policy (the rôle of the civil servant) is not as clear-cut as some people like to think.

In recent years some Ministers have become much more active in the work of their departments — evidenced by Michael Heseltine's introduction in the early 1980s of MINIS (the Management Information System for Ministers) into the departments for which he was responsible. This can raise the suspicion that individual Ministers are more prepared to interfere in the management of the department, past the level required to discharge their accountability to Parliament.

In the other direction, there was uncertainty about the obligations owed by a civil servant to a Minister, which came to a head in the trial of Clive Ponting in 1985 for passing classified information to an unauthorised person under the Official Secrets Act. Although Ponting was acquitted, this led to Sir Robert Armstrong (the Cabinet Secretary and Head of the Civil Service at the time) issuing a 'Note' emphasising that: *"The determination of policy is the responsibility of the Minister ... When, having been given all the relevant information and advice, the Minister has taken the decision, it is the duty of civil servants loyally to carry out that decision ... Civil servants are under an obligation to keep the confidences to which they become privy in the course of their official duties".*

That was in 1985. Since then, 'whistle-blowing' has become a more acceptable occupation, if the circumstances demand that exposure of malpractice is in the public interest. This is now taken into account, to some extent, in the Civil Service Code mentioned in the last section. The Code makes it clear that civil servants should keep official information confidential. However, it sets up a procedure for dealing with instances where a civil servant believes that he or she is being asked to act in a way which: is illegal, improper or unethical; is in breach of constitutional convention or a professional code; may involve possible maladministration; or is otherwise inconsistent with the Code. As a first step, the civil servant may report his or her concerns in accordance with departmental procedures. If that does not provide a reasonable response, then the civil servant may next report the matter to the Civil Service Commissioners. However, if that does not produce a result which satisfies the civil servant, he or she has one of two choices — either carry out the requested action; or resign.

Special Advisers, spin doctors and consultants

The rôle of Special Advisers is summarised in the Code of Conduct for Special Advisers produced in July 2001:

> *"As the Ministerial Code explains, the employment of special advisers on the one hand adds a political dimension to the advice available to Ministers, and on the other provides Ministers with direct advice of distinguished experts in their professional field, while reinforcing the political neutrality of the Permanent Civil Service by distinguishing the source of political advice and support.*
>
> *"Special advisers are employed to help Ministers on matters where the work of government and the work of the government party overlap and it would be inappropriate for permanent civil servants to become involved. They are an additional resource for the Minister providing advice from a standpoint that is more politically committed and politically aware than would be available to a Minister from the Civil Service".*

The Code also explains that special advisers are temporary civil servants appointed under the Civil Service Order in Council and are exempt from the general requirement that civil servants should be appointed on merit. They are also exempt from the requirement to behave with political impartiality and objectivity so that they retain the confidence of future governments of a different political complexion. Apart from that, they are required to comply with the Civil Service Code and their appointment comes to an end when the administration which appointed them comes to an end. Difficulties can arise in their dealings with civil servants; the line seems to be that special advisers can inform civil servants about a Minister's thinking on a particular issue, but they cannot issue instructions to civil servants on the Minister's behalf — the Minister himself or herself has to do that.

Particular rules apply to special assistants just before a General Election. If they wish to join their Minister in a campaign or help out at party HQ, then they have to resign first. Otherwise, they remain in post until automatically terminated on the day after polling day — but they have to be especially careful and are expected to consult the Cabinet Secretary's Office for advice about their conduct.

A colloquial name for special advisers or aides in the political context seems to be 'spin doctor'. Like other inelegant phrases such as 'sound-bite' and 'photo opportunity', the term originates in the US and was first coined, it is thought, in the 1980s. In this context 'spin' involves the manipulation of how something will be interpreted by the public. The word is usually accompanied by an adjective such as 'positive' or 'new'. The use of the word 'doctor' is usually regarded as a colloquialism — 'someone who fixes something' — rather than as a reference to a medical doctor or even a witch doctor!

Over the last few years, the number of special advisers in Whitehall, paid for out of public funds, has increased — to 38 towards the end of the Major government. Under the Blair government the number went as high as 74 (at a cost to the taxpayer of £3.6m a year) before falling back to the current level of 63. The fall in number has been attributed by some commentators to Tony Blair's announcement in June 2001 that "spin is dead" in New Labour's second term. That may well have been Tony Blair's aim, but then, in September, the Jo Moore episode occurred, as described later.

Simon Jenkins offered his own view of this growth in special advisers in the *Guardian* in December 1999 (in a piece commenting on Sir Richard Wilson's report on the future of the Civil Service mentioned later):

> "*Modern Ministers, Tory and Labour, are more interventionist than any in history. They have concentrated power in their own offices and found the resulting burden heavy to bear. They have turned to new sources of advice, and found it in consultants. Whitehall is now awash with policy consultants, financial consultants, publicity consultants. Their advice is expensive and inevitably partisan, influenced by the hope of patronage or a higher fee. But it fills a gap*".

Opinions differ about this growth in the number of special advisers and the rôle they appear to play behind the scenes — modern political reality (how can 480,000 civil servants be politicised by so few?); or the thin end of the wedge (towards the US model without proper debate by Parliament?).

The most recent and notorious example of a special adviser overstepping the mark was Jo Moore, special assistant to Stephen Byers. She sent an e-mail immediately after the events of 11 September 2001 suggesting that that would be a good time to 'bury' bad news emerging from the government. The existence of the e-mail rapidly became known and she was universally criticised as having a cynical approach to news manipulation; she was disciplined but Stephen Byers refused to sack her. He was supported in that by 10 Downing Street.

This approach towards the timing of the release of news so as to limit damage is not unusual. Bad news, at least from the government's point of view, is more usefully released when media and Parliamentary attention is directed elsewhere. For example, at a crucial stage of the Railtrack affair, there had been a meeting between the Chairman of Railtrack and Stephen Byers, of which Mr Byers gave one account and the Chairman gave another. Stephen Byers was under pressure to release a formal memo which existed and which minuted the meeting, so that people would be able to judge for themselves who was right. On the afternoon of 29 November 2001, Gordon Brown was delivering his Pre-Budget Report to Parliament. The DTLR decided to release the memo to journalists while Gordon Brown was still on his feet. Number 10 was not amused at this — they felt that the timing of the memo's release had contaminated the Chancellor's Report. Although Ms Moore did not brief about the memo, she was thought to have been involved in the timing of its release. Apart from 10 Downing Street's displeasure, the General Secretary of the First Division Association of Civil Servants, Jonathan Baume, was reported as calling on Ms Moore to "stand to one side and let the professionals get on with the job". Mr Baume was also reported as saying that his members had complained of routine intimidation by Ms Moore while she was at the DTI and the DTLR.

Prior to the Jo Moore episode, the Neill Committee on Standards in Public Life had published a report, *Reinforcing Standards,* in January 2000. Neill recommended that Westminster adopt the same procedure as Scotland and Wales and place an upper limit (100) on the number of special advisers. Neill commented: *"The considerable increase in numbers, particularly at No 10 where influential rôles are played by special advisers raises the question of whether their authority outweighs that of objective advisers".* Neill recommended that a new code of conduct should be adopted, making it clear that special advisers had a specific duty to uphold the impartiality of the Civil Service and defining and regulating their dealings with the media.

The Jo Moore episode prompted the Committee on Standards in Public Life, now under the chairmanship of Sir Nigel Wicks, to decide that the time had come to look at the matter again. Although the government had published the Code of Conduct for Special Advisers in July 2001, Sir Nigel felt that they had not gone far enough and he was disappointed that Parliament had not been given an opportunity to debate limits on the number of special advisers. He was also displeased that the government had not published a programme for the introduction of new legislation to regulate the Civil Service.

The use of government information for party political ends has become an increasingly grey area — and more recently so under the New Labour government. Fifteen of the 17 heads of information in the various government departments were replaced after New Labour came into power. One of the consultant spin doctors based in the Cabinet Office was charged with developing a new electronic information and rebuttal system called the *Knowledge Network Project* to which government departments are required to contribute, *"to explain the government's core message"* so that the public gets *"the full facts without going through the distorting prism of media reporting"*. The departments were required to feed in their 'lines to take' on key policy issues, with the three best arguments and five best facts — with an indication of which people outside the government support the policy, but not those who might disagree with it. Concern arose not only about the preoccupations about control which might be inferred from such a project but also the danger that the information may be transferred to Labour Party headquarters at Millbank prior to the next General Election. This concern was increased by the physical difficulty in preventing such a transfer from happening and the advertisement in January 2000 of the post of 'Head of Attack' at Millbank, co-ordinating New Labour attacks on Opposition parties and their policies, who would be required to liaise with the rebuttal unit in the Cabinet Office. The Cabinet Secretary, Sir Richard Wilson, was reported as seeking assurances from Tony Blair that there would be no transfer of information to Millbank.

The expression of unease and concern has not stopped there. The Commons Select Committee on Public Administration decided, at the end of January 2000, to summon Tony Blair to appear before it to explain and justify: his increasing power base at Downing Street; why he needs so many spin doctors and special advisers and whether he plans to recruit any more; and the Knowledge Network Project. This is reportedly the first time that a Commons Select Committee has decided to exercise its theoretical powers to interrogate a Prime Minister.

Political activities of civil servants

Civil servants are expected to implement the decisions of the government of the day, regardless of their own privately-held political beliefs and convictions — this is said to be a matter of public confidence in the political impartiality of the Civil Service. This does not mean, however, that civil servants are denied altogether the freedom to take part in the democratic political process which is enjoyed by others.

So, there is a set of internal rules which divides the Civil Service into three groups to determine the extent to which an individual civil servant can engage in political activity on a personal basis.

At one end is the 'politically free' group (mostly industrial or the non-office grades) who are free to engage in political activity, including standing as an MP or MEP. They do not have to resign from the Civil Service when they are adopted as a prospective candidate but they are required to resign when their election nomination papers are submitted to the Returning Officer. If they are unsuccessful, they can have their old job back, so long as they apply within one week of the declaration of the results.

At the other end there is a 'politically restricted' group, consisting of staff in the Senior Civil Service (Grades 1 to 5), in Grades 6 and 7 and members of the Fast Stream Development Programme who are banned from taking part in national political activities. They can, however, stand as MPs or MEPs, but they must resign as soon as they are adopted as a candidate — they cannot wait until nomination. They can apply for permission to engage in politics at a local level.

In between is the 'intermediate' group (everyone else) who can apply for permission to engage in political activity at national and local level. If they wish to stand as an MP or MEP, they are treated in the same way as the 'politically restricted' group.

Departmental management

The Civil Service has undergone a marked change in the past 20 years as a result of a series of management reforms aimed at providing the *'three Es'* — economy, efficiency and effectiveness.

There were two main milestones on this journey to more effective management. The *Efficiency Strategy* published in 1979 by Sir Derek (later Lord) Rayner, who was the Prime Minister's adviser on efficiency, started the process. In 1982 this impetus for change was reinforced by the *Financial Management Initiative* which sought to provide departmental managers with *"a clear view of objectives and performance"*.

More recent developments took the process one stage further, by transferring as much as possible of the executive work of government departments to separate executive units or agencies under the *Next Steps Programme* initiated in 1988.

This programme was mainly driven by the view that the volume of government services and the size of departments had become so large that management and supervision of them as single entities was no longer sensible. There was also the view that middle-ranking managers would be better able to develop the services which they managed, if they had more flexibility by being freed from hierarchical control by the centre of their department. It was also intended as the possible route to privatisation — and some of the Next Steps agencies have taken that step.

A White Paper, *The Civil Service: Continuity and Change,* was published in 1994 and discussed the rôle and future of the Civil Service. This led to the publication of a new Civil Service Code which came into force in January 1996. The Code provides a statement of the constitutional framework within which all civil servants work and the values which they are expected to uphold. The Code also includes an independent line of appeal to the Civil Service Commissioners on alleged breaches of the Code.

In July 1998, as part of the reorganisation of the Cabinet Office, the Civil Service Employer Group and Senior Civil Service Group were combined to form the Civil Service Corporate Management Command, with two Directorates — one to cover the recruitment and development of people and the other to cover performance management.

The present Cabinet Secretary, Sir Richard Wilson, has continued the process of modernising the Civil Service. In December 1999, in his report to the Prime Minister on *Building a Civil Service for the 21st Century*, Sir Richard wrote: *"Our aim is to help make the UK a better place for everyone to live in, and support its success in the world"*. The *Civil Service Reform Report* was published at the same time. In it the Civil Service Management Board adopted six themes to do with: stronger leadership with a clear sense of purpose; business planning; performance management; diversity; a more open Service which encouraged people with talent; and a better deal for staff. Some commentators fear that the jargon and terminology used in Sir Richard's report heralded the end of the politically neutral civil servant — rejecting the concept of the conduct of the nation's affairs as a profession and regarding it more like a business.

Executive Agencies

Agencies created under the *Next Steps Programme* are still part of the Civil Service, but enjoy greater delegated freedom on finance and pay under their framework documents. Each agency is headed by a chief executive (the actual job title may be different and the post-holder will probably not be a career civil servant) who is responsible for the day-to-day operations of the agency but is accountable to the supervising Minister.

The Next Steps Programme envisaged that an agency will not be created until some 'prior options' — abolition, privatisation or contracting-out — have been considered and rejected. These 'prior options' are also reviewed every five years once an executive agency has been established.

Market testing

The process did not stop at the Next Steps Programme — it went further. The Conservative government saw great value in the concept of the 'market place' and introduced a process for 'market testing', which can be viewed as an extension of the process of the privatisation of government services.

The original idea was to improve efficiency and customer responsiveness by comparing the in-house provision (often in a monopoly position and remote from commercial pressures) with competitive bids from the private sector. The process of comparison would force the in-house provider to find the true cost of what they did and shake itself up, in order to keep the right to continue providing the service.

This concept had first appeared in the form of Compulsory Competitive Tendering

(CCT) for certain blue-collar local government services in 1980. Its extension to the more significant parts of central government services was heralded in the government's White Paper, *Competing for Quality,* published in 1991, promising that before the next election, 25% of certain kinds of departmental work would have been exposed to competition, affecting over 130,000 civil servants overall.

In principle, the process looks to be a sensible one, but other views can be taken. The most important one is whether the service is to be awarded to the people who put in the lowest cash bid, regardless of the quality of the service they are likely to be able to deliver. Supporters of the change forget to take into account the costs of the necessary subsequent arms' length monitoring of the contractor's performance, when deciding whether the exercise has produced any worthwhile gain to the public purse. Another important point is the diversion of in-house resources and staff time (which is never truly costed) away from service delivery in order to compete in the market-testing process. Finally there will sometimes be distrust or even hostility about the process, leading inevitably to an adverse effect on staff morale.

Quangos and Task Forces

Although in theory not part of government, this chapter would not be complete without a comment upon the growth of the quango — *Qu*asi-*A*utonomous *N*on-*G*overnmental *O*rganisation. Many people do not realise how many quangos there are and how much public expenditure they control — all with no direct democratic control.

The massive growth in the number of quangos was a feature of the last Conservative government. The more cynical would say that they were the means by which criticism of government policies would diminish if those responsible for overseeing the delivery of services were appointees of the government, rather than local democratically elected representatives.

Examples of quangos at local level are Learning and Skills Councils and housing associations. At national (and local) level, the chance is that any body with the word 'Authority' in its name is probably a quango.

The scale of quangodom is difficult to gauge (different commentators will use different definitions) but the following figures from a *Democratic Audit* report published in July 1996 gave one view of the position then:

- there were between 66,000 and 73,500 people running quangos;
- there were about 26,500 local councillors running local authorities;
- there were 6,224 executive and advisory quangos;
- quangos spent £60.4bn in 1994/95, against a government estimate of £20.8bn; and
- local authorities spent £73bn in the same period.

The major point is the lack of direct democratic accountability of quangos for what they do. The National Audit Office produced a report in June 1996 in response to a government consultation paper on the spending of public money published in the previous March. The NAO emphasised the need for proper audit and accountability of quangos for the public money they spent. The NAO comment was consistent with the report published in May 1996 by the then Nolan Committee on Standards in Public Life which included the following comments on quangos at local level: *"More needs to be done to ensure that they all achieve the best standards on appointments procedures, openness, codes of conduct, training, whistle-blowing and local accountability"*.

Lord Nolan's letter to the Prime Minister which accompanied the report stressed: *"nothing ... points to any fundamental malaise in the sectors we have examined. But there is ... a tension between the management-driven and output-related approach which is central to many recent changes, and the need for organisations providing public services to involve, respond to, and reflect the communities which they serve"*.

Did the New Labour government increase accountability in line with the NAO and Nolan Committee comments? When visited in 1999 the Cabinet Office quango website (yes, there is one devoted to quangos — *www.cabinet-office.gov.uk/quango*), the New Labour government was committed to keeping the number of quangos "to an absolute minimum", but it has to be said that there is little evidence of any significant shift back to direct democratic control. The website indicated that during 1998/99 quangos spent about £23.5bn, significantly less than that found by the 1996 *Democratic Audit*. However, the definition of a quango now used by the New Labour government limits them to non-departmental public bodies (NDPBs), excluding NHS bodies, nationalised industries and public corporations. A visit to the website in early 2002 showed that there were said to be just over 1,000 NDPBs and around 500 NHS Trusts. So, in reality, has there been a reduction in the quangodom?

There have been concerns about some of the appointments made by New Labour to quangos — suggesting a politicisation of the bodies concerned, especially the NHS. It has to be said that when the Conservatives established the quangos they were not slow in appointing people with views sympathetic to their own.

The Neill Committee had identified the making of appointments to quangos as one area of concern and had recommended that an independent Commissioner should be appointed to oversee appointments to quangos by government departments. The office of Commissioner for Public Appointments *(www.ocpa.gov.uk)* was created by an Order in Council in November 1995. The Commissioner has produced a Code of Practice with which departments are expected to comply. No appointment can now be made unless it has been scrutinised by an Independent Assessor reporting to the Commissioner, to ensure that shortlist candidates have been chosen on merit. The Commissioner produces an annual report.

In fact, New Labour has gone further in conferring power and influence on groups of people appointed by Ministers with no direct democratic control — *Task Forces*. By the beginning of 2000 New Labour had created 44 Task Forces made up of people from industry and research bodies to consider problems ranging from social exclusion to housing. The report *Reinforcing Standards* published by the Neill Committee in January 2000 raised concerns about this new form of Labour political patronage implied by the existence of Task Forces. Neill suggested that Task Forces should have a specific task achieved over a limited life of not more than two years and if a Task Force exceeded that lifetime it should be converted to a quango, in which form it would then have a measure of accountability.

Parliamentary and Health Service Ombudsman

The Parliamentary Ombudsman *(www.ombudsman.org.uk)* (aka the Parliamentary Commissioner for Administration) investigates complaints from members of the public, not about Parliament, but about government departments or other specified bodies. Not all complaints are investigated. The basis of the complaint has to be that the individual has suffered some form of injustice because of maladministration (including delay, faulty procedures, mistakes, unfairness and bias). The Ombudsman cannot investigate complaints against judges, police or local authorities — which have their own complaints procedures.

If the Ombudsman investigates and finds the complaint of maladministration is justified, he can recommend that the organisation concerned provides a remedy — however, the Ombudsman cannot enforce his findings of maladministration.

Since devolution, there are similar arrangements for Scotland (the Scottish Parliamentary Commissioner for Administration) and Wales (Welsh Administration Ombudsman).

There is a separate Health Service Ombudsman (he shares the same website as the Parliamentary Ombudsman) who can investigate complaints about the NHS. However, there are limits, not all complaints are investigated and, again, his findings cannot be enforced.

7   The Political Process

Pressure Groups — Political Parties

As explained in the first chapter, the UK is a democracy. The political process within a democratic society is more than just participation in elections. Democracy is enhanced if individuals can express their views freely for a variety of causes — with the aim of influencing the views of other members of society and of those in government.

Pressure groups

Pressure groups are the means by which individuals seek to influence others. There are two main types of pressure group — a sectional or interest group; and a cause group.

Sectional or *interest groups* exist for the purpose of promoting and protecting the economic and other interests of their members. *Cause groups* exist to promote a much broader idea or issue which is not directly linked to the interests of their members.

Both types of pressure groups exist in the UK. Examples of sectional or interest groups are the various trade unions and professional societies and organisations representing the various sections of industry. Examples of cause groups are Greenpeace and CND.

Pressure groups vary enormously in their size and in the formality of their internal structure and organisation. At one end of the scale, there can be a fairly informal grouping of individuals with similar views on a single issue. At the other end, there can be large formalised organisations employing a significant number of people and with very substantial spending power (such as the CBI).

The more successful pressure groups will be those who follow the guidelines suggested by Des Wilson in 1986 during the Tyne Tees TV programme *Is Democracy working?*: *Identify your objectives; learn how the decision-making process works; formulate a strategy and campaign plan; undertake thorough and detailed research and preparation; mobilise as much widespread support as possible; understand how the mass media work and use them effectively; be professional; be confident about asserting your democratic rights; and be resilient and prepared for a long and difficult campaign.*

Pressure groups of whatever kind will seek to influence the legislative, government and political processes in much the same way.

Influencing others

Government will, more often than not, regard the influence of pressure groups in a positive, rather than negative, light. White and Green Papers are the more formal means by which views of pressure groups are sought in the legislative process. Although a pressure group's objectives may not match those of the legislature, nonetheless the knowledge and experience within the pressure group can be a valuable aid to the legislature. The end result is that the legislation, when passed, will work more correctly and efficiently to tackle the problem at which it is aimed.

The process of influencing government itself can be more subtle. The Executive has a wide discretion in the way it exercises its powers and pressure groups will seek to persuade those in government to use those powers in a way which is consistent with the group's aims and objectives. Ministers and civil servants are the more obvious targets, since they are part of the Executive. However, individual MPs, although properly speaking separate from the Executive, are also targeted because of the influence they can exert in monitoring the work of the Executive (see the sections on *Backbenchers* and *Early Day Motions* in earlier Chapters).

As a generalisation, the two aspects — legislative and governmental — come together in the political process itself. Many MPs will have some sort of connection with pressure groups. For example, many Labour MPs will be sponsored by a trade union. Many MPs (of any party) will be retained as paid or unpaid Parliamentary 'advisers' for pressure groups — so providing those pressure groups with direct access to the legislative and governmental processes.

Influencing the political process raises at least two interesting issues: Firstly, the extent to which the connection between a pressure group and an MP is disclosed by the MP when he or she deals with or raises an issue. Secondly, the recent rapid growth in the number of lobbying organisations whose sole purpose is to influence the political process (through hospitality at which introductions and meetings are arranged) often for quite lucrative fees.

In its report, *Reinforcing Standards,* published in January 2000 by the Neill Committee on Standards in Public Life, the Committee decided that it was unnecessary for lobbyists to be registered. However, Neill did recommend that a record of meetings between lobbyists and Ministers, civil servants and special advisers should be kept — but only where the lobbyist was seeking to influence government policy rather than just obtain information. Neill also commented on the increasing use of private company sponsors for conferences — Neill recognised the modern reality of this but recommended that the relevant Minister should be satisfied that the sponsorship was in the public interest and that all sponsorship deals over £5,000 should be published.

Political parties

The essential difference between a pressure group and a political party is simple to state: pressure groups exist to influence others, including those in government; political parties exist to take a direct part in the process of government itself.

Political parties will also differ from pressure groups in that their objectives will be bound up with a much broader set of ideas to do with society generally. One practical result of this will be that the party membership will consist of a range of interests — a range which may be reflected in the internal organisation of the party itself, on a geographical or other basis.

In the UK there is a number of parties — three relatively large; the remainder relatively small. One must appreciate that sometimes a small party can exert much more influence on government policy than its size might suggest — especially if the government of the day needs the votes from that smaller party to survive in Parliament.

As far as Wales, Scotland and Northern Ireland are concerned, there are other much smaller parties in those countries with aims connected with ideas of national identity or religion. Those parties are often sufficiently successful, in electoral success, to defeat one or more of the larger parties. See *Appendix A* for the reflection of this in the election results for the devolved bodies. This kind of electoral success is, however, diluted in the wider UK Parliament.

Each of the three larger parties will now be described in terms of its development and internal organisation. In all three cases, the party's history has had a formative influence on the way it is organised.

The Conservative Party — development

The modern Conservative Party *(www.conservatives.com)* can be said to have its origins in Parliament itself — growing out of the old Tory Party during the middle of the last century. Indeed, people who are members of the Conservative Party may still refer to themselves as being a 'Tory'. The initial preoccupation of the Tory Party was with supporting the established religious and political order, which also coincided with the interests of the landed classes. At that time, the landed classes were in a position to control a large number of MPs through the rotten borough system — but this was brought to an end by the Great Reform Act 1832. After the 1832 Act, the name 'Conservative Party' was adopted.

The abolition of the Corn Laws had the effect of splitting the party after 1846 and it only returned to prominence in the 1860s under the leadership of Disraeli. As subsequent electoral reforms extended the franchise beyond the initial 5% of the population, so the Conservative Party had to broaden its appeal downwards into the general population, if it was to retain its political position. In that sense, the development of the modern Conservative Party from the old Tory Party has been described as 'top-down'.

In 1921 those Liberals who were disenchanted with the idea of Irish Home Rule merged with the Conservative Party which changed its name to its present title of the Conservative and Unionist Party.

The Conservative Party — style of government

The modern Conservative Party has been in government for two-thirds of the time since 1918 and during that time has approached the business of government in different ways.

There have, in recent years, been tensions within the party. For many years during the 1950s and 1960s the Conservative Leaders took care to position the party in the centre of the political spectrum — sometimes referred to as 'One-nation Conservatism'. This approach was epitomised by the remark attributed to Harold MacMillan (Prime Minister 1957-163) when he led the Conservative Party to victory in the 1959 General Election by emphasising Britain's postwar full employment under the slogan *"You've never had it so good"*. They believed that there was a positive rôle for the State in providing welfare, full employment and taking care of the poorer and more vulnerable members of society.

However, the arrival of Mrs Thatcher as Leader saw a significant shift to the right, towards a more 'radical reforming' or 'neo-liberal' type of Conservatism — called 'Thatcherism'. In this context, the words 'radical' and 'liberal' had a different meaning from usual. Thatcherism gave prominence to the concept of the free market, regarding the rôle of government as often unnecessary or obstructive for the health of the economy and, therefore, society. Such Conservatism was prepared to accept a significant amount of unemployment and a reduction in public expenditure to a minimum, if that brought economic stability. The view was that people should themselves make provision to see them through adversity. One of the consequences of this type of

Conservatism was the increasing polarisation of UK society into 'two nations' — the 'Haves' and the 'Have-nots'. Indeed, a study published in January 2000 by the international Organisation for Economic Co-operation and Development (OECD) confirmed that two decades of Tory government had given Britain the worst poverty record in the developed world, with 38% of the population spending at least one year below the poverty line in the period 1991-96. Mrs Thatcher's model, the US, was the next worst.

Loyalty to the Leader is one of the features of the Conservative Party. However, that loyalty is not unquestioning. Even Mrs Thatcher was obliged to include in her Cabinet some people who were more inclined to support the greater public expenditure implications of a 'one-nation' approach — the so-called 'Wets'.

Most political parties, if they are realistic, will reposition themselves in the political spectrum if they see this as the best way of making themselves more attractive to the voters — especially after a bad election result. The Labour Party did this after their defeat in the 1992 General Election (becoming 'New Labour' in the process), effectively entering the middle ground vacated by the Conservatives. In modern Britain, it is probably the case that the party occupying the middle ground is most likely to be elected. The Conservatives are attempting, firstly under William Hague's leadership and now under Iain Duncan Smith's, to present themselves as a 'one-nation' party again (but, again, in this context the words have a somewhat different meaning than hitherto). However, to differentiate themselves from New Labour (and in Margaret Thatcher's words in an earlier context, to demonstrate 'clear blue water' between themselves and New Labour) they are having to adopt increasingly right-wing policies. Whether they are able to convince the voters in sufficient numbers to make a comeback in the next General Election remains to be seen. They seem to have failed for the 2001 General Election.

The Conservative Party — choosing the Leader

Before 1965 there were no formal selection procedures for Leader of the Conservative Party — the Leader just 'emerged' when a Conservative government needed to be formed.

In 1965, the party adopted an approach in which Conservative MPs elected the Leader from amongst their number following a secret ballot. In 1975, the process was modified so that the Leader had to seek re-election annually — making it easier to dispose of a Leader whose sell-by date had expired!

Prior to the 1997 General Election, the process was organised by the 1922 Committee. When there was a vacancy in the leadership, candidates had to be nominated by two MPs. When there was no vacancy (a challenge to the existing Leader), a candidate's nomination papers had be signed by at least 10% of the Parliamentary Party. Before balloting took place, although the views of Conservative constituency associations, MEPs and peers were collected by the 1922 Committee, the election of the Leader was still in the hands of the MPs themselves.

That process has now changed following the introduction of reforms by William Hague after the disastrous Conservative performance in the 1997 General Election. The 1997 General Election debâcle produced several results: the resignation of John Major as Leader; a delay in running the required leadership contest because most of the 1922 Committee (including its chairman) had lost their seats; and a call for the rules to be changed so that constituency representatives, MEPs and peers could take a more active part in voting for the choice of party Leader. There was some opposition towards the Hague reforms (notably from some members of the 1992 Committee who could see their control of the process slipping from their hands) and the system for electing the Leader which was finally adopted took into account the divergent views and retained some aspects of the existing procedure. The MPs, through ballot if necessary, would reduce the field to the two front runners; a ballot of the whole party on the basis of one member, one vote (OMOV) would then choose the next Leader of the Party from the two front runners.

The Conservative Party Leader can be removed from office only after a successful vote of no confidence. A vote of no confidence can only be proposed if 25% of Conservative MPs (or 45 such MPs, if a lesser number) requisition one. At least 51% of Conservative MPs must support the vote of no confidence to prevent the Leader from standing for re-election. Candidates must have the backing of 10% of the MPs before they can stand in a first ballot — and only MPs can vote in that ballot. Only those candidates with more than 25% of the votes in the first ballot can go on to stand in the final ballot. The final ballot (OMOV) is by the total membership of the Conservative Party. In other words, the grassroots members, rather than the MPs, now make the final choice.

The first time the Hague reforms were used to chose a new Leader was when William Hague fell on his sword following a similarly disastrous Conservative performance in the 2001 General Election. It was not a good PR exercise for the Conservative Party. There were so many candidates for the Leadership that several ballots had to be held — including one to decide who had come in last place in the first ballot. This was necessary because the new rules had not envisaged there being a dead heat for last place with neither of the 'last' candidates being willing to withdraw, even though their chances of a decent placing in the next ballot were slim. The exercise may well have produced a new Leader, Iain Duncan Smith, but it also served to illustrate the deep splits within the Conservative Party.

The Conservative Party — organisation

Because of how the Conservative Party developed, the 1922 Committee is very influential. The 1922 Committee represents Conservative backbench power in Parliament and any party Leader who disregards it will usually regret doing so later.

Outside Parliament, the National Union of Conservative Associations ('National Union') was established in 1867 to co-ordinate the work of the local constituency associations. It had a Central Council, consisting of Conservative peers, MEPs, prospective MPs and regional representatives. The Central Council met annually and its main job was to organise the annual party conferences of delegates of the constituency associations.

The arrangements for the top management of the party were changed by the Hague Reforms, adopted at the 1998 Annual Conference. The three strands of the party — grassroots, MPs and Conservative Central Office — were brought together in a 15 member Governing Board. Half of the Governing Board are appointed by the Leader and Central Office and the other half by the *Annual Convention*. The term 'Annual Convention', which was supposed to replace 'Annual Conference', did not come into common use; the 'Annual Conference' is still alive and well and is attended by the chairmen of the Conservative constituency associations. A *Conservative Policy Forum* (CPF) was set up with its own governing council consisting of members elected by the party, MPs and a number of people co-opted from business, the media and the Groves of Academe. The CPF runs two weekend policy conferences a year and brings together the views of 650 constituency-based discussion groups. The CPF is one of the means by which policy proposals reach the Annual Conference. The three previously separate youth movements — Young Conservatives, Conservative Students and Conservative Graduates — were merged to form *Conservative Future*.

The purpose of the Annual Conference in October is to inspire the party faithful and enable budding MPs to make their mark. There is a 'Spring Forum' in March each year. Both events are carefully orchestrated and provide a fairly anodyne public relations platform for the party leadership — especially the Leader, who always receives a 10 minute standing ovation! In real terms, the Annual Conference has little rôle in policy formulation and it is difficult to guess how much notice the party leadership actually takes of what is said at the Conference. Iain Duncan Smith has taken a leaf out of Tony Blair's book — he has established a Policy Unit within his office, supporting a Policy Board, in an effort to rekindle support for the party.

Central Office is the organisational core of the party. It is controlled by the party Leader who appoints the party Chairman and the several Vice-Chairmen who effectively run Central Office. The Party Treasurer is also appointed by the Leader. Following the revelations about the rôle played by the Party Treasurer Michael Ashcroft in propping up the party's finances, there have been suggestions that the senior party officers should be subject to an election process. Central Office co-ordinates the General Election campaign at national level and at other times provides policy advice and secretarial support to the leadership.

The Conservative Party — choosing the Parliamentary candidates

The constituency associations operate at constituency level with the aim of winning or retaining the seat. The process which finishes with the selection of a person to be the Conservative Party candidate for the constituency operates at national and then local level.

At national level, there is a screening process through which hopefuls have to pass. This involves the National Union's Standing Advisory Committee and Parliamentary Selection Board vetting people for inclusion in the Approved List of Candidates. The process is run by Central Office and managed by one of the party's Vice Chairmen. The candidates have to survive a 'candidates weekend' at which they have to demonstrate the appropriateness of their personality and their political and other skills.

At local level, the process starts with a vacancy being notified to Central Office, which in turn tells people on the Approved List. Anyone from the Approved List who then applies may be short-listed (about 20 applicants) and vetted by the constituency association's Executive Sub-committee (about 20 constituency association officers). People who are not named on the Approved List can still be considered, but specific clearance by the Standing Advisory Committee is needed.

The Executive Sub-committee will usually reduce, through a process of interviews, the shortlist to not less than three candidates. At this stage, the constituency association's Executive Council (about 60 constituency association officers) takes over and interview the survivors, with the aim of offering at least two of them for a final interview before the constituency association's General Meeting (all members of at least six months' standing).

Predictably, in safe seats the number of applications is usually high. Although loyalty to the sitting MP appears to be one of the tenets of the Conservative Party — at least in former times — in recent years constituency associations have shown themselves to be increasingly prepared to deselect a sitting MP if he or she has become an electoral liability.

Although the impression might be given that selection is a matter for the constituency association, occasionally the influence of Central Office can be seen in the final choice. Since 1948, the practice has stopped of according preference to those people willing to donate large sums of money to party funds.

The Conservative Party — finance and party funding generally

Individual constituency associations raise funds for their own activities and to meet a quota from Central Office for national funds. About 10% of national funds is raised in this way.

Traditionally, the larger companies made donations to the Conservative Party (which had to be listed in their annual accounts if they exceeded £200) but this source has diminished over the years. Money also flows into the party's coffers through a variety of sources, some of which are 'front' organisations set up for that purpose — such as Aims for Industry and British United Industrialists. The issue of party funding is dealt with in a later section in this chapter.

The Labour Party — development

If the development of the modern Conservative Party can be described as 'top-down', the development of the Labour Party can be described as 'bottom-up'. The origins of the Labour Party *(www.labour.org.uk)* are entirely different, evolving from a grass-roots movement outside Parliament.

In 1900 the trade unions, co-operative societies and socialist societies established the Labour Representation Committee to promote the entry of the working-class man into Parliament. The Committee changed its name to the Labour Party in 1906.

A written constitution was adopted in 1918. This constitution set out the party's objectives and the procedures for elections, appointments and decision-making within the party. For a time, the Co-operative movement fielded its own candidates but following its affiliation with the Labour Party, even though the Co-operative Party still exists as a separate entity, joint candidates are now usually fielded under the rubric 'Labour and Co-operative Party Candidate'. The federal origins of the Labour Party are still evident in its modern structure — with its emphasis on the National Executive Committee and the Party Conference as the mechanisms by which party policy is developed. The pre-eminence of the Conservatives' 1922 Committee is not replicated in the Parliamentary Labour Party's position in the Labour scheme of things.

The Labour Party — approach to policy formulation

If the Conservative Party is traditionally regarded as the party of the *status quo*, the Labour Party is the party of change — either gradual or root-and-branch.

The Labour Party has formed the government for less than one-third of the time since 1918. This period in Opposition has enabled the various interests within the party to assert themselves, with shifts towards the Left and, more lately, towards the Centre, being made. Given the history of the party, and the breadth and ideological differences of its membership, it is hardly surprising that the party was much more prone to internal factions and divisions than the Conservatives — although in recent years the Conservative Party has itself been increasingly riven by internal divisions. Being Leader of the Labour Party in Opposition was probably one of the toughest jobs in UK politics!

The 1918 Constitution also set out the Labour Party's ideology and this tended to limit the ability of the Labour Party, in and out of government, to modify its aims and policies to meet the prevailing conditions of the day — until recently. The public ownership of the major utilities — including the steel and coal industries — was for many years a major feature of Labour policies — as required by 'clause IV' of the party's constitution.

The relative importance of the trade unions within the Labour Party became more evident during the so-called 'winter of discontent' in 1979 when the industrial action taken by the trade unions on the collapse of Labour's incomes policy resulted in the paralysis of most of the UK's industry.

There has always been a tension between the leadership and the National Executive Committee. The Labour Party rules provided for the NEC to control the formulation of future party policy; and they also provided for a resolution passed by a two-thirds majority at Annual Conference to become part of the election programme, but not part of the manifesto. During the Wilson and Callaghan governments (1974-79) the respective Prime Ministers did not follow the path laid down by the NEC and the Annual Conference, with the result that they were dubbed 'revisionist' by some people in the party.

James Callaghan's style of government and his heavy defeat at the 1979 General Election gave rise to disillusion and a split in the party. This enabled the hard Left to gain significant influence within the NEC and at local level — but only for a time. Neil Kinnock is generally credited with reversing the trend towards the Left. By the mid 1980s he had secured the expulsion from the party of the supporters of *Militant Tendency*. *Militant Tendency* was ostensibly a hard Left periodical, the subscribers to which were regarded as being, in reality, a 'Party within the Party', which was contrary to Labour Party rules. He also restored the influence of the Leader on the party machine and particularly on the NEC. By the time he took office as party Leader, John Smith inherited a more centrally controlled party — the leadership was able to determine the party manifesto and election campaign.

The success of the Conservative Party in retaining the right to govern following their surprise victory in the 1992 General Election (and the fourth Labour defeat in a row) caused the Labour Party to review the way in which it formulated policy. There is now a National Policy Forum (of about 150 to 200 members elected biannually at the Conference) which, through its eight standing commissions, has the job of producing policy proposals for Conference consideration. All aspects of party policy (including suggestions from constituency parties) are examined on a two-year rolling programme basis.

The success of the National Policy Forum approach to policy formulation can be seen in the repositioning of the Labour Party to become New Labour. The ideological differences between Marxists and liberal socialists appear to have largely disappeared — an apparently united party with a sure sense of direction has now evolved, more attractive to the voters. The state ownership of the means of production, and socialism, are no longer serious issues (clause IV was modified at a special conference in April 1995); nor is there an open commitment to increase public expenditure. The political complexion of the NEC has shifted back towards the centre of the spectrum — indeed, some would say to the centre ground abandoned by the Conservatives when they adopted 'Thatcherism'. Some commentators have suggested that the Liberal Democrats are now more radical than New Labour.

Trade union leaders have seen their ability to influence the work of government through industrial action progressively diminish through a combination of rising unemployment and Conservative employment legislation. The voting power of the trade union leaders at the Annual Conference has also steadily been eroded (see later). In the past, trade unions have been portrayed as a having a close (some would say too close) relationship with a Labour government of the time. To counter this impression, in the run-up to the 1997 General Election Tony Blair made it clear that trade unions would not receive any special treatment from a New Labour government.

The Labour Party — choosing the Leader

After the fall of the Callaghan government in 1979, the Left wing increased its influence within the party with the aim of making it even more 'democratic' — in other words, moving control away from the leadership and the Parliamentary Labour Party and putting it firmly outside Parliament in the hands of the NEC.

This resulted in the 1981 Annual Conference changing the rules so that the Leader of the party would be chosen in future not by MPs but by an electoral college. The electoral college now consists of three groups: the trade unions; the individual membership of the Labour Party; and Parliamentary Labour Party/European Parliamentary Labour Party — each college accounting for one-third of the votes.

Individual nominations still need a significant level of support from the Parliamentary Labour Party — 12.5% if there is a vacancy; 20% if there is no vacancy. Because of the electoral college system, voting is by means of postal ballot. The successful candidate needs at least 50% of the votes in each college. If no candidate has 50% at the first count, the lowest candidate is eliminated from the contest and the votes redistributed until a winner is identified.

The Labour Party — organisation and policy formulation

The National Executive Committee runs the party's organisation and now consists of 33 members appointed in various ways:

12	elected by trade unions, of which six must be women (Div I)
1	elected by the socialist societies (Div II)
6	elected by CLPs, of which three must be women (Div III)
2	elected by local government (Div IV)
3	elected by PLP/EPLP, of which one must be a woman (Div V)
3	nominated by the Cabinet (Div VI)
1	Party Treasurer elected by the entire conference
1	Leader of the Labour Party ex-officio
1	Deputy Leader of the Labour Party ex-officio
1	General Secretary of the Labour Party ex-officio
1	Leader of the PLP ex-officio

The NEC composition described above was introduced following Tony Blair's 'Partnership in Power' proposals, approved at the 1998 Annual Conference. The proposals were not greeted with universal acclaim since they had the effect of reducing PLP influence (and increasing that of the Prime Minister) on the NEC. Other aspects of the proposals reduced trade union influence in policy formulation.

The 'Partnership in Power' proposals established a new National Policy Forum (NPF) which would be the source of proposals for consideration at future Annual Conferences. The 175 member (the trade unions only have 20 seats) NPF consists of seven sections (constituencies, regions, trade unions, the PLP/EPLP/councillors, socialist societies, the government, and the NEC) and is supported by a number of local policy forums. There are fairly complex rules which govern how issues can reach the Annual Conference and the extent to which amendments can be moved at the Conference itself. Some cynics amongst party members are suspicious of the control exercised by the Policy Unit at Millbank, to the extent that they are not convinced that 'Partnership in Power', while giving the appearance of widespread grassroots consultation, actually enables views contrary to those of the government to be fully aired at the Conference. The further development of the party was heralded in the consultation document *'21st century party members — the key to our future'* launched at the 1999 Annual Conference.

So, the organisation of the Labour Party from the grassroots upwards is: branch; then Constituency Labour Party (CLP); then the NEC; and finally the Annual Conference. All of these levels are involved in policy formulation and are supplemented by: local and regional policy forums; policy commissions (eight of these, covering specific policy areas such as crime and justice); and the NPF.

Labour Party — Annual Conference

OMOV is the acronym for 'one member, one vote' — a concept which (as will be seen) has gained increasing ground over the trade union 'block vote' within the decision-making processes of the Labour Party. The trade union block vote was wielded by trade union leaders on behalf of those members of their trade union who, as well as their union subscriptions, also paid the political levy to the Labour Party. These block votes collectively outweighed the votes of the smaller socialist societies and individual constituency members. Although there are 24 trade unions affiliated to the Labour Party, in practice the individual leaders of five of the largest unions (in descending order: Unison, Amicus, TGWU, GMB and USDAW) control a significant proportion of the votes. Amicus was formed on 1 January 2002 by the merger of AEEU and MSF, to form the second largest trade union.

The Annual Conference used to be altogether more lively than the Conservatives' equivalent and had a much more significant rôle in formulating party policy. Issues were debated, often with passion, and with the original proposal being substantially amended before the final vote. The Leader of the party, unlike his or her Conservative opposite number, could not usually expect an easy ride at the Annual Conference. That has changed since the advent of New Labour — recent Annual Conferences have been very carefully controlled occasions, regarded by some commentators (and some Labour Party members) as indicative of New Labour 'control-freakery' by party headquarters at Millbank to avoid contributions which are 'off-message'.

In an attempt to modernise the Labour Party, the NEC agreed in 1991 to reduce the unions' total voting strength from 90% to 70% of the total after 1993, and to 40% over the long term, linked to a commensurate rise in party membership. A long-term aim of John Smith, before he died, was to see the end of the union block vote altogether and its replacement by OMOV at the Annual Conference. His aim is well on the way to being achieved:

	unions	constituencies
1994	90%	10%
1995	70%	30%
1996	50%	50%

However, progress beyond the 50:50 split may be difficult, because the trade unions will be reluctant to reduce their influence further. The continuing effect of this voting influence was shown at the September 2000 Annual Conference where, despite some serious arm-twisting by government Ministers, the major unions stuck to their guns and produced a Conference vote against the government on the issue of State pensions. For its part, the government said that it would disregard the Conference vote on the grounds that it had been due to union voting power.

The Labour Party — choosing the Parliamentary candidates

The Left succeeded at the 1980 Annual Conference in securing the mandatory rese-lection of MPs during the lifetime of a Parliament. Some commentators argued that this made some moderate Labour MPs jump ship to the SDP when they realised that their position as a sitting MP was under threat from the Left at constituency level.

At constituency level, the trade unions had the power of a block vote at General Management Committee meetings in the selection of MPs and this tended to rein-force the view that the trade unions effectively controlled the party (through this and their block votes at the Annual Conference), no matter what impression the party's constitution might have given at that time.

Neil Kinnock had tried, unsuccessfully, at the 1984 and 1987 Annual Conferences to introduce OMOV as the sole means of candidate selection. The 1987 Conference introduced a compromise involving shifting selection from the constituency General Management Committee to a local electoral college — individual members accounting for at least 60% of the votes, with the trade unions having the remainder. This compro-mise turned out to be very difficult and confusing to operate in practice and was not popular.

At the Annual Conference in 1993, John Smith tried again by proposing that trade union block voting in the selection of MPs should go completely. The new method would be OMOV, with a 'levy plus' system, under which trade union members paying the party levy could become full members of the Labour Party (and able to vote for themselves) by paying an extra £3.

Some trade union leaders regarded this as a threat to their influential position and were determined to stop it — with a good chance of success due to their block vote at the Annual Conference itself. The vote appeared to be finely balanced, with the unions more or less evenly divided on the issue, and the outcome was uncertain.

John Smith had put his reputation as Leader on the line in trying to push this issue through: *"As the party of change we must surely be able to change ourselves"*. John Prescott is generally credited with just tipping the balance with a last-minute off-the-cuff speech: *"This man, our Leader, put his head on the block by saying 'I fervently believe in a relationship and a strong one between the trades unions and the Labour Party'. He has put his head there; now it is time to vote. Give us a little trust"*. This appeal won the day — but only just (47.5% for; 44.4% against).

The OMOV selection process, although more democratic than the system it replaced, has turned out to be somewhat more bureaucratic. The Labour Party maintains, like the Conservatives, a national list of approved candidates; the difference is that local constituency parties are not obliged to choose a candidate only from that source — although the person who emerges at the end of the selection process will still need NEC endorsement.

Prospective candidates have to have been members of the Labour Party for at least two years. They must be nominated by a 'nominating body' — ward and branch parties, affiliated trade unions and socialist societies, women's sections, Young Labour and the Executive of the Constituency Labour Party (CLP).

The General Management Committee of the CLP short-lists and then vets the hopefuls, who are required to write an election address of not more than 500 words. If the constituency is already represented by a Labour MP, that person must be short-listed; and if that person is nominated by two-thirds of the nominating bodies, he or she is automatically re-selected and the process goes no further. Any candidate receiving 25% of the nominations (must include one from a ward or branch party) is automatically short-listed. Guaranteed short-listing is also enjoyed by anyone receiving 50% of the nominations from affiliated organisations. The shortlist should contain at least one woman.

The survivors of the general management committee stage move on to a selection meeting of the whole constituency party at which there is an NEC observer and an OMOV ballot. The process is completed when the NEC endorses the preferred candidate. The NEC has greater influence at selection for a by-election, intervening at an earlier stage by approving the shortlist. The rôle of the NEC in candidate selection is important and can lead to disagreements with constituency parties which are intent on choosing someone who is regarded as unsuitable by the NEC — in the end, the NEC wins. In some instances, the NEC has even imposed its own candidate upon the local party.

In an earlier chapter reference was made to the results of the 1997 General Election and in particular the increased number of women MPs, especially on the Labour benches. This was no accident. For a time, 1993 to 1996, the Labour Party practised positive discrimination in favour of women through the use of women-only (or 'closed') shortlists. Initially the hope was that sufficient women-only shortlists would emerge through local consensus. In the event, progress was disappointing, so the NEC intervened by requiring specific constituency parties to adopt women-only shortlists. This element of compulsion led to increasing disagreement and the practice was under review for termination after the next General Election. It had to stop in January 1996, anyway, when an Industrial Tribunal in Leeds declared the practice to be unlawful under the Sex Discrimination Act 1975.

At the end of October 2001, the government introduced its *Sex Discrimination (Election Candidates) Bill* in the Commons. The purpose of this very short Bill was to remove the constraints imposed by the Sex Discrimination Act on any party which wanted to take positive action to increase the representation of women in Parliament and in the devolved bodies.

The Labour Party — finance

About half of the membership of the UK's trade unions pay a political levy as part of their union membership subscription. This is passed on to the Labour Party nationally and makes up about 80% of its finance. This explains, to some extent, the voting power of the trade unions.

The remainder of the party's finance is made up of membership subscriptions from individual members and from cash donations from companies and individuals.

The Liberal Democrats — development and policy

The Liberal Democrat Party *(www.libdems.org.uk)*, as such, is relatively recent, although the 'Liberal' part goes back as far as the Conservative Party — generally regarded as starting in June 1859 when Whigs, Peelites and Radicals joined together. Whigs represented the merchant classes; Peelites were supporters of Sir Robert Peel and his interests in an industrialised society and financial reform; and Radicals were supporters of Charles James Fox and interested in extending the Great Reform Act 1832 to cover the working classes.

Between 1867 and 1918 the Liberal Party was one of the two parties of government — the other was the Tories. By 1918 it had become the third party and its fortunes declined further over the next 30 years. In the 1970s the Liberal Party saw something of a revival and increased its share of the vote, achieving 19% of the poll in 1974. However, it then experienced another decline for several years.

After the Labour Party Annual Conference in 1980 when the Left strengthened its control over the Labour Party, Shirley Williams, David Owen, William Rodgers ('the Gang of Three') and Roy Jenkins joined forces to found the *Social Democratic Party* (the SDP). Over the following months they were joined by another 30 moderate Labour MPs and a significant number of peers.

Later in 1981, the SDP and the Liberal Party formed the *Alliance*, remaining separate but joining forces to fight General Elections. After disappointing results from the 1983 and 1987 General Elections, David Steel (the Liberals' Leader) called for the merger of the two parties, but David Owen (the SDP Leader) was against that course of action. In the event, the members of both parties voted for the merger.

In 1988, a new party was formed, the *Social and Liberal Democratic Party* (SLD or the Democrats). At the end of 1989, the SLD changed its name to the *Liberal Democrats*. The SDP rump carried on for a time under the leadership of David Owen with everdecreasing fortunes until it was wound up in 1990, by which time it had only three MPs.

The initial policy position of the Liberal Democrat Party was set out in its document *Democracy of Conscience.*

For the 1997 General Election campaign, the Liberal Democrats differentiated themselves from the other two parties by being explicit about their intention to increase the rate of income tax by 1p to finance their policy options. In some commentators' eyes the Liberal Democrats were now more radical than New Labour.

The Liberal Democrats — organisation and leadership

The Liberal Democrats have a federal structure, comprising three 'state' parties for England, Scotland and Wales and a federal organisation at national level.

Each 'state' party is responsible for its own organisation, finance and the selection of candidates within its 'state'.

At national level, the Federal Policy Committee (FPC) looks after policy formulation and consists of the Leader, the President (also elected by the party members), four MPs, one peer, three local councillors, two Scottish and two Welsh representatives and 13 other members elected by the twice-yearly Federal Conference. The FPC prepares the election manifesto in consultation with the Parliamentary party. Policy proposals endorsed by a two-thirds majority at the Annual Conference automatically become party policy.

The FPC can call a ballot of the whole party on *"any fundamental question where, in its judgement, the values and objectives of the party are at issue or it is otherwise in the essential interests of the party"*.

The Federal Executive Committee is responsible for national organisation and consists of the Leader, the President, three Vice-presidents, two MPs, one peer, two local councillors and 14 other members elected by the Federal Conference.

The party Leader must be an MP but is elected by an OMOV ballot of all the individual members of the party — a democratic approach achieved much earlier than the other two parties.

The finance for the party is raised by membership subscriptions and fund-raising at local level.

Party finance

For many years the source of most of the Conservative Party finance was unclear. The party steadfastly refused to disclose the sources of the largest part of its income — even when rumours persisted of large cash donations from foreign businessmen (with the implication that secret influence was being sought). In 1997 the Conservative Party was £10.8m in the red; but the situation subsequently improved. The 1998/99 accounts revealed that Michael Ashcroft (the Conservative Party Treasurer with dual Belizean/UK citizenship and resident in Belize and Florida) gave over £1.1m in cash and kind to the party during the year and had also made loans to the party of up to £2m at any one time. This information was published as a result of the Hague Reforms but was largely prompted by increasing unease over the secret sources of party funds and comments by the Neill Committee. Mr (now Lord) Ashcroft announced his intention to return to live in the UK as a tax-paying resident and declined to resign as Conservative Party Treasurer.

In 1997 Tony Blair referred the issue of party funding to the Neill Committee on Standards in Public Life. Neill recommended that political parties should not receive donations from people who were not registered UK voters or from companies not registered and doing business in the UK and that the source of all donations in excess of £5,000 should be published. Neill also recommended that there be a national spending limit on elections and referenda. The issues highlighted by Neill were covered by the Political Parties, Elections and Referendums Act 2000 described in the sections dealing with the *Electoral Commission* in the next Chapter.

8   Elections

The Franchise — Qualifications — How elections are run — European Elections — Electoral Commission

The Franchise

The UK has *universal adult suffrage* — in other words, all people over the age of 18 and qualified to vote can do so. It was not always so. In 1832 at the time of the Great Reform Act of that year, only 5% of the adult population was entitled to vote — and they were all men. The franchise was progressively extended during the 19th century. It was not until 1928 that the UK effectively achieved universal suffrage (99%), when the vote was extended to all men and women over the age of 21 (the age of majority then).

Boundary Commissions — Electoral Commission

The UK is divided into 659 constituencies, each containing around 65,000 electors, although many constituencies will depart from this average by as much as 15,000.

Reviewing these constituencies to take account of population increase and drift is the task of four permanent Boundary Commissions, one for each of the four countries in the UK. Each review is undertaken every eight to 12 years and the aim is to establish approximately equal constituencies, although this is difficult to achieve in practice. Changes which emerge from the Boundary Commission reviews can be politically sensitive, in that particular changes may favour one party or the other.

Scotland and Wales have long had more seats than the size of their populations would justify — partly because they were guaranteed a minimum number of seats in the Redistribution of Seats Act 1944.

Under the Political Parties, Elections and Referendums Act 2000 (see the last section of this Chapter), the responsibilities of the Commissions will ultimately be transferred to the new Electoral Commission.

Who can vote?

UK citizens, citizens of other Commonwealth countries, and citizens of the Irish Republic resident in the UK are entitled to vote if:

- their name is on the electoral register for the constituency where they live;
- they are over the age of 18; and
- are not disqualified from voting (as explained later).

Citizens of other EU States cannot vote in Parliamentary elections but can vote (and stand) in local and EU elections.

The register is compiled by the local council Electoral Registration Officer. Completing the electoral registration form is compulsory, although it is not compulsory to vote. When the Poll Tax (Community Charge) was introduced by the Conservative government, many people did not have their names put on the electoral register, preferring to lose the right to vote, in an effort to avoid paying the tax.

The key place and date for registration used to be place of residence on 10 October each year. The draft register was open for public inspection until 16 December, during which period people could apply to the Registration Officer to have mistakes (usually not appearing on the register at all) corrected. After that, the register came into effect usually on the following 16 February, although the date could change if there was a General Election. People changing address could not be registered at their new address until the register was next updated and published.

That all changed as a result of the Representation of the People Act 2000 (RPA 2000). The RPA 2000 introduced a new system of registration where entitlement to vote is not tied to residence on one specific date during the year. The electoral registration officer still carries out an annual canvass (on 15 October with a view to publication on 1 December) but it is now possible for someone to have their name added to the register — so-called 'rolling registration' — at the beginning of a month. Because the register can now be altered on a monthly basis, the old system of objection and correction between 10 October and 16 December is no longer necessary. The register cannot (except as a result of a formal appeal) be altered for the purposes of any particular election once the final date for nominations has passed.

People who are disqualified from voting are:

- peers retained in the House of Lords by the House of Lords Act 1999;
- foreign nationals (including the citizens of other EU states);

- some patients detained under mental health legislation;
- convicted (but not remanded) people detained in a penal or mental institution; and
- people convicted within the previous five years of corrupt or illegal election practices.

Members of the armed forces, Crown servants and staff of the British Council employed overseas (and their wives/husbands if they are with them) can be registered for an address in the constituency where they would normally live.

In addition, British citizens living abroad who have been resident in the UK and registered as electors within the previous 15 years can make an annual declaration, which allows their names to be included on the electoral register in the constituency where they were registered before going abroad. They can then vote by proxy at any Westminster, Scottish Parliament, Welsh Assembly and European Parliament (but not local government) election which occurs while they are on the register. The Political Parties, Elections and Referendums Act 2000 reduced the period from 20 to 15 years — the so-called 'Ashcroft clause' (see the last section of the previous Chapter). Ballot papers will not be posted to an address outside the UK, so electors resident abroad (for whatever reason) necessarily have to vote by using a proxy to vote on their behalf. Declaration forms are available from British consulates and diplomatic missions and the first time a declaration is made, it has to be attested by a consular official.

Holidaymakers are allowed an absent vote in national elections, following regulations approved on 24 June 1986 giving effect to the provisions of the Representation of the People Act 1985 to extend the franchise. If a voter expects to be absent from the constituency on polling day, he or she can apply for an Absent Vote. Under the Representation of the People Act 1985 an Absent Vote is allowed at a particular election if the electoral registration officer is *"satisfied that the applicant's circumstances on the date of the poll will be or are likely to be such that he cannot reasonably be expected to vote in person"*. There is a special exemption for electors who are taken ill prior to the poll. Their applications can be accepted up to the sixth day before the election.

Candidates

UK citizens, citizens of other Commonwealth countries, and citizens of the Irish Republic resident in the UK can stand for election as an MP, provided they are over _21_ years of age and are not disqualified from sitting in the House of Commons.

Those who are disqualified from sitting in the Commons are:

- peers retained in the House of Lords by the House of Lords Act 1999;
- Bishops currently sitting in the House of Lords;
- undischarged bankrupts;

- some patients detained under mental health legislation;
- people sentenced to, and currently serving, more than one year's imprisonment;
- people personally guilty of corrupt or illegal election practices — in the last 10 years (corrupt) or seven years (illegal) if the offence was in that constituency; otherwise in the last five years (corrupt and illegal) elsewhere; and
- holders of certain offices listed in the House of Commons Disqualification Act 1975:
  — holders of politically restricted posts within the Civil Service;
  — members of the regular armed forces of the Crown or the Ulster Defence Regiment;
  — police officers;
  — holders of judicial office;
  — members of specified commissions, tribunals and other bodies (for example: Commission for Racial Equality, Lands Tribunal and Police Complaints Authority).

The election process

At least 25 days' notice of a General Election must be given. Nominations close at noon on the 19th day before the day of election (excluding Sundays and Bank Holidays). A candidate's nomination must be proposed and seconded by two 'subscribing' electors and signed by eight other 'assenting' electors — all registered within the constituency.

The nomination will also usually include a description of the candidate, of up to six words, which will appear on the ballot paper and should be sufficient to identify him or her. Although the major party candidates' descriptions are predictable, those of many of the individual candidates in 1997 were not: 'Lord Byro versus The Scallywag Tories', 'The Mongolian Barbecue Great Place to Party' and 'Space Age Superhero from Planet Beanus' were some of the more inventive and obscure! On occasions, descriptions are chosen which seem to be intended to confuse the voters and divert votes away from one of the main parties or a particular candidate. Reference to spurious political parties should decrease in future as a consequence of the Political Parties, Elections and Referendums Act 2000, which is described in the last section of this Chapter.

Nominations can be withdrawn, provided this is done in writing by the candidate (with one witness) so as to reach the returning Officer by noon on the 16th day before the day of the election. A candidate does not have to be backed by a political party. The Returning Officer can refuse to accept nomination papers which appear to be out of order.

Tactical voting may arise in those elections where the system is something other than First Past the Post (FPTP). The judicious use of the second preference can secure that a particular party's candidate is not elected. There are other instances where this might happen, even where the FPTP system is in use. On occasions (quite rare, it has to be said), a particular party may reach an understanding with another party about fielding candidates. This is more likely to happen where the parties have a reasonable working relationship (they wouldn't offer to co-operate, otherwise) and one party knows that its candidate has no chance of winning a particular seat, but the candidate of the other party might be able to win that seat if he or she had less opposition. This happened during the Alliance phase of the development of the Liberal Democrats. The standing candidate could not necessarily be regarded as a joint candidate for both parties, but the co-operating parties might go so far as to recommend their voters to vote for that candidate in that election. That kind of arrangement would involve a measure of *quid pro quo*.

Tactical voting may also occur about a particular issue and this can produce that exceptional event — the election of a truly independent MP. Voters who, in other circumstances, would vote for a particular party may decide to vote differently, just to make a point. This happened in the cases of Martin Bell (1997 General Election) standing in Tatton as an independent against Neil Hamilton on an 'anti-sleaze' ticket and Dr Richard Taylor (2001 General Election) standing in Wyre Forest as an independent in protest against the downsizing of Kidderminster Hospital.

Each candidate must deposit £500, which is returned if he or she receives 5% or more of the total votes cast. The requirement for a deposit was first introduced in 1918 and the purpose behind it is to discourage frivolous candidates. The Treasury does rather nicely from forfeited deposits — it made just under £800,000 from the 2001 General Election.

Each candidate must appoint an election agent, with an office in the constituency, to which all formal communications are sent. The maximum amount which a candidate can spend on 'election expenses' is fixed by statute — a lump sum plus an amount per elector. A candidate can post one election communication to each elector free of charge. The election agent must submit a 'return' of the candidate's election expenses not more than 35 days after the election. Failure to do so (without an 'authorised excuse' approved by a court) is an election offence, as is exceeding the statutory maximum.

Voting

People will usually vote in person at a polling station which open at 7am and close at 10pm. People who cannot reasonably be expected to vote in person (for example, away on holiday) can apply for an *absent vote* for that particular election. People who

138

are physically incapacitated, or who cannot vote because of the nature of their work or because they have moved to a new area, can apply for an *indefinite absent vote*.

People entitled to an absent vote can either vote themselves by post or have someone else (their proxy) vote at the polling station on their behalf. Postal ballot papers cannot be sent to addresses outside the UK.

The ballot papers are issued to voters at the polling station by the election staff, who check the name of the voter against the electoral register. At this point, some people discover that their name is not on the register and they cannot vote. The polling staff are supposed to impress an *official mark* on each ballot paper before giving it to the voter, to guard against a voter introducing fake ballot papers.

At the close of the poll the ballot boxes are sealed and then taken to the counting place where they are counted either straight away or on the next day. The Returning Officer supervises the count and although the count is not open to the public, the candidates, their agents and a small number of scrutineers appointed by them can observe the count.

It is at this point that problems can arise — especially if the Returning Officer decides to disallow some ballot papers because they are spoilt or because they do not bear the official mark. Ballot papers are spoilt if the voter has put more than a cross on the ballot paper and this could lead to the voter being identified; or if the voter's intentions are unclear.

If the winner's margin is very small, the candidates can demand a recount (and more than one) until the Returning Officer decides that a demand for a further recount is unreasonable. If there is a dead heat, after recounts, then the result is decided by the drawing of lots.

If the result is particularly close, the disallowed ballot papers (if they had been allowed) might have produced a different result, and any candidate who is dissatisfied with the conduct of the election can apply to the High Court for an *Election Petition* against the Returning Officer. In the 1997 General Election, Gerry Malone lost his seat at Winchester by two votes and immediately launched an election petition to have the result overturned. His election petition succeeded but his victory in court was a Pyrrhic one, because when the election was re-run in November 1997, he was not elected.

Developments in voting

In the context of the next General Election, the arrangements for people to cast their votes may be a little different. For the local government elections in May 2000, 32 local authorities volunteered to take part in Home Office pilot studies running and evaluating different voting arrangements.

These pilots were authorised by the RPA 2000. The pilots included: electronic voting;

total postal voting; voting spread over a number of days; and voting on Saturdays. Similarly, in the elections for the Greater London Authority, voters were able to cast their votes over a number of days, in order to increase the chances of a reasonable turnout — in the event it was about 35%. The effect of these new arrangements was subsequently analysed by Colin Rallings and Michael Thrasher of the University of Plymouth, for the Local Government Association. Their conclusion was that only all-postal ballots had any consistently significant effect on turnout. Where there was a mix of traditional and experimental methods, their conclusion was that there was no consistent effect. Further pilots are planned for the local government elections in 2002. The experience gained in these pilots may then result in permanent changes to the voting arrangements not only in local elections but also in elections for Westminster, Scottish Parliament, National Assembly for Wales and the European Parliament.

In January 2002, Robin Cook mentioned the possibility of voting over the Internet as one means of engaging the younger voters. This is likely to be many years off, but does indicate a willingness on the part of government to consider non-manual methods of voting, so long as proper security measures are in place.

It used to be the case that it was simple to describe the electoral process in the UK — all elections were first past the post (FPTP). That is no longer the case — as appears in the following sections, there is now a slightly confusing mixture of FPTP and other systems. The best example of this confusing situation is the elections for the Greater London Authority. Voters have two votes: one for the elected mayor, elected under the Single Transferable Vote System; the other for the members of the Assembly, using lists for the Additional Member System.

First past the post (FPTP)

The FPTP system in the UK involves the candidate with the most votes winning the seat — runners-up count for nothing. This is called the *'first past the post'* system and it will always lead to the result that the number of seats won by a party will not match its share of the vote. This is illustrated by the 1997 General Election results described in Appendix A. These figures demonstrate two features of the FPTP system in the UK: the New Labour government may have an overwhelming number of seats, but it has less than half of the total votes cast in the UK. The substantial number of Conservative voters in Scotland and Wales have no MPs representing their point of view in Parliament.

Alternative systems

The essential feature of the various alternative systems is that they are intended to produce a closer correlation between the distribution of votes between the parties and the allocation of seats, than achieved through FPTP. Some of the alternative systems are forms of proportional representation (PR), while others do not amount to a form of PR in the strict sense.

The *Alternative Vote (AV) System* is used in Australia to elect the House of Representatives. Each elector puts the candidates in order of preference; the votes of those at the bottom of the poll are transferred (if necessary and in order of the voters' preferences) until one candidate has half of the total vote — that candidate is then elected.

The *Single Transferable Vote (STV) System* is used in the Republic of Ireland for large constituencies which may contain four or five members and was used for the first time in the UK in the elections for the New Northern Ireland Assembly. Like the alternative vote system, each elector numbers the candidates in order of preference. The minimum number of votes needed to win is regarded as a *quota* — for example, in a five member constituency the quota is just over one-sixth of the votes. Once a candidate has achieved the quota, any surplus votes for him or her are transferred to other candidates following the voters' second and lower preferences. This process continues until the required number of people have been elected. This process is now used for the election of the Elected Mayor component of the Greater London Authority.

The *Additional Member System (AMS)* is used in West Germany, Bolivia, Italy, Mexico, New Zealand and Venezuela; and for the first time in the UK, in the elections for the Scottish Parliament, the Welsh Assembly and the Greater London Assembly component of the Greater London Authority. A proportion of candidates is elected in single member constituencies (usually by FPTP); the second, or additional vote, is used to select from a list — usually regional — which are used to produce a degree of proportionality between the votes and successful candidates. The lists can either be *open* (as in Bavaria) or *closed*. Closed lists just involve choice of party; open lists give the voter more choice, with the ability to choose a preferred candidate, rather than party.

The *List System* is used extensively in western Europe and to elect the Knesset in Israel. Again, lists can be either *open* or *closed*. In the *closed* list system, the political parties control the lists and the order in which their candidates appear in those lists. A party which, say, wins 30% of the vote will claim 30% of the seats and work its way down its list to fill those seats. In other words, electors are voting for political parties rather than individual candidates. This system was used for the first time in the UK's MEP elections in 1999. The *open* list system enables the voter to vote either for the party lists (in the published order) or to vote for a specific candidate on the published lists, effectively reordering the party's priorities.

The *Supplementary Vote System* involves voters marking their first and second choices. A candidate who obtains over 50% of the vote is immediately elected. If that does not occur, all but the top two candidates are eliminated and second choices reallocated to produce a result.

FPTP versus alternative systems

Criticisms of the first past the post system include:

- the government often has a majority of the seats for a minority of the votes;
- large parts of the electorate are denied representation by an MP of their political persuasion and their vote is effectively wasted;
- the large number of safe seats for the incumbent party means there is less genuine choice;
- the change in government can bring abrupt changes and frequent reversals in policy; and
- as the main parties become more regionally based as between the north and the south and as between urban and rural areas, they may become less national in their policy approaches.

Criticisms of the alternative systems include:

- voters will be less able to hold a government responsible for its record by turning it out at the next election;
- the list system, especially a closed list, effectively breaks the connection between the constituency voters and the member finally elected;
- coalition government will be less stable;
- the policy of the coalition will be a series of compromises and will lack any sure sense of direction; and
- some unsatisfactory members of the ousted coalition will reappear again in the new coalition.

The UK General Election

The more astute reader will have realised that PR (of whatever version) has yet to touch the UK General Election! Will the General Election ever be run using PR or will the New Labour government be reluctant to dilute the size of its majority produced by the FPTP system?

Following a New Labour manifesto commitment and as a result of an agreement between the Labour Party and the Liberal Democrats (the *Cook MacLennan Agreement*), the *Independent Commission on the Voting System* was set up in December 1997 under the chairmanship of Lord Jenkins of Hillhead, Liberal Democrat peer and former Chancellor, Home Secretary and President of the European Union. The Jenkins Commission reported in 1998 and the options it looked most closely at were the AMS used for the Scottish Parliament and Wales and a new more pragmatic system called *Alternative Vote Plus* (AV+).

The AV+ System (and any other form of additional vote or member system) would involve a reduction in the number of constituencies to yield a similar number of MPs currently derived from FPTP. The majority of MPs (80%-85%) would continue to be elected on a constituency basis, with the remainder elected through a top-up process. The Commission recommended that the constituency MPs should be elected through the AV system. As far as the top-up element was concerned, the Commission recommended that it should be allocated 'correctively', that is on the basis of the second vote and taking into account the number of constituency seats gained by each party in each respective area. The 'respective areas' recommended by the Commission were the 'preserved' counties and the equivalently-sized metropolitan districts.

The recommendations of the Commission would involve primary legislation, which may be preceded by a referendum. The Labour Party will not be in favour of any alternative system, because anything other than FPTP will reduce the number of seats which New Labour is likely to be able to win in a General Election. The results of the 1997 and 2001 General Elections are ample proof of that. New Labour's experience in the first elections for the Scottish Parliament and National Assembly for Wales was not encouraging (it was forced to form a coalition as the only way to take part in government in those countries) and the June 1999 elections for the European Parliament were not much better for New Labour.

European Parliament elections

The European Parliament (EP) is directly elected by the member countries. In all countries (including the UK) some system other than FPTP is now used. Elections of Members of the European Parliament (MEPs) are held every *five* years — the last occasion being 1999.

There are 626 MEPs, allocated to member countries as follows:

Germany	99
UK, France and Italy	87 each
Spain	64
Netherlands	31
Portugal, Belgium and Greece	25 each
Sweden	22
Austria	21
Denmark and Finland	16 each
Ireland	15
Luxembourg	6

In the UK, the Boundary Commissions produce the MEP constituencies. MEP constituencies consist of groupings of whole UK Parliament constituencies. Each MEP constituency has to be as near as possible to the 'electoral quota' — the total relevant electorate divided by the number of seats (roughly equivalent to eight House of Commons constituencies grouped together).

For the 1999 EP elections, the UK (except Northern Ireland) was divided into 11 regions, each returning between four and 11 MEPs:

Scotland	8
Wales	5
East Midlands	6
Eastern	8
London	10
North East	4
North West	10
South East	11
South West	7
West Midlands	8
Yorkshire & Humber	7
total	*84*
Northern Ireland	3
total UK	*87*

The European election process in the UK is broadly similar to that for the UK Parliament — but there are some differences. Unlike the UK Parliament elections, peers (including those retained in the House of Lords under the 1999 Act) can vote. Peers, Ministers of religion and UK MPs can stand for election as MEPs. Any EU citizen can stand and vote in MEP elections. The candidate deposit is £600, rather than £500. Nominations have to be signed by 28, rather than eight, assenting electors.

As explained earlier, the UK 1999 European Parliament Elections were held using the Closed List System rather than FPTP used previously. It is generally assumed that this change in the electoral process was responsible for Labour losing half of the 62 seats which it held prior to the elections. This may well account for Labour's reluctance to abandon FPTP for the next UK General Election!

The Political Parties, Elections and Referendums Act 2000

As explained at the end of the previous Chapter, the reason for the Political Parties, Elections and Referendums Act 2000 (PPER 2000) lay in the way in which the Conservative Party had been funded in recent years and the New Labour government wanted greater control and transparency in party funding. The New Labour government extended the terms of reference of the Neill Committee on Standards in Public Life to study the funding of political parties. The Neill Committee's Fifth Report, the *Funding of Political Parties in the United Kingdom,* was published in October 1998 and the government published its response in a White Paper in July 1999 — the result was PPER 2000.

The Electoral Commission *(www.electoralcommission.gov.uk)* was established in November 2001 by PPER 2000. The Commission is independent of government, non-partisan and directly responsible to Parliament. The appointment of the Chairman and members of the Commission is subject to approval by the Queen.

The Commission has a wide-ranging rôle:

- maintaining statutory registers in connection with political parties and donations;
- monitoring compliance with campaign spending controls;
- advising on political broadcasting;
- piloting new electoral procedures;
- conducting national referenda;
- reviewing election and referendum law and practice;
- promoting electoral or democratic system awareness.

In 2002 the Commission is due to take over the functions of the *Local* Boundary Commission for England. Provided that the devolved institutions agree, the Commission will also assume similar responsibilities in Scotland and Wales. In due course, the intention is that the Commission will also assume the responsibilities of the four Boundary Commissions.

The Electoral Commission — Registers

The Commission maintains registers: for political parties; for recognised third parties; for permitted participants in a referendum; and in connection with political donations.

Political parties have to register with the Electoral Commission if they want to field candidates in elections. A party's name cannot be used on the ballot paper unless it is registered with the Commission. Once registered, a party's name is protected and cannot be used by any other party contesting seats in the same part of the UK. These formalities do not apply to parish or community council elections.

If an organisation or person wishes to campaign on behalf of a political party, then the PPER 2000 imposes limits on what can be spent by that organisation or person if it, he or she is unregistered — currently £10,000 in England and £5,000 in the other countries. Exceeding these limits is a criminal offence. If the organisation or person is registered as a 'recognised third party', then the limits are much higher and depend upon the nature of the election and the country involved — for example £793,500 for a General Election in England, £30,000 for an Assembly Election in Wales. The PPER 2000 is relatively new and few organisations have registered as recognised third parties — the trade union Unison is one.

Similar registration processes apply to any organisation or person who wishes to campaign for a particular result in a referendum. The limit on expenditure is £10,000 if not registered as a 'permitted participant'. Again, exceeding this limit is a criminal offence. Once registered as a permitted participant, the organisation or person can spend, for example, up to £500,000 on a UK-wide referendum. Separate rules apply to registered political parties during a referendum. In addition, the Commission can 'designate' a specific permitted participant to campaign for a 'Yes' vote and another permitted participant to campaign for a 'No' vote, if that is the choice offered by the referendum. A 'designated body' is eligible to receive financial assistance of up to £600,000 from the Commission and its spending limit is increased to £5m. So far, no organisation or person has registered as a permitted participant. This will obviously change once a referendum is in immediate prospect.

Donations to registered parties, if above specified limits, have to be notified to the Commission and they will then be entered in the registers maintained by the Commission. The obligation to notify the Commission rests not only on the registered party but also on the donor. The limits are either £1,000 or £5,000 and depend upon whether the recipient is:

- an 'accounting unit' (£1,000) or the 'central organisation' (£5,000) of a registered party;
- a recognised third party (£5,000);
- a permitted participant (£5,000);
- a 'members association' (an organisation whose members are wholly or mainly members of a registered party) (£5,000);
- a member of a registered party for political activities (£1,000); or
- the holder of a relevant elective office (MP, MEP, MSP, AM, MLA, local council/GLA member (not parish/community), Mayor of London or elected mayor).

The register will include anonymous donations and will not disclose the addresses of private individual donors. The limits cannot be evaded by splitting donations into smaller amounts — they have to be aggregated when being reported to the Commission.

Where a company makes a donation to a political party, the shareholders have to agree and the amounts must be disclosed in the directors' annual report to shareholders. Because of this, many companies have decided that making political donations is not worth the trouble.

146

The European Union

*The development of the European Union — the Treaties — the single market — economic
and monetary union — the EU institutions, budget and funds*

The first part of this Chapter relates to the establishment of the ECSC and its subsequent
development into the EC, then the EEC, and finally the EU; and the future enlargement
of the EU. The second part describes various aspects of the present EU and its institutions.

The Treaty of Paris 1951

Within a space of 30 years, Europe had been the centre of two World Wars, with all
the disruption such events entailed; something had to be done at the political level
to prevent that ever happening again. After the Second World War it was also necessary for the heavy industries of Germany and France to be reconstructed in a way
which would not threaten peace and which would ultimately lead to Franco-German
reconciliation. This was the basis for the development of the European Union.

In May 1950 Robert Schuman proposed the idea of the European Coal and Steel
Community (ECSC), which was later established by the Treaty of Paris (April 1951).
The Schuman Plan was adopted by six states: France, Germany, Italy, Luxembourg,
the Netherlands and Belgium. The ECSC was given a 'parliamentary assembly' which
met for the first time in September 1952 in Strasbourg.

The Treaty of Rome 1957

This supra-national approach was further developed by the Six adopting the
Treaty of Rome in 1957, establishing two further Communities — the European

Economic Community (EEC) and the European Atomic Energy Community (Euratom).

The Treaty of Rome provided for the harmonious development of economic activity, a continuous and balanced economic expansion and an accelerated rise in the standard of living. These aims were to be achieved by the creation of a common internal market; the elimination of tariffs between Member States; free movement of goods, people, services and capital; and the elimination of distortions in the operation of the market.

The attitude of the UK towards Europe at this time was ambivalent, if not decidedly cool. Although the Treaty of Rome was probably seen as an interesting development, the UK believed that its main interests still lay in what was then seen as its 'special relationship' with the USA (whatever that actually meant in practice) and in the Commonwealth (which was at least growing, as the British Empire dwindled).

By 1961 it was clear that the European Communities were helping the Member States to turn in strong economic performances, so four other states (the UK under Harold MacMillan, Denmark, Ireland and Norway) applied for membership. These applications coincided with the period of office of Charles de Gaulle as President of France and he effectively blocked the entry of the UK in 1963 and later, in 1967 (under Harold Wilson). Opinions differ about the reason for this hostility by de Gaulle towards UK membership, but fear of a still relatively powerful and influential rival for France within the EEC seems to feature in most of them.

Although de Gaulle also appeared to be antipathetic to supra-national institutions, it was possible to make some progress during the 1960s in implementing some of the EEC Treaty, including the establishment of the Common Agricultural Policy (CAP) and the removal of trade tariffs between the member countries.

Matters came to a head in 1965/66 when de Gaulle refused to send representatives to take part in Ministerial meetings of the three Communities — the so-called 'empty chairs' crisis. This had important consequences, because the solution to the problem was the 1966 Luxembourg Compromise, which was an informal agreement that, whatever the Treaties might say about majority decision-making, agreements between governments would be made only by unanimity or consensus. The implication underlying the Luxembourg Compromise is still important — at least for the UK, if not for some of the other members.

In 1967 the three Communities — ECSC, Euratom and EEC — were merged and became collectively known as the European Community (EC).

The first increase in the EC came in January 1973 when the UK (under Edward Heath), Ireland and Denmark joined the Six. By this time, de Gaulle had been replaced by Georges Pompidou. The 1970s saw little in the way of further progress in integration, apart from the establishment of the European Monetary System (EMS) in 1979.

There followed two further enlargements: in 1981 Greece joined; and Spain and Portugal acceded in 1986.

The Single European Act 1986

A more significant development, in terms of supra-national integration, came with the 1986 Single European Act (SEA), taking effect in 1987. The SEA was the first comprehensive revision of the original 1957 treaties, confirming their aims and objectives. Further integration was promoted in two ways — the speeding-up of economic integration; and the strengthening of the supra-national institutions to speed-up the decision-making process. The enthusiasm generated by the SEA in turn led to pushing on with other earlier ideas for integration, such as European Monetary Union (EMU), which had been under discussion for some years.

The reunification of Germany, in October 1990, effectively added the former Democratic Republic of East Germany to the EC.

The Maastricht Treaty 1992

The next treaty revision exercise took place in December 1991 and led to the new all-embracing Treaty on European Union (popularly known as the Maastricht Treaty, from the name of the Dutch city where it was signed), signed in February 1992. However, this time, the process was not entirely smooth.

The Maastricht Treaty provisions had to be ratified at national level and there were difficulties in this in two countries — Denmark and the UK. Was this due to the supra-national policy-making élite being out of touch with the true wishes of the people of the nation states, who viewed further integration with some suspicion — especially given the uncertainty about some fundamental questions in Europe?

The result of the first Danish referendum in June 1992 was against ratification and this was seen as a threat to the whole process, until the second Danish referendum in May 1993 supported ratification. But the Danish experience had the knock-on effect of prolonging the process of ratification by a UK Parliament which was reluctant to cede sovereignty to the EU ('the European Super State' was one of the pejorative terms used by Mrs Thatcher while she was Prime Minister).

The UK eventually ratified the Maastricht Treaty, but only after securing the Social Protocol. This Protocol enabled the UK to opt out of the extension of EU social policy (usually called the 'Social Chapter') into areas of UK economic activity over which the then UK Conservative government preferred to retain national control. These opt-out provisions might be viewed as repeating the safeguards of the informal 1966 Luxembourg Compromise and they reflected continuing unease in the Conservative UK Parliament about the sovereignty issue. The New Labour government opted into the Social Chapter, as explained in the *Social Chapter* section, below.

The Maastricht Treaty summary

This treaty eventually came into effect in November 1993, after ratification by the Member States. The treaty had various effects:

- introduced new commitments, moving toward economic and monetary union (EMU) in three stages, the third stage being a single European currency, the euro;
- established the European Union (EU) from a combination of the European Community (EC) and the inter-governmental arrangements for a common foreign and security policy (see the later section *Decision-making in the EU*);
- set up the framework for a common foreign and security policy (CFSP, with its own Secretariat) under which inter-governmental decisions were to be taken only on a unanimous basis;
- increased co-operation on interior/justice policy issues;
- codified the principle of *subsidiarity* (action should be taken at European level *only* if its objectives cannot be achieved by Member States acting alone and can be better achieved by the Community — a principle which is of particular importance to the UK, reluctant to see the centralisation of power in Brussels; but which is also important for other member countries which view the principle as authorising devolution of power to regional level within Member States); and
- introduced the concept of European Union citizenship, supplementing national citizenship.

The Maastricht Treaty had some other implications which are mentioned in some of the sections which follow.

Corfu Treaty 1994

By a further treaty signed at Corfu in June 1994, Austria, Finland and Sweden joined the EU in January 1995. The Corfu Treaty also envisaged the accession of Norway, but they decided not to join. A number of the emerging democracies in central and eastern Europe applied to join and have agreements with the EU which may lead to membership. The Enlargement of the EU is discussed in the Agenda 2000 section, below.

The Amsterdam Summit and Amsterdam Treaty 1997

In March 1996 an Inter-Governmental Conference (IGC) was convened by EU heads of Government to consider further treaty amendments.

The approach now adopted within the EU is for treaty changes to be considered by an IGC first. The IGC's conclusions are then considered by the European Council. In fact, although technically one of the EU institutions, the European Council is seldom referred to by that name. Instead, the practice is now to describe the meeting by reference to the place where it takes place, calling it either the [place] Summit or the [place] European Council — for example, the 'Amsterdam Summit' or the 'Göteborg European Summit'. The next IGC to consider treaty revision is planned to take place in 2004.

The Amsterdam Summit met in late June 1997, to consider how to convert the IGC conclusions into a further treaty. The result was the Amsterdam Treaty which came into effect on 1 January 1999. This treaty provided new powers for the EU in a range of areas to protect EU citizens and to improve their standard of living — in relation to consumer protection, the fight against crime and drugs, the protection of the environment, recognition of the Charter on Fundamental Workers' Rights and giving the EU new powers to fight poverty.

The Amsterdam Summit, however, failed to agree a common EU-wide policy on immigration and asylum. The UK, Ireland and Denmark opted out, leaving the remainder to form the *Schengen Group* which adopted a common policy for their own countries. The UK was invited to join the Schengen Group at the Nice Summit in 2000.

Agenda 2000

On 16 July 1997, the European Commission published *Agenda 2000: For a stronger and wider Europe.* The aim of the document was to provide a blueprint for the EU for the next century. It outlined changes in the development and simplification of EU policies such as CAP and the Structural Funds, and it gave the Commission's Opinion on the accession applications from 10 countries in Central and Eastern Europe. Agenda 2000 also proposed a new budgetary framework for the EU for the period 2000-06, with a budget not exceeding 1.27% of the EU's GNP.

The proposed simplification of policies involved reducing the number of Objective areas from seven to three — two Regional Objectives and one Objective relating to human resources. Transition from the existing system to any successor system (assuming that the Agenda 2000 proposals were agreed) would be phased. The number of EU Initiatives would be reduced from 13 to three. A proportion of the Structural and Cohesion Funds would be reserved for EU Enlargement.

Any State wishing to join the EU would need to meet the economic and political criteria for membership and adopt the *aquis communitaire* (the laws and policies of the EU) before it could become a member. Cyprus having already received approval, Agenda 2000 proposed that accession negotiations start with Poland, Hungary, Estonia, Slovenia and the Czech Republic.

The Helsinki Summit 1999

The extension of the EU beyond that described in Agenda 2000 was discussed at the Helsinki Summit. The Helsinki Summit decided to avoid target accession dates for specific countries. Instead, it was suggested that by the end of 2002 the Commission should be in a position to admit any candidate country which met the qualifying conditions.

Accession talks would be opened with Slovakia, Romania, Bulgaria, Latvia, Lithuania and Malta. The list was also extended to include Turkey. The possible accession of Turkey (an important member of NATO) raised some interesting issues. Turkey had been rejected in 1997 but the EU was keen to encourage the accession of Turkey, provided some preconditions were met. Turkey would have to improve its human rights record and it would have to agree to refer its disputes with Greece over territories in the Aegean to the International Court of Justice in the Hague if they had not been settled by 2004. Turkey's case was not improved by the May 2001 finding of the European Court of Human Rights that Turkey had violated the human rights of thousands of Greeks when it invaded northern Cyprus in 1974.

The accession of these smaller States has implications for the voting system at meetings of the Council of Ministers. These implications are discussed in the later section *The Council of Ministers — voting*.

The Nice Summit and Treaty of Nice 2000

The five-day Nice Summit in December 2000 will be remembered as one of the more frustrating, largely due to the behaviour of Jacques Chirac, pursuing his own domestic French agenda. Indeed, he managed to strain Franco-German relations almost to breaking point.

The Summit 'proclaimed' (as a political declaration and not included in the Treaty of Nice) the new *EU Charter of Fundamental Rights*. The Charter is different from the European Convention on Human Rights, but could be viewed as a compilation of existing rights generally accepted within the EU. The 53 Articles of the Charter covered such issues as: equality between men and women; fair and just working conditions; right of collective bargaining and action; access to EU documents; and rights of elderly people to a life of dignity. There was an immediate dispute amongst the 15 Member States about the Charter's legal status — that would be reconsidered again at the 2004 IGC. The UK made it clear that it considered that the Charter had no legal authority but most commentators expect that the Charter will start to have some influence on the EU Court of Justice when reaching its decisions.

At this Summit, the implications of the (by now) 12 prospective EU members

(Bulgaria, Cyprus, Czech Republic, Estonia, Hungary, Latvia, Lithuania, Malta, Poland, Romania, Slovakia and Slovenia) joining the EU were discussed. Turkey had, for now, dropped by the wayside. The implications were related to Council membership and voting (the voting weights, the extension of Qualified Majority Voting (QMV) and the reduction of the right of veto).

The decision-making structures designed for the EU when it consisted of the six original Member States needed to be changed — if there was no change, as more members joined, the EU would grind to a halt. In addition, the size of Germany had increased significantly when reunification took place. After some hard bargaining, the larger Member States protected their positions *vis-à-vis* the smaller existing and new Member States. The Treaty of Nice 2000 proposals for the voting arrangements to apply when the EU has been enlarged to 27 are described in *Appendix C*. The Qualified Majority would be 258 (73%) votes and would need to represent a minimum of 62% of the population. This would mean that three large and one small Member States could block developments and Germany's 80m population would give it the edge over the UK and France, with 60m each.

The EU Commission currently numbers 20, with the UK, France, Germany, Italy and Spain having two Commissioners each. As the EU enlarges, the Commission would be capped at 27, with each Member State having just one Commissioner. Any new members beyond 27 would have to take turns on a rota basis. This was interpreted as confirming power in the hands of the Council of Ministers, leaving the Commission with little more than a back-up rôle.

Some commentators believe that it is unlikely that any of the candidate members will have been able to become full EU members by the 2004 IGC, so the position described in the second part of this Chapter should be taken to reflect the current position.

EU immigration and asylum policy was also considered at this Summit (see the earlier section on the *Amsterdam Treaty 1997*). Joining the Schengen Group would give the UK access to the Schengen database of people who have been refused entry by other countries. The UK tended to cherry-pick those EU Directives on immigration which suited its fairly negative attitude to immigration. A more liberal view might acknowledge the overall EU need to import more skilled workers to fill gaps in the EU workforce.

However, all of this will be reconsidered at the 2004 IGC, which promises to be a fundamental review of the EU — including whether the EU needs a formal Constitution. Two possible Constitutional models have been suggested: either a legally binding written Constitution; or a more flexible one, based on individual treaties, laws and cases. This is discussed further in the following section on the *Commission's 2001 White Paper on EU Governance*.

The Göteborg Summit 2001

This Summit was a disappointment to its Swedish hosts, who had hoped to push forward the enlargement issue, so that at least Poland and Hungary could join by the 2004 IGC. Several factors worked against this: Because the Treaty of Nice was regarded as implicitly impinging on the Irish Constitution, especially with regard to neutrality, the Irish government was compelled to put the treaty to a referendum (all of the other EU countries would ratify it through their respective Parliaments). The result of the referendum was 'No', albeit a slim one on a poor turnout. This tended to overshadow the discussions and raised the question of whether other countries might start to lose enthusiasm for enlargement. For example, enlargement might mean that the French would not benefit so much from the Common Agricultural Policy subsidies, and the Spanish might see their EU grants being redirected to the poorer Czechs and Slovaks.

The Summit was unusual in that the newly-elected President Bush took part at its beginning (billed as an EU-US Summit) and the second disappointment was the continued refusal of the US to ratify the Kyoto Treaty on gas emissions. Finally, the level of violence shown by anarchist demonstrators was so great that security at future Summits became a matter of concern — to the extent that the practice of Summits being held in the home country of the current EU President might be abandoned, with all future Summits being held in more secure conditions in Brussels.

The Commission's 2001 White Paper on EU Governance and the IGC 2004

The 'No' result in the Irish referendum on the ratification of the Treaty of Nice must have come as something of a shock to the Commission and the Council. Was this a rerun of the difficulties which faced the ratification of the Maastricht Treaty in 1992 — a possible illustration of the EU supra-national policy-making élite being out of touch with the true wishes of the people of the nation states?

So, in July 2001, the Commission published its White Paper *European Governance*, with responses before the end of March 2002. The White Paper's Executive Summary puts the problem succinctly:

> *"Today, political leaders throughout Europe are facing a real paradox. On the one hand, Europeans want them to find solutions to the major problems confronting our societies. On the other hand, people increasingly distrust institutions and politics or are simply not interested in them. The problem is acknowledged by national parliaments and governments alike. It is particularly acute at the level of the European Union. Many people are losing confidence in a poorly understood and complex system to deliver the policies that they want. The Union is often seen as remote and at the same time too intrusive...*

Yet people also expect the Union to take the lead in seizing the opportunities of globalisation for economic and human development, and in responding to environmental challenges, unemployment, concerns over food safety, crime and regional conflicts. They expect the Union to act as visibly as national governments. Democratic institutions and the representatives of the people, at both national and European levels, can and must try to connect Europe with its citizens. This is the starting condition for more effective and relevant policies".

The Commission suggested a new approach within the EU — less top-down, through:
- better involvement and more openness;
- better policies, regulation and delivery;
- global governance; and
- refocused institutions.

The 'global governance' was an explicit reference to the wider international rôle which the EU now saw itself as having.

On the specific subject of EU Governance, the White Paper identified five principles which were thought to underpin good governance:

- *Openness:* The institutions should work in a more open manner.
- *Participation:* The quality, relevance and effectiveness of EU policies depend on ensuring wide participation throughout the policy chain.
- *Accountability:* Rôles in the legislative and executive processes need to be clearer.
- *Effectiveness:* Policies must be effective and timely, delivering what is needed on the basis of clear objectives, an evaluation of future impact and, where available, of past experience.
- *Coherence:* Policies and action must be coherent and easily understood.
- *Proportionality and subsidiarity:* From the conception of policy to its implementation, the choice of the level at which action is taken (from EU to local) and the selection of the instruments used, must be in proportion to the objectives pursued. This means that before launching an initiative, it is essential to check systematically: (a) if public action is really necessary; (b) if the EU level is the most appropriate one; and (c) if the measures chosen are proportionate to those objectives.

The results of this consultation exercise will be analysed by the Commission and any proposals considered at the 2004 IGC.

The Single Market

The Single Market provides for the free movement of people, goods, services and capital, as envisaged by the Treaty of Rome in 1957.

This is achieved by removing customs tariffs, liberalising the movement of capital, opening up public procurement to all Member States and the mutual recognition of professional qualifications. The object of all of this is to reduce business costs and increase efficiency, widen consumer choice and create jobs and wealth.

The first stage of European Economic and Monetary Union (EMU) as envisaged by the Maastricht Treaty was the completion of the Single Market by 31 December 1993. By the European Economic Area (EEA) Agreement, which came into force on 1 January 1994, most of the EU Single Market provisions were extended to Iceland, Norway and Liechtenstein.

That is the theory. In practice, individual countries can find ways of inhibiting trade between Member States, often to protect domestic industries. Germany used its strict brewing laws, at least for a time, to prevent the sale of 'poor quality' UK beer in Germany.

Following the BSE outbreak in the UK, the export of UK beef to other EU countries was banned on grounds of 'public health' — probably, it has to be said, understandably at the time. By June 1997 the UK government believed, on the basis of expert technical advice, that its slaughtering and animal health arrangements had become the best in the EU.

The UK government was disappointed that the ban on UK beef imports to other EU countries had not been lifted, despite requests for this to happen. It therefore felt justified in threatening to ban the import into the UK of beef from those EU countries with 'inferior' arrangements, on 'public health' grounds. Banning such imports for 'tit-for-tat' or for purely trade reasons would have contravened the EU treaties. The BSE issue is still unresolved since although the formal legal action started by the Commission against France for its refusal to lift its ban on British Beef was decided in the UK's favour, the final stage, the imposition of some form of sanction, could take years.

European Economic and Monetary Union (EMU)

Given the reasons for the original foundation of the EC/EU, it is hardly surprising that the idea of monetary union was on the agenda for many years — at least since the 1970s. A start was made by establishing a currency unit (the European Currency Unit or *ecu*) which was used only for internal EU purposes.

EMU was originally due to have been achieved by 1980, at least in theory. However, the programme was effectively stopped by a combination of the 1973 oil crises and the wild fluctuations in the international monetary system which that crisis caused.

In 1979, another attempt was made but this time it was more modest — the European Monetary System (EMS). A component of EMS was the Exchange Rate Mechanism (ERM) which the UK did not initially join, because it was felt at that time that membership of ERM would constrain UK domestic economic policy.

However, by October 1990 the then Chancellor of the Exchequer, John Major, was able to persuade Mrs Thatcher that it would be a good idea for the UK to join the ERM, because of low inflation in Europe. However, John Major (as Prime Minister) was later forced to take the UK out of the ERM because the money markets decided that sterling was overvalued in relation to the other currencies in the ERM. This withdrawal took place on 16 September 1992 ('Black Wednesday') after a phenomenal amount of the UK's reserves (£4 billion) had been spent in trying (and failing) to maintain the value of sterling within the ERM limits, in the face of widespread and determined currency speculation and in spite of a 5% increase in UK interest rates to 15% during the course of the day. The Italians also had to withdraw the Lira from the ERM at the same time. Its ERM experience goes a long way towards explaining the UK's subsequent, and continued, scepticism about EMU envisaged by the Maastricht Treaty and participation in the euro.

The Maastricht Treaty, following the earlier *Delors Report* (1989) on the achievement of economic union, plotted the progress towards full EMU in three stages:

- *Stage 1* began on 1 July 1990, aimed at the abolition of all restrictions on the movement of capital between Member States; and concluded at the end of 1993 with the practical completion of most of the Single Market;
- *Stage 2* began on 1 January 1994, with the establishment of an advisory and consultative European Monetary Institute (EMI) to strengthen central bank co-operation and monetary policy co-ordination and to prepare for the establishment of the European System of Central Banks (ESCB); monetary policy remained with national governments who co-ordinated their economic policies within agreed, but non-binding, guidelines; and
- *Stage 3* began on 1 January 1999, with the creation of a single currency, the *euro* (€); exchange rates within Euroland were locked together at that date, but the euro only came into public use on 1 January 2002.

The UK negotiated a special Protocol (an 'opt-out') to the Maastricht Treaty, which recognised that the UK was not obliged to move from stage 2 to stage 3 of the EMU.

The European Council, on the advice of the EMI, adopted in June 1997 the principles and fundamental elements of the new Exchange Rate Mechanism (EMI II). Those Member States who wished to move to stage 3 had to satisfy certain *convergence criteria* on inflation rates, government deficits, currency fluctuation margins and interest rates — and those convergence criteria were the source of some of the problems. The governments of Germany and France expressed complete confidence that they would achieve stage 3 by the Maastricht deadline. However, the economic measures that they were obliged to impose on their people in order to meet the inflation and public deficit criteria, were not very popular amongst their electorate.

Euroland and a two-speed Europe

The *euro* (€) and *Euroland* is now a reality. In May 1998, the Council of the European Union decided that 11 Member States — Belgium, Germany, Spain, France, Ireland, Italy, Luxembourg, Netherlands, Austria, Portugal and Finland — had complied with the convergence criteria and could participate in stage 3. The European Central Bank (ECB) came into operation in June 1998 and its predecessor, the EMI, having completed its work, started to liquidate itself. On 1 January 1999, stage 3 was initiated with the irrevocable locking together of the exchange rates of the currencies of the 11 participating Member States and with the ECB assuming responsibility for the single monetary policy.

The monetary policy included more than exchange rates — it also involved a single interest rate across Euroland. The issue here was that, traditionally, interest rates are used to control inflation and regulate growth within the economy. Difficulties were experienced in countries like Ireland (high inflation, Euro interest rate too low) and Germany (stagnation in the economy, euro interest rate too high).

Greece joined the preparations for Euroland in January 2001, bringing the number of participants up to 12. The three non-participating Member States — the UK, Denmark and Sweden — have limited rights to participate in ECB meetings and their currencies remain free to fluctuate against the euro.

During the transitional period, in participating Member States prices were quoted in the relevant national currency as well as in euro and cent. The first euro banknotes and coins came into public use on 1 January 2002 — the delay was due to the fact that over 10 billion new banknotes needed to be printed and over 70 billion new coins minted, to replace those in circulation in Euroland.

At its initial launch in January 1999, the euro was presented as a currency which would be strong enough to hold its own against the US dollar. However, in exchange rate terms, the euro soon progressively declined in value against both sterling and the US dollar. The euro started trading at about $1.18, but by 3 December 1999 it had dropped in value to parity with the US dollar, a position not thought possible at its launch — and by the end of January 2000, it had dropped further to $0.98. Many thought that the ECB would intervene in the money markets to prop up the value of the euro, but at that stage, doubtless mindful of the UK's previous experience on 'Black Wednesday', the ECB appeared to believe that no national authority could win against the money markets and left the euro to find its own level. The money markets were concerned about Italy being allowed a less rigorous application of the convergence criteria and about Germany's internal economic difficulties and willingness to use public money to support ailing industries.

However, the euro continued to slide until it had reached $0.84 by September 2000 — a loss of 27% of its launch value. At that point the International Monetary Fund (IMF) *(www.imf.org)* decided that something had to be done to protect the world economy, which would slow down if any further decline in the value of the euro led to rising inflation in Euroland and artificially strong currencies elsewhere. So, on 22 September, the G7 group of leading industrialised countries responded to the IMF's call. The ECB led a surprise assault on the money markets and started to buy the euro soon after 10.30am. The Bank of England, Bank of Japan and the US Federal Reserve rapidly intervened to lend support and started to buy the euro themselves. The Central Banks of Canada and France also lent support. It was estimated that up to £5.5 billion was spent, globally, in supporting the euro. The decline was halted, with the euro ending the day at $0.88. The position was stabilised — at the beginning of 2002, the euro was trading at $0.86 (equivalent to £0.62). Some commentators thought that the timing of the ECB action was no coincidence — in the following week Denmark was due to vote in a referendum on whether or not to join Euroland. In the event, although the result was close, the Danish people decided that they did not wish to join the euro.

The significance of the Danish result was that it was the first time that a referendum had been held on the issue — no national referendum had been held within the 12 participating states before their entry. Commentators suggested that the Danish people were influenced more by issues of loss of Danish national identity within the EU than by the economic arguments. The next promised referenda are due to be held in Sweden and the UK, although precisely when those referenda are attempted may be influenced (and delayed) by the Danish result.

In the meantime, if Denmark, Sweden and the UK remain outside the euro for any length of time, this may raise the prospect of the core countries of the EU within Euroland deciding to go ahead with greater political integration between themselves — in effect creating a two-speed Europe. The credibility of the euro in the world money markets may not be improved if the candidate countries mentioned in the *Nice Treaty 2000* section earlier also join the euro when they join the EU — because their economies are amongst the weakest in Europe. However, they are unlikely to be able to meet the convergence criteria, precisely because their economies are so weak.

The UK, the Euro and the 'Five Tests'
The timing of the referendum on UK membership of the euro was raised by the Tories in their 2001 General Election campaign, although it failed to interest the voters in

supporting their party. The issue was first raised shortly after the 1997 General Election and in October 1997 the Chancellor of the Exchequer, Gordon Brown, announced his 'Five Tests' which would need to be satisfied if the UK felt able to join the euro:

- Would joining the euro create better conditions for firms making long-term decisions to invest in the UK?
- How would adopting the euro affect the UK's financial services?
- Are business cycles and economic structures compatible so that the UK and the other EU countries could live comfortably with euro interest rates on a permanent basis?
- If problems emerge, is there sufficient flexibility to deal with them?
- Will joining the euro help to promote higher growth, stability and a lasting increase in jobs?

The continued strength of the pound against the euro could also be an obstacle. The Treasury would not look kindly on having to take action to diminish that strength to facilitate UK entry into Euroland.

Cynics suggest that these Five Tests are largely meaningless and can justify continued delay in putting the issue to a UK referendum. In any case, economics is hardly an exact science, so the timing of the UK referendum will almost certainly be a political, rather than economic, decision. The climate of opinion within the UK population may become more positive as they experience the advantages of a single currency when on cross-border holidays in Euroland.

In addition, some concern exists about whether the EU Commission could resist interfering in the internal economies of the countries in Euroland. For example, in May 2001, Gordon Brown issued a strongly-worded warning to the Commission when it attempted to make 'recommendations' about UK fiscal policy, especially holding the level of public spending at 37.3% of output, when New Labour intended to increase it by £51bn.

The Social Chapter

The 'Social Chapter' of the Maastricht Treaty comprised a Protocol and Agreement setting out a basic framework for the adoption of minimum standards of social protection at work and provided for measures agreed by all Member States to be brought forward in the form of Directives. There are certain work-related issues which are specifically excluded from the Social Chapter as being matters for individual Member States: employees' pay, the right to strike, the right to impose lock-outs and freedom of association.

As explained earlier, the UK opted out of that part of the Maastricht Treaty, so the other 14 Member States adopted a separate Agreement on Social Policy. The New

Labour government adopted the Social Chapter when it came into office, so it now applies to the UK. So far, three Directives, derived from the Social Chapter, were adopted following the Treaty of Amsterdam: the *Parental Leave Directive* (right to unpaid leave of up to three months for parents of both sexes with a new child within the first eight years); *European Works Councils* (right of workers to consultation in works councils in large firms with over 1,000 employees in one EU Member State and 150 employees in another); and the *Part-time Work Directive* (right of part-time workers to comparable pro-rata employment rights as those enjoyed by full-timers, unless there is an objective justification for different treatment),

The Parental Leave and European Works Council Directives came into force in 1998 in the other 14 Member States — the UK was given two years to implement those Directives in UK law. The Parental Leave Directive was implemented in the UK on 19 December 1999 but the right to take leave only existed in relation to children born or adopted after its implementation and then only during the first *five* years after the child's birth or adoption, because of the age at which the UK education system starts. The right is to take 13 weeks' parental leave, acquired after the completion of one year's service with the employer. As far as the Part-time Work Directive was concerned, the UK had until 20 January 2000 to implement it, although, in the event, negotiations with unions and employers delayed its introduction until 1 July 2000. Part-timers acquired the right to the same hourly rate as comparable full-timers, the same access to pension schemes, the same access to training, and the same entitlement to annual leave as well as parental and maternity leave, on a pro-rata basis with comparable full-timers.

The Three Pillars of the Union

The European Union is said to rest on three pillars:

The first pillar (Pillar 1) is the *European Community* itself, derived from:
- the Treaty of Rome, as revised by the Single European Act;
- the European Institutions;
- European Economic and Monetary Union;
- European Citizenship.

The second pillar (Pillar 2) is a *Common Foreign and Security Policy,* achieved through:
- systematic co-operation, common positions and joint action on foreign policy.
- common defence policy based on the Western European Union (WEU).

The third pillar (Pillar 3) is *Home Affairs and Justice,* involving closer co-operation on:
- asylum policy.
- rules on crossing Members States' external borders;

- immigration policy;
- combating drug addiction;
- combating international fraud customs, police and judicial co-operation.

The European Institutions

The main European Institutions are:

- European Commission *(www.europa.eu.int)*
- Council of the European Union *(www.ue.eu.int)*, which is different from
- European Council *(www.ue.eu.int)*
- European Parliament (EP) *(www.europarl.eu.int)*
- European Court of Justice (ECJ) *(www.curia.eu.int)*
- European Court of Auditors *(www.eca.eu.int)*
- European Investment Bank (EIB) *(www.bei.org)*, which is different from
- European Central Bank (ECB) *(www.ecb.int)*
- Economic and Social Committee *(www.ces.eu.int)*
- Committee of the Regions *(www.cor.eu.int)*
- European Ombudsman *(www.euro-ombudsman.eu.int)*.

Issues of national pride would suggest that a single location was not an achievable objective anyway, but one of the aspects which tends to make the EU seem rather remote from the ordinary people is the location of its various institutions. The European Commission is based in Brussels. The EP has its plenary sessions in Strasbourg and Brussels, its committee meetings in Brussels, and its Secretariat based in Luxembourg — the logistics must be horrendous. The ECJ and EIB are based in Luxembourg. The European Council meets in each Member State according to the rotation in the Presidency of the Council.

There are currently 12 European Agencies, Foundations and Centres established by the European Commission or European Council which are spread around the Member States. For example, the European Agency for the Evaluation of Medicinal Products (EMEA) is based at Canary Wharf; the European Environment Agency (EEA) is based in Copenhagen; the European Centre for the Development of Vocational Training (CEDEFOP) is based in Thessaloniki; and the European Monitoring Centre for Drugs and Drug Addiction (EMCDDA) is based in Lisbon.

The European Commission

Put simplistically, the *European Commission* is, in effect, the EU Civil Service — but it is far more than that. Unlike national equivalent organisations, the Commission can initiate policy, proposing legislation without waiting for instructions or guidance from Ministers. The Commission carries out the decisions of the European Council and checks that EU rules are observed by the Member States. The Commission can also develop ideas which transcend national interests — sometimes described as being 'the conscience of the European Community' — but their initiatives must be sensible if they are to survive the legislative process.

The Commission operates on a collegiate basis and is organised into *Directorates-General*, the equivalent of Whitehall ministries. Each policy area is overseen by one of 20 *Commissioners* (one per member state, except for the five most populous, UK, France, Germany, Italy, Spain, which have two each). One of the Commissioners acts as *President of the Commission*.

The Commissioners are expected to support the interests of the EU rather than their own nation states. Their period of office is, as a result of the Maastricht Treaty, now five years to synchronise with the EP electoral cycle, and their appointment is subject to EP approval. As demonstrated in 1998, when some individual Commissioners were found to have indulged in nepotism in their area of responsibility but were reluctant to resign, the EP is, however, not very effective in removing individual unsatisfactory Commissioners from office — the whole Commission has to be dissolved.

The Council of the European Union — the Council of Ministers

The Council of the European Union (usually called the *Council of Ministers* to avoid confusion with the European Council) comprises the *Ministers* of the 15 Member States, representing the subjects under discussion, so its precise membership (and name) will vary according to the subject-matter being discussed; for example 'the Council of Agriculture Ministers' will include the UK Minister for Rural Affairs within the Department for Environment, Food and Rural Affairs, and 'the Council of Economic and Finance Ministers' will include the UK Chancellor of the Exchequer. The Council of Ministers now meets in about 25 different guises and includes Ministers from all UK Ministries except Defence — some (e.g. Economy and Finance) meet monthly, while others (e.g. Transport, Environment and Industry) meet two to four times a year.

The Council of Ministers exercises legislative and decision-making powers within the EU. It is also a forum in which the representatives of the governments of the Member States can assert their interests and attempt to reach agreements on any differences. Its other rôles include general co-ordination of EU activity (for example, the internal market and single currency) and inter-governmental co-operation.

The main task of the Council of Ministers is to take policy decisions which are political in nature and its work is supported by the Committee of Permanent Representatives (COREPER). Like the Council, the precise membership of COREPER will vary according to the subject matter under discussion — and will consist of permanent civil servants from each Member State, or each Member State's ambassador to the EU.

The *President of the Union* is responsible for chairing all meetings of the Council of Ministers and COREPER, and holds office for six months (starting in January and July each year), on a pre-determined rotational basis between the Member States (from 1 July 1995: Spain; 1996: Italy then Ireland; 1997: Netherlands then Luxembourg; 1998: UK then Austria; 1999: Germany then Finland; 2000: Portugal then France; 2001: Sweden then Belgium; 2002: Spain then Denmark; 2003: Greece). The UK last held the Presidency in the first half of 1998 and the European Summit (see next section) meeting in June 1998 met in Cardiff. Because of the relatively short period of office (six months is hardly long enough to learn the ropes), the *General Secretariat* of the Council, nationals of the Member States, provides a large degree of continuity, in much the same way as the UK Civil Service.

The Council of Ministers — voting

A distinctive feature is the system of voting — by weighted majority voting. The size of each member State's weighted vote is approximately proportional to its population:

Germany, France, Italy and UK	10 each
Spain	8
Belgium, Greece, Netherlands, Portugal	5 each
Austria, Sweden	4 each
Ireland, Denmark, Finland	3 each
Luxembourg	2
total votes	*87*

As explained in the section on the *Treaty of Nice 2000*, these figures (and the QMV described in the next paragraph) are set to change as the EU is enlarged from 15 Member States towards 27.

The voting depends on the issue involved. Although the Council tries to reach a consensus, within Pillar 1, where a European Commission proposal is involved, at least 62 votes must be cast in favour. In some cases *qualified majority voting* (QMV) operates — 62 votes from at least 10 Member States are needed. In other cases (e.g. taxation) a unanimous vote is needed — this is why the UK was able to veto the proposal for a *withholding tax* (all income in the EU taxed at source at a standard rate, to eliminate tax evasion; largely a German problem but which had been agreed by the other Member States) on the grounds that the lucrative Eurobond market would be driven from the City of London (and outside the EU), with the consequent loss of jobs and prestige. Issues within Pillars 2 and 3 require unanimity, except where a joint action is proposed, where a qualified majority is sufficient.

What this means is that, in theory, the UK can sometimes be outvoted and be expected to implement the legislation agreed by the majority. Little use was made of the feature until the SEA and Maastricht. However, it is still not as simple as the treaties might suggest — only consensual policy stands the best chance of implementation throughout the EU.

Voting was one of the issues which came to the fore when the expansion of the EU was discussed at the Nice Summit 2000 (see earlier section). There were serious concerns that the smaller countries, once admitted to the EU, would be able to veto and effectively stultify any development of the EU along the lines desired by the original Member States. The Treaty of Nice 2000 effectively safeguarded the rights of the larger Member States.

The European Council — European Summit

The European Council (as already explained, now usually called the *European Summit*) was established in 1974 and comprises the Member States' Heads of State or Government (France sends its President), their foreign Ministers and two Commissioners (the President and one other). The President of the EP is invited to make a presentation at the opening session of each meeting. Of all the EU institutions, the European Summit is probably the best placed to initiate major policy developments, if only because of its composition.

The European Summit meets at least twice each year, with venues following the Presidency rota (e.g. June 1998: Cardiff; December 1998: Vienna; March and June 1999: Berlin and Cologne; October and December 1999: Tampere and Helsinki, Finland). However, after the violence at the Göteborg Summit in June 2001, the venue may become fixed in Brussels for security reasons. The European Summit decides broad policy lines for EU policy and for matters of foreign and security policy and co-operation in justice and home affairs. The European Summit has some significant policy developments to its name; for example: the SEA, EMU and Maastricht.

The European Parliament (EP)

Between 1952 and 1958, the EP was known as the *Common Assembly* of the ECSC. From 1958, its name was changed to the *European Parliament* as a result of the Treaty of Rome — at that time the 142 MEPs were *not* elected but were *delegates* of their national parliaments. As provided by the Treaty of Rome, the EP was directly elected for the first time in 1979, by which time the number of MEPs had increased to 410 from the nine Member States. Its current membership is now 626 directly-elected MEPs from the 15 Member States, of which the UK has 87.

Elections take place every four years, the last being in 1999. Prior to the 1999 EP elections, UK (except Northern Ireland) MEPs were elected by the 'first past the post system' — the MEPs of the other Member States were elected by some form of proportional representation. The UK system changed as a consequence of the European

Parliament Act 1999, which provided for a regional list system of proportional representation. In each region, parties would win a share of seats which was broadly proportional to their share of the vote in that region.

For the 1999 EP elections, the UK (except Northern Ireland) was divided into 11 regions, each returning between four and 11 MEPs:

Scotland	8
Wales	5
East Midlands	6
Eastern	8
London	10
North East	4
North West	10
South East	11
South West	7
West Midlands	8
Yorkshire & Humber	7
total	84
Northern Ireland	3
total UK	87

In the EP, MEPs sit in political groups rather than in national delegations. There are currently seven political groups, together with some 'non-attached' MEPs. The minimum number of MEPs required to form a political group is: 29 if they come from a single Member State; 23 if they come from two Member States; 18 if they come from three Member States; and 14 if they come from four or more Member States. The political groups have ostensibly similar political ideologies but from markedly different national political traditions; they have to learn to live with their internal differences:

- Group of the Party of European Socialists (PSE);
- Group of the European People's Party and European Democrats (PPE-DE);
- Group of the European Liberal, Democratic and Reform Party (ELDR);
- Confederal Group of the European United Left/Nordic Green Left (GUE/NGL);
- Group of the Greens/European Free Alliance (Verts/ALE);
- Union for Europe of the Nations Group (UEN);
- Group for a Europe of Democracies and Diversities (EDD).

The rôle of the EP is to be consulted about major decisions and has shared power with the Council over the EU budget. It is interesting to see how the powers of the EP have developed.

The EP was first directly elected in 1979 and had fairly limited powers. At that time these were confined to giving non-binding opinions on proposed EC legislation; the right to examine the work of the Commission and the Council; and the ability to dissolve the Commission.

However, the rôle of the EP was enhanced when it gained some influence over the EC (now EU) budget. The SEA introduced some further development by giving the EP a part to play in the legislative process in certain policy areas — the 'Co-operation Procedure' — and thus enabled it to influence the Council in those areas.

This process of developing the power and influence of the EP was taken one step further by Maastricht, by introducing a new power of 'Co-decision' — put simply, this new power can enable the EP to reject legislation, rather than comment upon it. Much of EU legislation now goes through either the co-operation or co-decision procedure.

The EP is a unique multi-national Parliament representing the interests of 370 million European citizens. It meets in public and its debates, opinions and resolutions and published in the *Official Journal of the European Communities*. There is simultaneous translation of all parliamentary and committee debates in the EU's 11 official languages: Danish, Dutch, English, Finnish, French, German, Greek, Italian, Portuguese, Spanish and Swedish. All EP documents are translated and published in these languages.

The activities of the EP and its bodies are the responsibility of the *Bureau*, which consists of the President and 14 Vice-Presidents and, in a consultative capacity, five *Quaestors* responsible for administrative and financial matters directly affecting MEPs. The members of the Bureau are elected for a two year period of office. The EP's work and plenary agenda are organised by the Conference of Presidents which consists of the President of the EP and the chairmen of the political groups.

Outside the plenary sessions, the EP's detailed work is done in its committee system — there are 17 standing committees specialising in particular fields such as: agriculture and rural development; fisheries; regional policy, transport and tourism; and women's rights and equal opportunities. These standing committees are supplemented by subcommittees, temporary committees or committees of inquiry. Joint Parliamentary Committees handle relations with parliaments of States linked to the EU under *association agreements*. Inter-parliamentary delegations maintain relations with a large number of parliaments in other states and with international organisations.

The European Court of Justice (ECJ)

The ECJ comprises 15 judges and nine advocates-general, appointed for a renewable term of six years, chosen by common accord of the governments of the Member States. The judges choose one of their number to be *President of the Court* for a renewable term of three years. The President of the Court directs the work of the ECJ and presides at hearings and deliberations.

The work of the ECJ is assisted by a *Court of First Instance*, which deals with certain types of cases brought by companies and individuals. The ECJ itself can sit in plenary session or in chambers of three to five judges. Plenary sessions are normally used when a Member State or EU Institution is involved and so requests; or in very complex or important cases.

The process in the ECJ or the Court of First Instance is rather different from UK courts. The procedure starts with a written stage and a *Judge-Rapporteur* and *Advocate-General* are appointed. The Judge-Rapporteur summarises the facts alleged and the arguments of the parties and any interveners. The oral stage then starts with the judges sitting in public and questioning the parties. Some weeks later, in open court, the Advocate-General analyses the facts and the legal aspects and proposes a solution by means of an *Opinion*. The judges then deliberate in private until they reach a majority decision on a judgment initially drafted by the Judge-Rapporteur — the final judgment is usually consistent with the Advocate-General's earlier Opinion. The judgment is later read in open court, in the language of the case, which can be one of the 11 official languages or Irish.

The importance of the ECJ should not be underestimated — not least as a vehicle for UK constitutional change. The body of EU law and treaty provisions is increasing, as is its impact on the citizens of the Member States and the rights which they enjoy. The important point is that EU law now has precedence over domestic UK law and its implementation within the UK can be enforced by the ECJ.

The nature of EU law is also important — its terminology is necessarily general because it needs to make some sort of sense for all of the different internal arrangements within the 15 Member States. So, this broad-brush approach enables the ECJ, in interpreting what EU law actually means, to *make* law to a greater extent than any of its national counterparts.

European Court of Auditors

As its name suggests, the Court of Auditors checks that the EU's money is spent according to its budgetary rules and regulations and for the purposes for which it was intended. It has 15 members, one from each Member State.

European Investment Bank (EIB)

The EIB was created in 1958 under the Treaty of Rome to finance capital investment furthering European integration by promoting EU economic policies. It is the EU's long-term lending institution and the Member States contribute to its capital. As a result of the Lisbon European Council in March 2000, the EIB Board of Governors decided to establish the 'EIB Group' (consisting of the EIB and the EIF) to provide increased support for small to medium enterprises in the EU.

The EIB *Board of Governors* consists of Ministers designated by each of the Member States, usually the Finance Ministers; one of the Board's members is appointed as *President of* the EIB. The Board of Governors determines credit policy, approves the balance sheet and annual report, commits the EIB in respect of financing operations outside the EU and decides on capital increases. The Board of Governors appoints the Board of Directors, the Management Committee and the Audit Committee.

The EIB *Board of Directors* consists of 25 members, of which 24 are nominated by Member States and one by the European Commission. The Board is responsible for the management of the EIB, including lending and borrowing operations.

The EIB *Management Committee* is a collegiate executive body controlling the day-to-day activities of the Bank. The EIB President or one of the Bank's seven Vice-Presidents presides at Management Committee meetings.

In 1994, the *European Investment Fund* (EIF) was established to provide guarantees to facilitate the financing of trans-European infrastructure and capital investment. In June 2000, as a result of a restructuring, the EIB became the majority shareholder (60%) of the EIF; other shareholders are the European Commission (30%) and some 80 banks (10%) across the EU. The President of the EIB is Chairman of the EIF's Supervisory Board.

European Central Bank (ECB)
European System of Central Banks (ESCB)

The ECB is the product of the Maastricht Treaty and the three stage process of monetary union and the single unit of currency, the euro. The ECB came into existence in June 1998 and is part of the European System of Central Banks (ESCB). The ESCB consists of the ECB and the EU national central banks (NCBs). The NCBs of the 11 Member States participating in the euro are full members; the NCBs of the other four non-participating Member States are still members, but with a special status.

The primary objective of the ECB is to maintain price stability and it does this through:

- defining and implementing the EU monetary policy;
- conducting foreign exchange operations;
- holding and managing the official foreign reserves of the participating Member States; and
- promoting the smooth operation of the payment systems.

The ECB has a Governing Council and an Executive Board. The Governing Council has a supervisory rôle and because it still has responsibilities for completing monetary union, the three non-participating Member States are members of the Council on the grounds that they may join the euro.

The ECB's capital is €5,000m, subscribed by NCBs — non-Euroland NCBs subscribe at a lower rate. In order to provide the ECB with foreign reserve assets, the NCBs can provide up to €50,000m, should the need arise.

European Economic and Social Committee (ESC)

Established by the Treaty of Rome, the ESC advises the Commission, the Council and the EP. It now consists of 222 representatives, divided between the 15 Member States according to a given quota. The representatives are drawn from employers' organisations, trade unions, farmers, consumer groups, professional associations etc. The Committee 'grassroots' views in a formalised and institutional way, on draft EU legislation.

Committee of the Regions (COR)

This was established in 1994 as a consultative body responsible for bringing forward local and regional viewpoints on EU legislation and policy. It consists of 222 members (and 222 alternate members) who are elected officials from cities and regions across the EU, appointed by the Member States. COR is based in Brussels and its work is divided between five 'commissions' and a 'study unit'.

The COR produces *Opinions* which are adopted at one of the COR's four-yearly plenary sessions, at which the COR's President presides.

European Ombudsman

Every citizen of each Member State is both a national and a European citizen. One of the rights of a European citizen is to apply to the European Ombudsman if he or she believes that they have been the victim of maladministration by the EU institutions or bodies. In carrying out his investigations, the Ombudsman can require relevant EU institutions and national authorities to supply him with information. The Ombudsman may make recommendations to the EU institutions and he can refer a case to the EP for consideration at a political, as opposed to an administrative, level.

Decision-making in the EU

Put simply, proposals usually originate from the Commission, which by then will have consulted interested parties and groups, often through the extensive lobbying arrangements which exist at EU, as well as national, level. A recent example of the consultation process is the Commission's 2001 White Paper on *European Governance*.

Proposals from the Commission are sent to the Council of Ministers and are usually looked at first by COREPER, on behalf of the Council. At the same time the proposals are also sent to the EP and the Economic and Social Committee, each of which makes its views known to the Council.

Finally, the Council will reach a decision (taking into account the advice it has received from the EP and the Economic and Social Committee), using whatever voting method is relevant for the particular policy area involved.

However, there are important areas of policy which are deliberately *not* handled through the mechanisms set out in the Treaties. This approach started in 1970 with foreign policy but has since been extended to police co-operation, drug-smuggling, cross-border crime and immigration. For these particular issues, member governments have wanted to retain an element of national sovereignty, preferring to deal with them at inter-government level — effectively keeping them out of the hands of the Commission and the EP; and largely out of the public arena.

The Maastricht Treaty to some extent gave formal authority to this inter-governmental activity by recognising it as providing, with the EC, two of the Three Pillars of the EU. One was the Common Foreign and Security Policy (CFSP) and the other was Judicial and Home Affairs (JHA) co-operation. Decisions within these two Pillars are, unlike the other EU Treaty-based arrangements, unanimous only — so national sovereignty in these areas of policy is preserved. There is no accountability to the EU institutions — information, only, is supplied.

The product of the decision-making process emerges from the Commission or the Council of Ministers in different ways. *Regulations* are of general application and are, in effect, EU law, binding as such. *Directives* are also of general application and are binding, but only in relation to the objective to be achieved, leaving the means of doing so up to each member state within its domestic law. *Decisions* are directed towards specific bodies and are binding only on those bodies. Finally, *Recommendations* and *Opinions* can be issued — which, as their name suggests, are not binding.

The Community budget

The Community's income consists of:

- levies on agricultural imports;
- customs duties;
- proceeds of a notional rate of VAT of up to 1.4% on a standard 'basket' of goods and services; and
- contributions from members states based on their gross national product (GNP).

In the case of the UK, it has an annual rebate worth £2bn because, without a rebate of that value, its net contribution would be much more than was justified by the UK share of the EU GNP.

The future shape of EU finance was reached at a European Council Summit in Edinburgh in 1992, because of concerns about the future size of the EU budget. The overall revenue ceiling was kept at 1.2% of EU total GNP until 1995. Since 1995, the ceiling rose, in steps, with the aim of reaching a new limit of 1.27% of EU total GNP by the end of 1999. The 1.27% target was continued by the Agenda 2000 document. The Edinburgh Summit also agreed to allocate more funding to the poorer regions of the EU.

By the end of 1999, agricultural spending was planned to be less than 50% of the total budget — compared with 80% in 1973 and 60% in 1996.

Community Policies and Funds

The *Common Agricultural Policy* (CAP) is designed to secure food supplies and stabilise markets — it has, however, in the past led to over-production (various food 'mountains' and 'lakes') and put pressure on the EU budget. The operation of the CAP seems to excite universal criticism, but the aim of Agenda 2000 is to bring EU prices down to world market levels, against the background of World Trade Agreements. Existing price support measures have to be reduced because of GATT (General Agreement on Trade and Tariffs) rules but direct aid to agriculture might be the preferred future alternative.

The *Common Fisheries Policy* (CFP) concerns the conservation and management of fish stocks. This is achieved by setting annual total allowable catches (TACs) for different species of fish which are then allocated to EU Member States, taking account of traditional fishing patterns. The phenomenon of *Quota hopping* appeared whereby UK registered fishing boats are, in fact, wholly or partly owned by foreign interests but use up the UK fishing quota and then land most of their catch outside the UK.

The EU also operates four *Structural Funds* (about one-third of the total EU budget) aimed at:
- promoting economic development in underdeveloped regions;
- regenerating regions adversely affected by industrial decline;
- combating long-term unemployment and helping young people to enter the labour market;
- helping workers to adapt to changes in industries and systems of production;
- streamlining agricultural production, processing and production systems; and
- promoting rural area development.

The *European Regional Development Fund* (ERDF) finances infrastructure projects and industrial investment — with the ERDF providing 75% and the Member State 25%. The *European Social Fund* (ESF) supports training and employment initiatives aimed at young people and unemployed people. Agricultural restructuring is funded via the *European Agricultural Guidance and Guarantee Fund* (EAGGF). The modernisation of the fishing industry is supported by the *Financial Instrument of Fisheries Guidance* (FIFG). The Agenda 2000 European Commission discussion document puts forward a proposed reduction in the number of Structural Funds, involving a reclassification of EU areas.

The Structural Fund which is most often referred to in the UK is the ERDF. The ERDF has a number of eligibility criteria and the Regional Government Offices act as co-ordination centres in the UK. As far as the UK is concerned, the most relevant ERDF Objectives are 1, 2 and 5a:

- *Objective 1*: To promote the development and structural adjustment of regions whose development is lagging behind (Merseyside, Northern Ireland and the Highlands & Islands);
- *Objective 2:* To convert the regions, frontier regions or parts of regions (including employment areas and urban communities) seriously affected by industrial decline (various areas);
- *Objective 5a:* To promote rural development by: speeding up the adjustment of agricultural and fisheries structures in the framework of the common agricultural policy and of the review of the common fisheries policy (various areas).

About £7 billion is made available to the UK from the Structural Funds.

The Maastricht Treaty set up a *Cohesion Fund*, designed to reduce the differences between levels of development in richer and poorer Member States, to facilitate monetary union — this is becoming more important as the EU increases in geographical size. Initially, the Cohesion Fund was reserved for four Member States (Spain, Portugal, Ireland and Greece) to improve their infrastructure, provided their GNP was less than 90% of the EU average.

10 The National Health Service

Administrative structure and finance

Development

The National Health Service (NHS) *(www.nhs.uk)* was created in July 1948 as part of the social welfare policies of the Labour government (under Clement Attlee) immediately after the Second World War. The social welfare policies went beyond the NHS and were aimed at providing universal and free welfare benefits for those people who were in need — *'from the cradle to the grave'*. Such an approach had been envisaged by William Beveridge's 1942 Report on *Social Insurance and Allied Services*, which provided the plan for the development of the UK's welfare state.

Since the 1940s, the original 'free of charge' approach has been significantly modified, so that many aspects of the NHS are now paid for — by those deemed able to afford to do so. In January 2002, New Labour announced proposals which would have a fundamental impact on the NHS — see the later section on *The end of the NHS as we know it?*

Administration at national level

The Secretary of State for Health in England and the relevant Ministers in Scotland, Wales and Northern Ireland are responsible for the administration of the NHS in their areas.

The departments supporting the Secretary of State and Ministers are:

England	Department of Health *(www.doh.gov.uk)*
Scotland	Health Department *(www.scotland.gov.uk)*
Wales	Health and Social Services *(www.wales.gov.uk)*
Northern Ireland	Department of Health, Social Services and Public Safety

The *NHS Executive* in the Department of Health has the rôle of developing and implementing policies for the provision of health services in England. The NHS Executive is responsible for planning, resource allocation and major capital projects. The eight regional offices of the NHS Executive replaced the 14 regional health authorities (RHA), which were abolished in April 1996. They, in turn, are due to be replaced in 2003 (see the section on *The NHS Plan*).

Administration at local level

In England and Wales, prior to April 1996, the NHS was administered by District Health Authorities (DHA) which were responsible for hospital-based services and by Family Health Service Authorities (FHSA) which were responsible for community-based services. Their responsibilities were combined and given to all-purpose Health Authorities (HA), whose boundaries largely reflected the former DHA boundaries — covering populations ranging from 125,000 to 1 million.

The rôle of the new HAs was to assess the needs of their population and to produce plans (with local people, local authorities, hospitals, community health services and GPs) and then buy in services from GPs, pharmacists, opticians and dentists, to meet the needs identified in the plans. That has now changed again under New Labour, as will be seen later (the sections on *The New NHS* and *The NHS Plan*). In Scotland, Health Boards carried out similar responsibilities.

Community Health Councils (CHCs)

In each HA area there are Community Health Councils (CHCs) which enable local opinion to be expressed on the HA's plans and the standard of service being provided. The CHC comprises representatives of local authorities, voluntary organisations and other people with an interest in local health services. CHCs usually produce annual reports. The equivalent to CHCs in Scotland are Local Health Councils.

However, the days of CHCs are numbered. At the time that the New Labour government announced its intention to abolish CHCs, some commentators suggested that CHCs had been rather too successful in highlighting problems in the NHS. The government's idea was that local government could assume the 'community champion' rôle of the CHCs, even though local authorities already had more than enough to do.

These changes were highlighted in the consultation documents *Involving Public and Patients in Healthcare* and *Shifting the Balance of Power within the NHS*. The abolition of the statutory CHCs required legislation and the CHC staff would transfer either to a Primary Care Trust (PCT) or a Health Authority — including the new Patient Advocacy and Liaison Services (PALS), which the government planned to be in place in all NHS Trusts and most PCTs by April 2002.

NHS Trusts

The NHS and Community Care Act 1990 introduced the idea of NHS Trusts. A hospital or health service unit (for example: an ambulance service or a community health service) could apply to become a self-governing NHS Trust, independent of direct local health authority control. Similar arrangements were introduced in Northern Ireland for Health and Social Services Trusts, which had more responsibilities because of the greater integration of health and social services there.

NHS Trusts are still part of the NHS, accountable to the relevant Secretary of State and have to produce business plans, annual reports and accounts; and hold at least one public meeting each year. A board of directors runs the Trust, which can employ staff, set its own pay and conditions, carry out medical research and even treat private patients. By the middle of 1996 there were over 520 NHS Trusts — by 1999 their number had been reduced to 450, mostly through amalgamations creating larger Trusts. A visit to the quango website *(www.cabinet-office.gov.uk/quangos)* in January 2002 showed that their number had again increased to 500.

NHS Trusts derived most of their income from providing services under contracts with health authorities and GP *fundholders* — the so-called 'internal market'. There were problems with Trusts and the internal NHS market. Some of the smaller Trusts rapidly realised that they were not viable and had to be taken over by larger Trusts, presumably to gain from economies of scale. Mergers brought with them 'rationalisations' of hospital and even ambulance services — including the closure of complete hospitals or A&E departments, provoking much, but largely ineffectual, public anger. However, on occasions, that public anger can be effective. At the 2001 General Election, the electors of Wyre Forest, in protest at the downsizing of Kidderminster Hospital, voted for Dr Richard Taylor as their Independent MP, unseating a junior New Labour Minister in the process.

The operation of the NHS internal market led to a burgeoning bureaucracy within the NHS, diverting resources away from clinical and nursing services. The Conservative government's preoccupation with demonstrating the benefits of the internal market for reducing waiting lists for certain kinds of surgery led, it is said, to a skewing of surgical services so that waiting lists for other kinds of surgery lengthened.

The NHS Trust process was seen as one of the ways of encouraging private sector participation in capital development in the public sector — through the Private Finance Initiative (PFI). The Conservative government made much of its scheme to promote the design, construction and operation of new hospitals through PFI. Although many PFI schemes were approved (50 since 1992), the programme in the NHS effectively stalled due to the complexity of the negotiations. There were also doubts within the private sector financiers about whether the NHS Trusts had the necessary legal power to enter into PFI agreements at all — without that power, the agreements would be unenforceable.

The New Labour government is no less enthusiastic about PFI schemes as a means of creating the appearance of limiting public expenditure, given the limitations on public expenditure which it has accepted. New Labour took two courses of action to get the programme going again — the responsibility for pushing schemes forward was transferred from NHS Trusts to the NHS Executive; and legislation was passed to remove any doubts about the legal powers of NHS Trusts (and other public bodies) to complete PFI/PPP agreements. For a critique of the impact of PFI/PPP on the NHS, see the section on *Public Private Partnerships* in the later Chapter *Industry and Commerce.*

GP Fundholders

As a result of the 1990 Act, in England and Northern Ireland, GP practices with more than 5,000 patients were eligible to apply for 'fundholder status'. In Wales and Scotland, the threshold was 4,000 patients.

The object of this scheme was to give GPs the opportunity to manage a proportion of the NHS budget allocated to them, leading (it was said) to better management and control of costs and innovative methods of patient care. The budget was used to buy non-urgent hospital services from any hospital in the UK, public or private. Community nursing services could be bought from the NHS and the budget covered the charges for the cost of drugs issued on prescription by the practice and the costs of running the practice itself.

The points made earlier about the consequences of the internal NHS market applied here as well — there were over 3,500 GP fundholding practices involving 15,000 GPs and other commissioning groups involving 7,000 GPs. The potential for bureaucratic waste in running the internal market was not lost on the New Labour government, which produced a White Paper *The New NHS* overhauling the administration of the NHS.

The 'New' NHS

The 'internal market' was replaced with 'new financing and accounting arrangements'. GP fundholding was replaced with *Primary Care Groups.*

Under the *New NHS,* HAs (under a phased transition which started in April 1999) lose their direct commissioning responsibilities and, instead, concentrate on drawing up three-year *Health Improvement Programmes* in consultation with local authorities, NHS Trusts and Primary Care Groups. The rôles of the three levels of the 'New' NHS — Primary Care Groups, NHS Trusts and the Department of Health — are considered in turn.

Primary Care Groups and Primary Care Trusts

Primary Care Groups (PCG) consist of all the GPs in a given area and assume responsibility, with community nurses, for commissioning services for their local community. The aim is that PCGs cover about 100,000 patients and each has a capped unified budget, to provide a measure of flexibility. PCGs are able to choose one of four models for their individual rôle, while the GPs within them retain their independent contractor status:

- in an advisory capacity in support of the HA in commissioning care;
- as part of the HA, assuming devolved responsibility for managing the healthcare budget for their area;
- as a free-standing Primary Care Trust (PCT), accountable to the HA for commissioning care; or
- as a PCT, with extra responsibility for providing community services for their area.

Each PCG is managed by a board, consisting of between four and seven GPs, one or two community nurses, a representative of the local social services authority, a lay member and the chief executive of the PCG. By April 2001, half of PCGs had become PCTs; the remaining half are expected to become PCTs by April 2002. The future rôle of PCTs is discussed in the later section on *The NHS Plan*.

NHS Trusts

NHS Trusts have devolved operational responsibilities within the local Health Improvement Programme and have long-term service agreements with Primary Care Groups. The service agreements can either relate to a particular care group (such as the elderly) or a particular disease (such as heart disease) and will be linked to new *National Service Frameworks*.

The NHS Plan

In 2000, New Labour announced its 10 year NHS Plan — *"to give the people of Britain a health service fit for the 21st century"*. The Plan was linked to the March 2000 Budget settlement which was aimed at increasing NHS expenditure by one third in real terms over the next five years. That aim might turn out to have been a little ambitious, and actual progress will depend upon the state of the government's finances and the other calls on public resources.

To lead the changes, a new *Modernisation Board* was established under the chairmanship of the Health Secretary and including health care professionals and patient representatives. The rôle of the Modernisation Board is to advise the Secretary of State.

In addition, the Department of Health set up 10 Task Forces to drive the change required by the NHS Plan. Six of the Task Forces concentrate on particular service issues (such as mental health, and waiting times and access to services), while the remaining four concentrate on methods for improvement (such as quality and investment in IT).

The actual work of ensuring that the NHS Plan is delivered is given to the Modernisation Agency, which works with the NHS Executive Regional Offices and NHS Trusts.

All of this is accompanied by a massive restructuring of the NHS, some of which requires legislation. The intention is that the existing 95 English HAs will be replaced by 28 larger (and more remote?) Strategic Health Authorities (StHAs). The StHAs will be responsible for the strategic development of health services and the management of the performance of PCTs and NHS Trusts in their area. StHAs will be established in April 2002, although the NHS regional offices will continue for another year. The local PCTs will become the lead NHS organisation in assessing need, planning and securing all health services in their area, and in providing most community services and developing primary care services, such as GPs and dentists. The plan is that by 2003/2004, 75% of NHS resources will be spent through PCTs. NHS Trusts will continue to provide most secondary care and specialist services in hospitals. From April 2003, the NHS Executive's eight regional offices will be abolished and be replaced by four new Regional Directors of Health and Social Care, who will supervise the development of the NHS. These Regional Directors will provide the link between the various NHS organisations and the government. Whether these changes in structure actually produce any benefit in terms of service delivery remains to be seen.

The end of the NHS as we know it?

The NHS, as originally envisaged and managed, is a monolithic organisation and has always been regarded as separate from, and alternative to, the private medicine sector. However, in 2001 the NHS waiting lists were becoming longer, rather than shorter, and New Labour started to examine ways of improving matters — including using the facilities within the private sector. In late 2001, the Secretary of State, Alan Milburn agreed a concordat under which the NHS would arrange for patients who had been on a waiting list for more than six months to have their operation done in a private sector hospital — or even in a hospital elsewhere in the EU. A private sector representative was also appointed to the NHS Modernisation Board.

In mid-January 2002, the Secretary of State, Alan Milburn, made a rather surprising announcement about New Labour's latest view of the future shape of the NHS and, in particular, the future involvement of the private sector. Apart from the content of what he said, the method by which his views became public was surprising — he chose to make the announcement in an interview with the *Times*. In doing this, he breached the understanding that Ministers would announce major changes first in

Parliament. Mr Milburn was summoned to the Commons by the Speaker, Michael Martin, to explain himself and answer MPs' questions. Tony Blair was reported as having an equally difficult time at the Parliamentary Labour Party meeting later that week. The proposals, it was reported, had received no prior consideration by either the Cabinet nor the NHS Modernisation Board before Alan Milburn gave his *Times* interview.

In his interview with the *Times* (15 January 2002), Alan Milburn described the NHS as Britain's *"last great nationalised industry"*, a model which he regarded as unsuitable for the 21st century. The best hospitals (those with three stars under the government's NHS Trust league tables system) would be given greater management freedom as 'foundation hospitals' (similar to 'foundation schools'). The idea might also be extended to PCTs. The management of the poorer performing hospitals could be awarded as 'franchises' to charities or even the private sector. Some of the immediate criticism suggested that this arrangement was not totally dissimilar to the Railtrack arrangement on which Stephen Byers had pulled the plug. Alan Milburn explained that the legal and financial framework was being examined and that proposals would be announced within three months.

Department of Health

The Department of Health and the NHS Executive retain those responsibilities more appropriate for national level. These include producing the new National Service Frameworks (at the rate of one new Framework a year) which are intended to promote consistent access to services and quality of care. Frameworks are intended to set national standards, put in place strategies to aid implementation, and make arrangements for monitoring performance. Frameworks which have been published include those for mental health, coronary heart disease, cancer, and older people. Future Frameworks will include those for diabetes, renal services, children services and long term conditions.

The Secretary of State will be able to intervene where a particular health authority, Primary Care Group or NHS Trust is not working satisfactorily. The NHS itself overall will be held to account by the government through a new *National Performance Framework* which will be used to measure NHS performance.

The *New NHS* White Paper also set up some initiatives (in addition to the National Service and Performance Frameworks) aimed at securing quality within the NHS, including:

- a new *National Institute for Clinical Excellence* (NICE), set up as a Special Health Authority on 1 April 1999, to provide specialist guidance on best practice within health technologies and clinical management; and

- a new *Commission for Health Improvement* to support and supervise the quality of clinical services at local level — and to intervene if necessary.

Health Action Zones

Health Action Zones (HAZs) are 'partnerships' between the NHS, local authorities, the voluntary and private sectors and local communities, to find solutions to inequalities in health and to develop services which are more responsive to patients and users.

More than £274 million was made available to help HAZs in 1999-2002. The 26 HAZs (established in 1998 and 1999) cover populations from 180,000 to 1.4 million and cover over 13 million people in total. HAZs are located in some of the most deprived areas in England, including inner cities, rural areas and ex-coalfield communities. HAZs test joint working and pooled budget arrangements between the agencies involved in the 'partnership'. HAZs are co-ordinated locally by a 'Partnership Board' and their performance is monitored by the NHS Executive regional offices.

The HAZ 'partnerships' represent a new approach to public health — linking health, regeneration, employment, education, housing and anti-poverty initiatives, to respond to the needs of vulnerable groups and deprived communities within the area they cover. The objective is that the services and approaches pioneered and developed by HAZs are, if successful, adopted for mainstream activity.

How the NHS is funded

Just over 80% of NHS expenditure is met through general taxation. The remaining 20% comes from:

- the NHS element of National Insurance contributions;
- charges to patients for drugs and treatment;
- income from land sales and income generation schemes; and
- funds raised from voluntary sources.

Health Service Commissioners

There are three *Health Service Commissioners* (one each for England, Scotland and Wales). In practice, the three posts are held by one person who is generally called the *'Health Service Ombudsman'* and who is also Parliamentary Commissioner for Administration (the Parliamentary Ombudsman). In Northern Ireland, the Commissioner for Complaints undertakes a similar rôle.

The Commissioner handles complaints made by members of the public that they have suffered injustice or hardship as a result of:

- failure in service from an NHS body;

- failure to provide a service which the person was entitled to receive; or
- maladministration by an NHS body.

The Commissioner produces an annual report for Parliament.

In 1996, the scheme was extended to cover complaints in respect of all family health service practitioners and about the exercise of clinical judgment. Under the *New NHS* White Paper, the complaints procedure has been revised (in line with most other complaints processes) so as to promote resolution at the lowest possible level, by adopting a three-stage approach:

- Stage 1: called *Local Resolution* — the complainant and the *complaints manager* of the local health care provider (NHS Trust, GP etc) involved attempt to resolve the complaint at local level. If that fails, then:
- Stage 2: called *Independent Review* — a specially trained member of the NHS Trust or Health Authority called a *convener* becomes involved, who will consult an independent lay person to see if local resolution is still possible. The convener may decide to go further and convene a local three person lay panel (the convener, an independent lay person acting as chairman and one other) to consider specific issues raised in the complaint. The complainant does not have the right to demand that the convener sets up a panel. If that fails, then:
- Stage 3: the complaint is referred to the *Health Service Commissioner* or Ombudsman. The Ombudsman is interested not only in the substance of a complaint but also in how it was handled — for example, the Ombudsman might investigate the refusal of a convener to set up a panel.

Patient's Charters

The Patient's Charter was an extension of the Citizen's Charter programme. The aim of the Charter is to describe the rights of patients and the standard of service which they can expect to receive from the NHS. Each of the four countries in the UK has its own Patient's Charter.

The first English Patient's Charter came into force in 1992 and was extended in 1995 to cover dental, optical and pharmaceutical services as well as the hospital environment. The standards of service cover:

- respect for the individual patient;
- ambulance waiting time;
- A&E clinical assessment;

- out-patient clinic appointments; and
- cancellation of operations

In addition, there were separate charters on maternity services (1994), blood donation (1995) and hospital and community services for children and young people (1996).

Another aspect of a quality service was the provision of appropriate information. The NHS *Code of Practice on Openness* came into force in 1995. The Code applied to NHS Trusts, health authorities and local health practitioners (GPs, dentists and pharmacists). The Code described the information which should be published or made available about:

- the services provided, their cost and effectiveness and the performance targets set and results achieved;
- proposed changes in health policies or the way services will be delivered; and
- access to one's own health records.

Greg Dyke was asked by the New Labour government in 1997 to review the existing patient charters and these were consolidated in a *New Patient's Charter* which covered patients' entitlements in relation to:

- access to service;
- personal consideration and respect; and
- provision of information.

NHS Trusts and GP practices are also encouraged to produce their own charter covering the standards of the services which they provide.

Social Welfare Services

Administrative structure and benefit system

Administration

The present system of social welfare services also has its roots in the 1942 Beveridge Report. Immediately before July 2001, the main government department overseeing the system was the Department of Social Security (DSS), although the actual work was carried out by a number of executive agencies, including one (Employment Services Agency) based in the Department for Education and Employment (D*f*EE) as it then was, and by another government department, the Inland Revenue. This multi-departmental approach meant that the dividing line between pure social welfare, on the one hand, and employment and training, on the other, was at times difficult to see. This may well have been one of the reasons for the reorganisation after the June 2001 General Election, under which the DSS became the Department for Work and Pensions (DWP), taking over responsibility for the Employment Services Agency and the D*f*EE was renamed to become the Department for Education and Skills (D*f*ES). For the purposes of this book, social welfare and training are dealt with in separate chapters, although in the last analysis they all have an impact on public expenditure.

The relevant executive agencies within the DWP are:

- *Benefits Agency* (BA) — administers and delivers most benefits;
- *Employment Services Agency* (ES) — pays benefit (Jobseeker's Allowance) to unemployed people on behalf of the Benefits Agency;
- *Child Support Agency* (CSA) — assesses and collects maintenance payments for children;

- *Information Technology Services Agency* — computerises social security administration; and
- *War Pensions Agency* — services to war pensioners.

However, since the principal aim of the DWP is to implement the government's 'welfare to work' strategy, the benefit and jobsearch services for working-age people previously provided through the BA and ES are to be combined in a new agency *Jobcentre Plus,* to come into full operation by April 2003. At the same time, a new agency, the Pension Service, has been established to take over responsibility for pensions. Finally, the CSA is to be radically modernised.

The *Inland Revenue (www.inlandrevenue.gov.uk)* now collects National Insurance (NI) contributions and deals with claims for the recently-launched Working Families' Tax Credit (WFTC), Disabled Person's Tax Credit (DPTC) and Children's Tax Credit — the payments are actually made by employers through the PAYE system.

The Housing Benefit and Council Tax Benefit schemes are run by local authorities which recover most, but not all, of the cost from the government.

The CSA had the dubious distinction of having alienated practically everybody with whom it had had contact. The agency was beset with administrative problems right from the start and failed to meet the performance targets set for it. To improve its chances of meeting its targets, it concentrated on the 'easy' absent fathers, leaving the 'difficult' ones for later. The single mothers saw no real advantage from the payments extracted from absent fathers, because these were used to offset the cost of benefit payments made to the mothers. Indeed some suffered hardship — the CSA was so inefficient that mothers often found their benefits quickly reduced by the more efficient BA, with the CSA failing to make up the shortfall by collecting the absent father's assessed contribution on time. Even some of the absent fathers had cause for complaint — when the CSA assessed them for payments, even though they had earlier reached what they thought was a 'clean break' divorce settlement, often approved by the court. In some cases, the additional unlooked-for payments threatened the stability of the father's second family.

Social Security benefits — summary

There are three main types of social security benefit (contributory or non-contributory):

- *contributory benefits* — available to people with a satisfactory history of payments into the National Insurance Fund;
- *income-related benefits* — available to those people whose income falls below a specified threshold — not dependent upon the claimant's NI contribution record (non-contributory); and
- *other benefits* — available to those people who satisfy specified tests — for example, disability or family needs.

Social security is the largest public expenditure programme, accounting for almost one-third of the total. The relative size of the benefit programmes can be judged from the fact that contributory benefits take up about one-half of the expenditure, income-related benefits almost one-third and other benefits about one-sixth.

As far as funding for the social security programme is concerned, general taxation provides over one-half, employers' NI contributions about one-quarter and employees' NI contributions about one-fifth.

The whole social security benefit system is complex and only the more significant types of benefit are described later in this chapter. Since most benefit rates are changed annually in line with inflation, no rates are given. Current benefit rates can be obtained from any local BA office. Some benefits are tax-free; others are taxed.

National Insurance (NI)

The *National Insurance Fund* is a statutory fund which receives all NI contributions from employers, employees and self-employed people and meets expenditure on contributory benefits. Originally run as part of the DSS, then as an executive agency (the Contributions Agency) within the DSS, the collection of NI contributions is now part of the Inland Revenue — at last giving final recognition to the fact that for many years NI has just been another form of general taxation.

There are five classes of NI contributions:

- *Class 1* — paid by both employers and employees, where employees are paid above a specific threshold. An *employee's* contributions are based on a percentage of his or her pay up to a specified upper limit. The *employer's* contributions are also based on a (higher) percentage of the employee's pay and there is no specified upper limit. The contribution can be lower if the employer operates a 'contracted-out' occupational pension scheme;
- *Class 1A* — paid by an employer who provides the benefit of a car and/or fuel to an employee, for private use. The amount is related to the cash equivalent of the benefit provided;
- *Class 2* — paid by self-employed people earning above a specific threshold. Paid at a flat rate per week (see Class 4);
- *Class 3* — paid voluntarily to safeguard one's rights to some benefits. Paid at a flat rate per week;
- *Class 4* — paid by self-employed people in addition to Class 2 contributions if their taxable profits exceed a specified threshold. Based on a percentage of those profits up to a specified upper limit.

Employees who work after reaching pensionable age (women at 60 and men at 65 as the law currently stands, but this discriminatory anomaly will have to disappear) do not pay NI contributions, but the employer does. Self-employed people over pension-able age do not pay NI contributions.

Contributory benefits

These benefits are available only if NI contributions have been paid. The individual concerned must have paid (or been credited with) a minimum number of contributions to obtain any benefit at all; and the amount of benefit depends on the number of contributions actually paid. Many people receive less than the maximum benefit.

There are five main contribution-based benefits *(other benefits of a related kind appear in brackets after each description)*:

Basic Retirement Pension

This is payable to women at the age of 60 and to men at the age of 65. UK domestic law, the Sex Discrimination Act 1986, did not prevent the different treatment of men and women within the state pension scheme. However, EU legislation does and the UK government had to respond by the Pensions Act 1995. Retirement ages for men and women will be equalised (to 65), the change being phased in over 10 years from April 2010. Women born before April 1950 will still retire at 60; those born after April 1955 will retire at 65; those born in between 1950 and 1955 will retire between 60 and 65 according to the year of birth. The New Labour government has introduced the idea of the 'stakeholder pension', which is described in more detail in a later section. *(Over 80 Pension, Graduated Retirement Benefit and Additional Pension (SERPS))*

Widow's Payment

This is a lump sum payable to widows under the age of 60 or to widows over that age whose husbands were not entitled to a state pension when they died. *(Widowed Mother's Allowance, Widowed Parent's Allowance and Widow's Pension)*

Incapacity Benefit

This is payable when any statutory sick pay paid by an employer ceases or to those who do not qualify for sick pay at all. There are three rates of benefit which vary according to the period of the incapacity and the age of the claimant (short-term below pension age, short-term above pension age, and long-term). Stringent tests have been introduced to ensure that only those people incapacitated for *any* type of work will receive this benefit after an initial period.

Maternity Allowance

This is payable (for up to 18 weeks) to women who are not eligible to receive statutory maternity pay from their employer or who are self-employed or who have recently left or changed their job.

Jobseeker's Allowance

This was introduced in October 1996 to replace unemployment benefit and income support for unemployed people. There are *two* types of Jobseeker's Allowance: contribution-based and income-based (non-contributory); both are paid by the D*f*EE Employment Services Agency on behalf of the DSS. The allowance is paid to unemployed people who are actively seeking work, are capable of work and are available for work. The *contribution-based* Jobseeker's Allowance is payable for up to six months and takes into account other available income; people may then move onto the income-related version if their means justify it. The *income-based* Jobseeker's Allowance is payable to those on low income and is means-tested, taking into account family circumstances and commitments. All Jobseeker Allowance claimants have to appear fortnightly at the relevant Employment Office to 'sign on' and notify any change in circumstances. Periodic interviews are held with claimants to check their efforts to find suitable work. Claimants suspected of fraud (working for cash while claiming the allowance) may be required to 'sign on' each day. *(Back to Work Bonus, and for people just entering work: Lone Parent's Benefit Run-on, Housing Benefit/Council Tax Benefit Extended Payment).*

Income-related benefits

These are not dependent upon the claimant's NI contribution record, are paid to people whose family income falls below a specified threshold and are means-tested, particularly in relation to any savings or capital. Family Credit has been replaced by Working Families' Tax Credit. The application of a means-test will often result in no benefit being payable *(other benefits of a related kind appear in brackets after each description):*

Income Support

This is payable to people who are not expected to be available for work: lone parents, pregnant women within 11 weeks of the birth, pensioners, carers and long-term sick and disabled people. The amount received depends upon family income (including other social security benefits), savings and commitments, and is made up of a personal allowance, premium payments and housing costs, including help with a mortgage. This used to be available to unemployed people on low incomes, but was replaced in October 1996 by the income-related Jobseeker's Allowance. In order to encourage people to work to support themselves — at least to some extent — claimants can still remain eligible even if they work part-time for less than 16 hours a week (24 hours in the case of a partner). *(Help with health costs, help with prison visits, and for people just entering work: Housing Benefit/Council Tax Benefit Extended Payment).*

Housing benefit

This is payable (by local housing authorities on behalf of the DWP) to people having difficulty paying their rent. The amount received is calculated taking into account factors similar to those for Income Support but is available to people in work if their income is low enough. The payment does not cover mortgage payments, fuel costs and some service charges. In relation to private sector tenants, benefit is based not on the actual rent paid but on average rents for property of that size in the area — to encourage people to move to more cost-effective accommodation and to avoid the artificial inflation of private sector rents. The Housing Benefit paid to single people under the age of 25 will usually be limited to the average rent of a self-contained single room in the area. *(Extended Payment Scheme).*

Council Tax Benefit

This is available to people having difficulty paying their Council Tax and is awarded by the local authority responsible for collecting Council Tax allowing a percentage rebate (up to 100%) on the council tax bill. The amount of the rebate is calculated taking into account factors similar to those for Income Support and is paid to eligible people in work as well as those who are unemployed. *(Extended Payment Scheme).*

Child Benefit

This is paid for each child under the age of 16; each child under the age of 19 in full-time education; and each child under the age of 18 who has registered for work, or training with the Careers Service or Connexion Service, and is actively seeking work or training. The payment is not means-tested but is taxable. There are three rates (eldest qualifying child, other qualifying child, and lone parent with eldest qualifying child). Child Benefit has been joined, since April 2001, by the Children's Tax Credit (see later) — Tax Credits are New Labour's preferred mechanism for directing some social security payments towards lower paid people in work — to achieve the government's strategy of 'welfare to work'. *(Guardian's Allowance, Child Support Maintenance and Child Maintenance Bonus).*

Family Credit

This was paid to low-income employed and self-employed working families with children, with the objective of encouraging them to stay in work. The amount depended upon the family net income and the number and ages of dependent children within the family. *(Help with health costs, help with prison visits).*

After October 1999 no new Family Credit applications were approved; instead, new applicants claim Working Families' Tax Credit (WFTC) from the Inland Revenue. People already receiving Family Credit could not switch to WFTC until their existing Family Credit award expired. For a description of WFTC see the later section on *Tax Credits.*

The Social Fund

This fund covers a range of additional benefits, most of which are means-tested and, therefore, may not be paid. The benefits are payable to people receiving some of the income-related benefits described in the last section and entitlement varies. In one case (the discretionary crisis loan) receipt of another income-related benefit is not required to qualify.

The main point is that the Social Fund consists of two types of payment: *regulated* and *discretionary.* There is no financial limit on the regulated payments, but the discretionary payments come out of a capped part of the Social Fund and when the money runs out, that may be it — although the BA says that a crisis loan will rarely be refused for that reason alone.

Regulated payments are:

- *maternity payment:* a lump sum for each baby born or adopted;
- *funeral payment:* a lump sum to meet specified expenses; and
- *cold weather payment:* a weekly payment towards heating costs in very cold weather from November to March (0°C or below for seven consecutive days), payable only to those on Income Support who are elderly, disabled or have children under the age of five years.

Discretionary payments are:

- *community care grant:* to help people remain in the community, or resettle into the community after a period in care;
- *budgeting loans:* a lump sum loan for important intermittent expenses; and
- *crisis loans:* a lump sum loan for help in an emergency or disaster, where there is a serious risk to health or safety.

Benefits related to disability or illness

As mentioned earlier, there are other benefits which are payable to people who satisfy specific tests other than income — for example disability *(other benefits of a related kind appear in brackets after each description):*

Attendance Allowance

This is payable to people over the age of 65 who need help with their personal care because of illness or disability. To claim, the person concerned usually has to prove that they have needed the help for the last six months — that is, they have to wait six months before they can receive Attendance Allowance. However, special rules enable expedited payment for people who are terminally ill. There are two rates (higher and lower) payable, depending on the person's care needs during the day and night. *(Constant Attendance Allowance and Exceptionally Severe Disablement Allowance; Pneumoconiosis, Byssinosis and Miscellaneous Diseases Benefit; Workmen's Compensation (Supplementation) Scheme; Industrial Injuries Disablement Benefit)*. (However, social security benefits for industrial injuries may disappear from the social security scene and be replaced by insurance policies paid for by employers, as New Labour announced in December 1999 as part of its welfare reforms).

Disability Living Allowance
This is payable to people who became severely disabled before the age of 65 who have personal care needs or who need assistance with mobility. The allowance has two components: the care component and the mobility component. People usually have to wait three months after the onset of their condition before they can start receiving DLA and their condition must usually be expected to last for at least another six months. However, again, there are special rules for people who are terminally ill. The amount depends upon the level of attention they need. People who are terminally ill receive a higher amount.

Disability Working Allowance
This was payable to people who were aged 16 or over; who were working at least 16 hours a week on average; but who had an illness or disability which put them at a disadvantage in getting a job. The allowance was means-tested and income-related and was only paid if the applicant qualified, but did not depend on NI contributions. To qualify, the applicant had to have been receiving the Disability Living Allowance (or an analogous benefit under the war pensions or industrial injuries schemes); or had a invalid three-wheeler or other vehicle under the NHS Act 1977; or had received one of several specified benefits but at their higher rates.

Like Family Credit, Disability Working Allowance was replaced, in October 1999, by a tax credit arrangement run by the Inland Revenue, with similar transitional arrangements. The replacement, Disabled Person's Tax Credit (DPTC), is described in the section on Tax Credits.

Severe Disablement Allowance
This is payable to people who are not eligible to receive Incapacity Benefit because they have a poor NI contribution record. Claims can be made by people aged between 16 and 65, but is payable beyond the 65th birthday. There are stringent medical tests.

Invalid Care Allowance

This is payable to people between 16 and 65 years old who are spending at least 35 hours a week caring for someone who is receiving the *middle* or *higher* rate of the Disability Living Allowance care component or the Attendance Allowance. Claimants cannot earn more than a specified amount per week after allowable expenses or be in full-time education. *(Vaccine Damage — lump sum payments).*

Statutory Sick Pay and Statutory Maternity Allowance

Although both of these payments started life as part of the former DSS system, their administration has now been transferred to employers.

Statutory Sick Pay is paid to people who are off work sick for more than four consecutive days and is payable for a maximum of 28 weeks. Employers with more generous sick pay arrangements (either amount or length of time) will abate payments under their contractual scheme to offset any Statutory Sick Pay which they pay to the employee.

Statutory Maternity Pay is paid for a maximum of 18 weeks to pregnant employees who satisfy continuous employment and earnings tests. There are two rates — *higher* (90% of average earnings or the statutory level, whichever is the higher) for the first six weeks and *lower* (the statutory level for the remainder of the period). Claimants have to produce a certificate of pregnancy from their GP or midwife.

Tax Credits

The New Labour government decided that it was more appropriate to regard social security benefits paid to people already in work as an aspect of the fiscal, as opposed to social welfare, system — and, therefore, in October 1999 replaced Family Credit with Working Families' Tax Credit (WFTC) and the Disability Working Allowance with the Disabled Person's Tax Credit (DPTC) and transferred responsibility from the DSS and BA to the Inland Revenue (which had earlier assumed responsibility for collecting NI contributions).

Working Families' Tax Credit

This is means-tested method of topping up the earnings of employed or self-employed people on low or middle incomes, who: work for 16 hours or more a week; have one or more dependent children under the age of 16 (or 19 if in full-time education and still living at home); and have savings of £8,000 or less.

There are various elements to WFTC: *basic* (one per family); *extra 30-hour* (where at least one family member works for at least 30 hours a week); *child* (depends upon age of each child); *disability* (depends on whether adult or child is disabled); and *childcare* (up to 70% of eligible approved childcare costs up to specified maxima depending on number and ages of children requiring childcare). There can also be extra help for new parents, people on statutory maternity leave, people with disabilities, and people on widowed maternity leave, provided that they meet eligibility criteria.

Until April 2000 WFTC was paid to the claimant direct. Since that date, WFTC has been paid via the PAYE system in the claimant's wage packet. Self-employed people in receipt of WFTC continue to receive it direct after April 2000. Since April 2000, providers of childcare services for older children have been able to attain *Approved Provider* status from *Accredited Organisations* and are able to advertise that their services are eligible for WFTC.

Disabled Person's Tax Credit

This is also means-tested and is designed to encourage disabled people to return to, take up, or stay in work — disabled people who have an illness or disability which puts them at a disadvantage in the labour market. DPTC differs from DWA which it replaced, by including an element for childcare costs. Similarly to WFTC, DPTC tops up the earnings of employed or self-employed people on low or middle incomes but the qualifying conditions are slightly different — people who: work for 16 hours or more a week; are already in receipt of one of a range of incapacity or disability benefits (broadly similar to those previously required for DWA); and have savings of £16,000 or less.

There are various elements to DPTC: *basic* (depends on whether single, couple or lone parent); *extra 30-hour* (as for WFTC); *child* (as for WFTC); *enhanced disabled child* (for each child in receipt of DLA or who is registered blind); *enhanced disabled adult* (depends on degree of disability); and *childcare* (as for WFTC).

The payment and childcare accreditation arrangements are similar to those for WFTC described above. In addition, since April 2000 there is a new *Fast Track Gateway* offering an alternative route to DPTC, avoiding the need to obtain the specified qualifying incapacity or disability benefits first. To qualify for access to DPTC through the Fast Track Gateway, the person must: have received Statutory Sick Pay (or equivalent) for 20 weeks; pass a disability test; produce evidence from their GP that the illness and disability will continue for at least another six months; and show that, when they return to work, their earnings will be at least 20% less than they would have earned but for the illness or disability.

Children's Tax Credit

This is a new tax credit introduced from April 2001. It differs from Child Benefit in several ways: it is means tested, but only for higher rate taxpayers; there is only one credit per family, irrespective of the number of eligible children; and it can be claimed by married or unmarried couples and single parents who have at least one child under the age of 16 living with them — no extension to cover under 18 or under 19 children.

Reviews and appeals

By now the complexity of the scheme, if not much else, will be clear. The entitlement rules are complex and will be applied by thousands of individual officers in the various executive agencies. Previously, the decisions were technically taken by individual Adjudication Officers and there was a system of reviews and appeals against their decisions, ultimately reaching the Central Adjudication Service. That has now changed as a consequence of the Social Security Act 1998 and the *Decision Making and Appeals* (DMA) initiative. The 1998 Act provides that all decisions taken after 28 November 1999 will technically be taken by the Secretary of State, even though the decisions will, in reality, be taken by individual 'Decision Makers' at local level. The Act also enables decisions to be made by computers acting on behalf of the Secretary of State — the electronic age has finally arrived! This technical change enables the review/appeal processes to be streamlined and dealt with within a target of one month.

Not all decisions made by or on behalf of the DSS are susceptible to appeal anyway — for example, a decision made about a Social Fund *discretionary* payment can only be *reviewed* by the decision maker who made it; that is as far as the process goes.

People (or customers, as they are now called) are encouraged to try to settle the matter locally, without going to formal appeal, by asking for their case to be looked at again — a *review*. This can now be done by telephone rather than in writing.

If the claimant remains dissatisfied after the review, then he or she can proceed to *appeal*, if there is the right to do so. The appeals will be handled by The Appeals Service (TAS) managed as an executive agency of the DSS. The 1998 Act replaced the previous three-member appeals tribunals (with a legally qualified chairman) with new tribunals consisting of one, two or three members. The size and composition of each tribunal will depend upon the qualifications and expertise needed to determine the appeal. A particular tribunal can call on expert, including medical, assistance — and can insist on the appellant being medically examined (but not by the tribunal). Cases with no reasonable prospect of success will be rejected through an initial sifting process before TAS decides to convene a tribunal.

The tribunal phase of the appeal process is not necessarily the end, but nearly always is. It is possible to take an appeal one stage further — to a *Social Security Commissioner* — but only on a point of law; not on a point of fact or on a medical issue. The Social Security Commissioner is a lawyer who is independent of the DWP, the Employment Service agency of the DWP and the tribunals. Both sides, the appellant and the decision maker, may appeal to a Commissioner.

War pensions

War pensions have a history which predates the Welfare State — the first scheme for war pensioners dates back to the reign of Elizabeth I. Inadequacies in the system were highlighted by the enormous number of casualties in the First World War (particularly in the Battle of the Somme) and this led, in 1917, to the rationalisation of the existing arrangements into a new War Pensions Scheme under a new Ministry of Pensions.

The scheme is now administered by the War Pensions Agency within the DSS, which makes payments to about 327,000 war disabled and war widows in over 100 countries. Despite the name, qualification for a war pension does *not* depend upon service in HM Forces during time of war. A war pension can also be paid for disablement or death in peacetime service. The Agency also runs schemes for Second World War civilians, merchant seamen and Polish Forces who served under British command during the Second World War. In addition to assessing, awarding and paying pensions, the Agency also runs the War Pensioners' Welfare Service (WPWS) and a residential and nursing home for people who qualify under the Polish Resettlement Act 1947.

The future of the State pension

The basic State pension has existed in its present form since the introduction of the Welfare State in 1948. This basic pension, paid for through NI contributions, was supplemented in 1978 when the second State pension was introduced — the State Earnings Related Pension Scheme (SERPS). At that point it became compulsory for most employees to contribute to a second pension. Occupational pension schemes had been available for many years (since the early 1900s, in fact) and it was possible for people in those schemes to 'contract-out' of SERPS. Finally, many people chose to make voluntary personal pension arrangements — and were encouraged to do so by successive Conservative governments. Of the 35 million people currently in work, about 7 million are in SERPS, about 10.5 million are in occupational schemes and about 10 million have personal pensions.

For the past few years, there has been a greater awareness of the demographic problem facing State provision for people in their old age. The New Labour government published *A New Contract for Welfare: Partnership in Pensions* and followed it with the Welfare Reform and Pensions Act 1999 which paves the way for pension reform.

A new *State Second Pension* replaced SERPS in April 2002, aimed at people not able to save much for their old age but who should be able, through their NI contributions or credits, to receive a pension at or above the 'minimum income guarantee in pension'. The State second pension is aimed to extend entitlement to carers and disabled people who have broken work (and, therefore, NI contribution) records. The government believed that some 18 million people (14 million low and moderate earners, 2 million carers and 2 million disabled people) would gain more from the State second pension than they would have made from SERPS.

For people who are able to save more and who are not already in an occupational scheme, a new flexible low-cost *Stakeholder Pension Scheme* has been created (from April 2001), provided through the private sector. People are encouraged to take out a stakeholder pension by being offered increased NI rebates. Providers of stakeholder pensions have to comply with compulsory government standards (similar to the government's voluntary CAT standard for ISAs — no Charges, ease of Access and fair Terms) and are subject to regulation by the *Occupational Pensions Regulatory Authority* (Opra). Stakeholder pensions are 'portable' — that is, people will be able to take their pension with them, as they move from job to job. These pensions are of more interest to people on moderate and higher earnings. The stakeholder pension arrangements will take many years to take full effect, as the existing workforce progressively retires under their existing pension arrangements.

Employment, Training and Economic Development

Helping unemployed people to find work — the promotion of industry and employment

Helping unemployed people to find work

The previous chapter was about the social welfare system although it is evident that that system has close links with the system for finding people work, to avoid recourse to the social welfare system. The government department most involved in finding people work is the Department for Work and Pensions (DWP) *(www.dwp.gov.uk)*. The DWP executive agency involved in the transition from *Welfare to Work* is the Employment Services Agency (ES). Department for Education and Skills (DfES) *(www.dfes.gov.uk)* is the government department most involved in providing people with appropriate skills to make them more employable.

The point of contact with employers and people seeking work is in one of over 1,000 Jobcentres country-wide — although a new service, *Employment Service Direct,* enables people to check up on available vacancies over a local call rate telephone, in much the same way as telephone banking. Employers are helped to advertise their vacancies in the local Jobcentre and are given advice about employing people with disabilities. The DWP is developing *Jobcentre Plus,* a new service involving combined offices where both welfare benefits and job search services are provided in the same place. This service development arose out of the ONE Service (through which people of working age were able to access information about work, benefits and other welfare services) piloted in 12 areas. The aim is that the office environment should be more open, on the basis that if the surroundings are friendly so might the clients be. The staff from the ES were already used to this approach; those from the BA were more used to having security screens to protect them from their clients and were reluctant to work in a less controlled environment.

Jobseeker's Agreement

Before an unemployed person can receive the Jobseeker's Allowance (JSA), they must complete a *Jobseeker's Agreement* with their ES adviser. The purpose of the Jobseeker's Agreement is to focus the claimant's mind on the search for unsubsidised work. The claimant's attempts to fulfil the terms of the Agreement will be reviewed from time to time and certainly after three months.

At the three month stage, additional facilities become available. The claimant may also be able to claim travelling expenses to attend job interviews and have access to the *Employment on Trial* arrangement — JSA will not be lost, provided the job is given a fair chance (at least four weeks).

At the six month stage (and still unemployed), a Restart Interview is held to refocus the search for work and give access to further facilities: *Job Interview Guarantee, Work Based Learning Programme, Work Trials, Starting Your Own Business, Career Development Loans* and *New Deal*. The Restart Interview process is repeated after 12 and 24 months unemployment. After 18 months, claimants over 25 years old will be asked to attend a series of *Jobfinder Plus Interviews*. At any stage, uncooperative claimants may find their JSA stopped.

The *Job Interview Guarantee Scheme* involves an employer giving the ES a guarantee that they will interview people with the right skills and experience, selected by the ES. The *Work Based Learning Programme* is made available through local Learning and Skills Councils (these replaced Training and Enterprise Councils) and can involve job-specific training, work towards an NVQ or SVQ or actual work experience or a combination of them. Pre-vocational training may also be available to people who lack basic literacy and numeracy skills. *Work Trials* involve the claimant doing a real job for a potential employer wanting to fill a vacancy. The trial can last up to three weeks (at no cost to the employer) and during that time the claimant continues to receive JSA and additional travelling and meals expenses. The *Starting Your Own Business* scheme involves the provision of advice and help through the Jobcentre or the local Learning and Skills Council. Deferred payment *Career Development Loans* can be made available through four major banks to pay for vocational courses lasting up to two years, to provide the person with additional skills to make them more employable. *New Deal* is an initiative which deserves a section of its own.

New Deal, Employment Zones and Action Teams for Jobs

New Deal is an important part of New Labour's *Welfare to Work* Agenda. Initially available to unemployed people between 18 and 24 years of age, it is now available to unemployed people aged 25 plus and 50 plus. The New Deal programme is co-ordinated by the ES but is actually provided through local companies, voluntary organisations, training providers, local authorities, Jobcentres, and a range of other organisations which form New Deal partnerships. There are specialised New Deal programmes for lone parents and people with disabilities. By the beginning of 2002, just under 9,000 companies had signed New Deal agreements.

People eligible for New Deal have an initial interview with their ES New Deal Personal Adviser who will provide help and advice through this initial, or *Gateway*, period. The primary aim is to find an unsubsidised job. If such a job cannot be found after a few months within New Deal, then four options are made available: a job with an employer for up to six months subsidised by the government or help in setting up a business; work with the Environment Task Force improving the local environment; work for a voluntary organisation; or full-time education or training to obtain appropriate skills. At last one day each week will be spent on appropriate training. During New Deal, the claimant will receive an amount at least equivalent to JSA and can receive more.

Employment Zones are a new initiative aimed at helping long-term unemployed people with complex social problems to improve their employability. The programme is delivered by a series of partnerships with local authorities or local Learning and Skills Councils and was based in 15 zones from April 2000, aimed at helping 48,000 people.

An initiative launched in 2001 was *Action Teams for Jobs*, with special funding, to help people back to work in those areas with the lowest employment levels, including Employment Zone areas. The Teams provide help which is tailored to meet the needs of the individual. By January 2002, there were 53 Action Teams throughout the UK (excluding Northern Ireland), one of which was working with a prison to ensure that the inmates had access to job and training opportunities when they were released.

ES services for disabled people

Specialist services are available for people with disabilities, who have access to *Disability Employment Advisers* in Jobcentres. The specialist advisers are part of integrated teams — *Placing Assessment and Counselling Teams*. The specialist services include: *Access to Work* — helping young people with disabilities to overcome barriers to employment; and the *Supported Employment Programme* — providing opportunities to over 20,000 people with severe disabilities whose productivity levels would make it difficult for them to keep a job in an open placement — similar to a sheltered employment scheme where specific employers receive payments to compensate them for the low productivity of their disabled employees.

Learning and Skills Councils

The functions of the Training and Enterprise Council (TEC) and the Further Education Funding Council (FEFC) were combined in April 2001 and given to a new

Learning and Skills Council (LSC) at national level, responsible for all post-16 education and training. The LSC has a budget of £5.5bn and works through a network of 47 local offices.

LSCs are an important instrument of government training policy. They manage the provision of training and enterprise programmes for several government departments under contracts which are supervised by the Government Offices for the Regions. The programmes are diverse and the range of providers under LSC contract include most Further Education Colleges — with the result that LSCs now control the supply of virtually all work-related further education. In addition to the DfES training programmes delivered through LSCs, the DTI provides funds to LSCs to deliver its enterprise programmes. Many of the projects funded through the Single Regeneration Budget (SRB) have LSCs as their lead organisation.

Training Access Points (TAPs) in local libraries and some Jobcentres, provide information about local and national training and education opportunities.

Industry Training Organisations (ITOs) exist to deal with training issues (including ensuring that needs are met and standards maintained) for a particular sector of industry, commerce or the public service. They have a rôle to play in developing occupational standards and NVQs and their Scottish equivalent, SVQs. Examples of ITOs are: the Construction Industry Training Board, the Law Society and the Newspaper Society.

Modern Apprenticeships

This is a government initiative to improve the range of training available to young people, so that every young person, who is not in full-time education or who does not have a job, can be offered a suitable training opportunity. Through this scheme, trainees can gain skills and qualifications in a working environment. The previous system of *National Traineeship* has now been integrated into Modern Apprenticeships, essentially as the 'Foundation Modern Apprenticeship' leading to an NVQ level 2 qualification.

Modern Apprenticeships came into full operation in 1995, after pilot schemes had been run in some areas, and now cover over 80 industrial sectors, including some with no previous experience of apprenticeships. Over the previous 10 years or so, traditional apprenticeships on offer had rapidly declined and these Modern Apprenticeships are seen as a means of reversing that trend and producing a supply of young people trained to technician, supervisor or equivalent level.

Successful completion of the Foundation Modern Apprenticeship can lead on to the Advanced Modern Apprenticeship which leads to an NVQ level 3 qualification. Progression from the Advanced Modern Apprenticeship can lead to an education to degree level at a university.

The employer side of industry and commerce

Chambers of commerce are locally-based organisations established to promote the economic development of local businesses and are a focal point for the exchange of information and ideas at local level.

Employers' organisations usually exist on an industry basis — for example the Engineering Employers' Federation — and although they may have interests in pay-bargaining and industrial relations, they also have interest in training within the relevant industry.

Trade associations tend to consist of businesses which produce a specific product or specific range of products. They aim to provide support services to, and act as spokesman for, their members.

The Institute of Directors (IOD) provides business advisory services to its 48,000 company director members. Its members include directors of 75% of the FTSE 100 companies, while 65% are directors of small and medium sized businesses. Like the CBI, the IOD holds an annual conference.

The Confederation of British Industry (CBI) was founded in 1965 as a non-profit-making and non-party political organisation funded by member subscriptions. The CBI represents, directly or indirectly, 250,000 businesses. It is the largest organisation of its type in the UK and many chambers of commerce, employers' organisations and trade associations are in membership. The CBI has 12 UK regional offices and an office in Brussels for EU matters. It offers its members a forum (including an annual conference) where issues can be debated, a lobby for influencing government and a range of support services.

Investors in People

LSCs provide information and advice to the organisations which participate in the *Investors in People* Scheme. The Investors in People Standard was developed during 1990 by the National Training Task Force in partnership with organisations such as the CBI, TUC and the Institute of Personnel and Development and was tested the following year through the former TECs. Investors in People aims, through the application of rigorous standards, to improve the performance of organisations by linking the training and development of all employees with the achievement of specific business objectives. About 25,000 organisations employing more than 5 million people have agreed to participate in the scheme — the incentive to do so is that the Investors in People logo indicates a quality organisation and is good for business!

Promoting industry and employment

The economic health of the UK depends upon a variety of factors, the more important of which are industrial activity and the employment of people. Apart from issues of self-esteem, people who are in work do not generally require social welfare benefits, so reducing public expenditure and the need for additional taxation. Therefore, an important part of government policy is the encouragement of new industry (especially to replace old industries) within the UK to improve its trading position in the world.

This encouragement takes two forms: the improvement of the physical industrial plant and environment to meet modern standards and to create or retain jobs; and the improvement in the training of the potential workforce so that its skills match those currently required by industry. Some of the training schemes have had varying degrees of success — often young people go through a training course (including work experience) only to find no suitable work waiting for them at the end. Because of this, the range of training initiatives (including those already described) is continually changing in the search for greater success.

Job creation through regeneration

The next few sections deal with the various government schemes (some with EU assistance) which, over a period of years, have been aimed at improving and regenerating the industrial infrastructure. Most of these schemes have been under the auspices of the DoE/DETR, although in recent years there has been greater emphasis on using the integrated Government Offices for the Regions.

Previous initiatives

There were 12 *Urban Development Corporations* to tackle large-scale urban decline — Bristol, Leeds, Central Manchester, London Docklands, Merseyside, Birmingham Heartlands, Black Country, Plymouth, Sheffield, Trafford Park, Teesside and Tyne and Wear. They were wound up by March 1998. Public expenditure in 1996/97 was £208 million, including the London Docklands Light Railway.

The *City Challenge* initiative was started in 1991 — local authorities were asked to submit bids in partnership with the private and voluntary sectors, local communities and government agencies. The objective was to deal with problems of physical decay, lack of economic opportunity and poor quality of life in key neighbourhoods within the local authority area. The financial objective was to use government funding to attract a larger amount of private finance. The City Challenge experience was valuable in developing the Single Regeneration Budget Challenge Fund and any continuing City Challenge commitments were subsumed in SRB funding.

Enterprise Zones were designated as an experiment to see how far private sector industrial and commercial activity could be encouraged by the relaxation of some tax and administrative red tape. Altogether, 28 enterprise zones were designated, mostly in the period 1981-84. Each zone had a life of 10 years. The facilities available in an enterprise zone were: exemption from national non-domestic rates; 100% corporation and income tax allowances for new industrial and commercial development; and a simplified land-use planning system. Enterprise zones should be distinguished from the new *Employment Zones*.

Task Forces were intended to have a limited existence — the aim was to deal with the problem and strengthen local organisations which could then take over future management. Task Forces were small teams (about five or six people) from government departments, local authorities and the private and voluntary sectors. The objective was the economic regeneration of specific inner-city areas with an emphasis on improving local employment and training opportunities.

English Partnerships was a government regeneration agency which concentrated on the development of vacant, derelict or contaminated land. As its name suggests, the agency worked in partnership with other public bodies and the private and voluntary sectors. The objective was to stimulate local enterprise, create jobs and improve the environment. The programme was itself eligible for help from the European Regional Development Fund. The regeneration work of English Partnerships outside London transferred to the new *Regional Development Agencies* in April 1999.

The *Rural Development Commission* undertook a similar rôle in the countryside where problems of social and economic decline were often as acute as those in urban areas. The Commission's programme was delivered largely through the 312 *Rural Development Areas* which it established.

There were some parts of the UK where additional help with economic growth and enterprise was thought to be necessary. These were identified as *Assisted Areas (Development Areas* and *Intermediate Areas*) and covered about 35% of the UK working population. Some areas were identified as having been adversely affected by colliery closures or the decline in the shipbuilding industry. Inward investment into these Areas, especially to create jobs, was encouraged by a system of grants: *Regional Selective Assistance, Regional Investment Grants* and *Regional Innovation Grants*. The grants were administered by the Government Offices for the Regions, the Scottish Office Industry Department and the Welsh Office Industry and Training Department.

Single Regeneration Budget

The *Single Regeneration Budget* (SRB) *Challenge Fund* came into existence in April 1994, bringing together 20 programmes from five government departments — including those mentioned in the previous sections. The idea of combining resources to deal with regeneration problems had been piloted under the 'City Challenge' initiative and was found to be successful. The main programmes funded through the SRB were administered by the integrated Government Offices for the Regions, combining the previous regional offices of the DETR, DfEE, DTI and DoT. Since April 1999, the administration of the SRB outside London is with the Regional Development Agencies (RDAs). Regional Development Agencies and the Government Offices for the Regions are described in the earlier Chapter on *Devolution*.

The priority aim of the SRB was to enhance the quality of life of people in areas of need — by supporting initiatives aimed at: enhancing the employment prospects, education and skills of people; promoting sustainable regeneration and local economies and businesses; and tackling a range of social exclusion problems. The SRB programme was (and still is) actually delivered through local partnerships from the public, private and voluntary sectors.

Since its inception the SRB had six bidding rounds. Under these rounds, over 900 schemes were approved, with a life of up to seven years. The SRB support was worth over £5.5bn, which in turn attracted a further £10bn of private sector finance and even more EU funding.

From April 2001 the SRB system has been replaced by a single RDA budget which brings together all of the funding streams (including SRB) previously made available to RDAs. The idea is that RDAs will be able to use their single integrated budget in a flexible way to meet the needs of their area, under management arrangements agreed by the Department for Transport, Local Government and the Regions (DTLR) *(www.dtlr.gov.uk)*.

Regional Development Agencies will be expected to work within their Regional Strategy and, in particular, take account of proposals put forward by the emerging *Local Strategic Partnerships* (LSPs). LSPs are multi-agency umbrella partnerships leading action to:

- develop and implement community strategies;
- regenerate deprived neighbourhoods, through local neighbourhood renewal strategies;
- rationalise existing strategic partnership working; and
- co-ordinate the activities of operational partnerships.

Wales

Since devolution, the National Assembly for Wales, through its various divisions, is now the co-ordinating body for regeneration activity. In 1994 a new *Strategic Development Scheme* (SDS) was established, taking over the previous Urban Programme. *Urban Investment Grants* were used to encourage private sector investment in derelict and run-down sites in urban areas. The SDS resources were transferred to Welsh local authorities in April 1999 and at least 20% is spent in collaboration with the Wales Council for Voluntary Action.

The *Welsh Development Agency* (WDA) *(www.wda.gov.uk)* was established by the UK government in 1976 with the aim of regenerating the economic prosperity of Wales following the significant industrial decline in Wales over the preceding decades. Its land reclamation programme is the largest and most sustained in Europe, having produced over 8,000ha of land suitable for recreational and commercial use. Its capital development programmes and Regional Initiatives provide readily available industrial premises. The WDA claims to have created over 90,000 new jobs, saved 50,000 existing jobs and attracted over £12bn inward investment through its *Investors in Wales* scheme. The WDA is now responsible to the National Assembly for Wales, following devolution.

Development was also encouraged by the former *Land Authority for Wales*, a self-financing statutory body which ploughed back its profits into further schemes. The aim was to assemble land for development where the private sector would find it difficult to do so.

The first *Programme for the Valleys* (1988-93) was a scheme for the economic and physical regeneration of the South Welsh valleys, co-ordinating the activities of the WDA and other public and private sector bodies. This was followed by a second five year programme (1993-98) with broader objectives to do with housing, health, training and job-creation. The interests of the Valleys (in particular the use of EDRF Objective 1 funding) are now considered through *The Valleys Forum* launched in August 1998. In addition, Wales benefits from the £50m *Great Britain Coalfield Regeneration Trust*.

The *Cardiff Bay Development Corporation* was set up in 1987 to revitalise the south part of Cardiff, especially its docks. The Cardiff Bay barrage scheme created a large freshwater lake, although there were concerns about its environmental impact. The Development Corporation's aim was the creation of 25,000 new jobs and the construction of 6,000 new homes. The Development Corporation was wound up in March 2000, when its job was largely completed.

Scotland

Since devolution, the Scottish Executive is responsible for regeneration coordination. There have been initiatives in Scotland similar to those in England, the most notable being a partnership approach, using *Urban Programme* funding (the Urban Programme funding disappeared into the SRB in England), on which detailed decisions were taken by the local partnership. The comprehensive regeneration strategy was based on the experience gained from four Partnerships — Dundee, Edinburgh, Glasgow and Paisley — which were set up by the Scottish Office in 1988.

Scottish Enterprise (the Lowlands) *(www.scottish-enterprise.com)* and *Highlands and Islands Enterprise* (the Highlands) *(www.hie.co.uk)* are two bodies which manage government and EU support to industry and commerce. They aim to attract inward investment and encourage new businesses, as well as improve the environment by reclaiming derelict and contaminated land.

Northern Ireland

Since devolution, the Northern Ireland Executive is responsible for regeneration and industrial development coordination, principally through two departments: Enterprise, Trade and Investment; and Social Development. Job creation and improvement in the environment in Northern Ireland was achieved through the *Urban Development Grant,* which was directed towards the partnership schemes in the inner-city areas of Belfast ('Making Belfast Work') and Londonderry ('Londonderry Initiative').

The smaller towns were covered by the *Community Regeneration and Improvement Special Programme* which was jointly funded by the Department for the Environment for Northern Ireland and the *International Fund for Ireland,* established by the UK and Irish governments in 1986 (under the Anglo-Irish Agreement), whose donors include the US, EU, Canada and New Zealand.

Industrial development and international investment in Northern Ireland is promoted by a combination of the *Industrial Development Board, the Local Enterprise Development Unit* and *the Training and Employment Agency.*

EU Programmes

The EU Structural Funds and their purpose have been described in the chapter on Europe. The most relevant of the EU Structural Funds for regeneration is the *European Regional Development Fund* (ERDF) — particularly for areas affected by industrial decline.

13 Industry and Commerce

Industrial relations — health and safety — forms of corporate organisation — the London Stock Exchange — FTSE — competition

Industrial relations

Industry will operate more efficiently if there are arrangements in place for maintaining good industrial relations between the two sides: employers and the workforce. Industrial relations include not only collective bargaining but also the settlement of 'collective disputes' (involving groups of workers) and ensuring a safe working environment. Trade unions also assist particular members in resolving 'individual grievances' with their employer.

Industrial relations is in essence a voluntary process, affected in some respects by the forces of the marketplace: shortage of labour possessing the required skills; shortage of jobs. However, over time, successive governments have underlined the importance of good industrial relations by intervening and putting in place a degree of regulation on both sides and a means by which the resolution of disputes can be helped.

The employer side is regulated by the health and safety legislation and the employee side is regulated by the progressive limitation on the ability of trade unions to take industrial action. The resolution of disputes is helped by the government's Arbitration, Conciliation and Advisory Service (ACAS).

Trade unions — the national scene

In the previous Chapter mention was made of the employer side of industry and the representative organisations fulfilling that rôle. The employee side has also evolved its own means of representation — the trade unions.

It is often forgotten that for many years before the middle of the 19th century, trade unions were illegal — 'combinations' of labour were outlawed by successive Acts of Parliament. As the 20th century progressed, especially with the advent of Labour governments, trade unions became more powerful and the previous statutory limitations on their freedom of action were progressively eliminated. With the arrival of the Thatcher Conservative government, the pendulum started to swing back again (but not as far) as limitations were reimposed on the ability of trade unions to disrupt industry through industrial action.

Trade unions are not just about pay and conditions bargaining, they will aim to provide their members with benefits and services, including educational and social facilities, and legal and financial advice.

Over the past few years, the overall picture of trade unions has been changing. The total number of trade union members nationally has declined and the proportion of male trade union members has also declined. This has been put down to two main factors: the shift in the scope of industry away from manufacturing to service industries, where unionisation is less prevalent; and the shift in the nature of work from full-time to part-time, in which women are more represented.

The number of trade unions has declined by about one-third over the past 20 years, mostly by mergers. Most trade unions are affiliated to the TUC. The largest trade union (1.3 million members), UNISON, was produced from three public sector unions: COHSE, NALGO and NUPE. The next largest union, Amicus, was produced by a similar merger on 1 January 2002 of AEEU and MSF. Two other unions have over 500,000 members: TGWU and GMB. The smallest trade union affiliated to the TUC is SWSWU, the Sheffield Wool Shear Workers Union, with just 20 members.

As explained in a later section, trade unions have privileges (e.g. rights to recognition and time off work for officials) and immunities from legal action. Those privileges and immunities are, however, only available to 'independent' unions. In this context 'independence' means a union which is truly independent of the employer and thus more likely to represent the interests of its members fearlessly, rather than a fairly weak staff association which is dependent upon the employer. This independence is 'certified' by the *Certification Officer*, a statutory office created in 1975, appointed by the Secretary of State for Trade and Industry and based at ACAS HQ. The Certification Officer receives annual reports from trade unions and makes his own annual reports to the Secretary of State and ACAS. The Certification Officer can also examine the internal activities of any trade union which is thought to be breaking the rules, including processes for electing the union's officers. The Certification Officer also lists the employers' organisations.

Trade unions — the local scene

Although the internal organisation of trade unions varies, there will usually be a national executive committee and there may be a regional or district organisation, if the union is large enough to need it.

Unions usually have to be 'recognised' by the employer for collective-bargaining purposes and once recognition is granted, a workplace organisation will be set up by the union to handle formal relations at that level. Only independent trade unions, with certified status, can be recognised.

A union will have a branch organisation which may cover more than one workplace. Where an employer has recognised more than one union for the same workplace, there is usually a 'shop stewards' committee' to iron out any differences. 'Shop stewards' are workplace representatives elected at local level and should be distinguished from the full-time paid officials of the union.

Trades Union Congress

Most (but not all) independent trade unions are affiliated to a national organisation called the *Trades Union Congress* (TUC) *(www.tuc.org.uk)*. The TUC was founded in 1868 and its affiliated membership consists of 76 trade unions, representing 6.8 million people or 80% of trade union members nationally.

The aims of the TUC are to promote the interests of its affiliated organisations and to improve the economic and social conditions of working people generally, both in the UK, the EU and internationally. The TUC is the mechanism through which inter-union disagreements (sometimes about poaching each others' members!) are settled and is the primary representational and lobbying interface between the UK workforce and the government. The questions it deals with tend to be broad ones, affecting trade unions generally, both in the UK and internationally and are debated at the four-day TUC Congress held in September each year. Affiliated trade unions send delegates to the annual Congress, the number depending on the size of the union.

The TUC has six regional councils in England and a single one for Wales — the *Wales Trades Union Council*. There is a body equivalent to the TUC in Scotland: the *Scottish Trades Union Congress*. In Northern Ireland, the trade unions there are represented on the *Northern Ireland Committee* of the *Irish Congress of Trade Unions* (ICTU).

The TUC is itself affiliated to various international labour organisations: the *International Confederation of Free Trade Unions* (ICFTU) and the *European Trade Union Confederation* (ETUC). The International Confederation of Free Trade Unions *(www.icftu.org)*, established in 1949, links over 220 affiliated organisations in 148 countries. The TUC also nominates the British workers' delegation to the *International Labour Conference*, which takes place each June in Geneva, attended by delegates (two government, one employer and one worker) of states in membership of the *International*

Labour Organisation. The International Labour Organisation *(www.ilo.org)* was founded in 1919 as part of the League of Nations and is now an agency of the UN.

Industrial action — trade union immunities

As mentioned earlier, some statutory limitations have been imposed on the ability of trade unions to call upon their members to take strike action whenever they want. Strike action by an employee amounts to an unlawful breach of contract, upon which the employer can act — either by firing the employee or by suing for damages. Industrial action falling short of strike action may or may not amount to breach of contract. When a trade union instructs its members to take strike action, the union is *inciting* breach of contract and can also, in theory, be sued for damages by an employer. In many cases, employers will be more interested in getting their employees back to productive activity than in starting theoretical legal proceedings, but the important point is that employers can go to court to obtain injunctions if unions are acting unlawfully — a much more effective weapon, because the union's own assets could be at risk if the injunction was ignored.

However, trade unions can claim immunity from legal action, but only in specific circumstances. The most important point is that the industrial action must be *"wholly or mainly in contemplation or furtherance of a trade dispute"* between workers and *their own employer*. Striking about something unrelated to a trade dispute (for example, the company's activities in another country) is unlawful. It is also unlawful for trade unions to involve workers who have no dispute with their own employer — *'Secondary picketing'*. There is also a limit on the number of picketers who may be placed outside a workplace, to avoid intimidation of those workers not in sympathy with the dispute.

The union also has to go through the correct procedure before the industrial action can proceed — any mistakes and the industrial action is unlawful. The process involves a secret postal ballot of its members to obtain support for the proposed action (the union can reclaim from the government the costs incurred in the postal ballot) and it must tell the employer of the holding of the ballot. If the ballot authorises industrial action, then the union must give the employer at least seven days' written notice of the intended action and the details of the ballot result.

Advisory, Conciliation and Arbitration Service

The *Advisory, Conciliation and Arbitration Service* (ACAS) *(www.acas.org.uk)* is a quango appointed by the DTI *(www.dti.gov.uk)* but independent of it, with the rôle of promoting the improvement of industrial relations in the UK except Northern Ireland. In Northern Ireland the analogous body is the *Labour Relations Agency*.

The title of ACAS indicates its various functions:

- *advice* — aimed at preventing industrial action in the first place;

often general advice developed jointly with employers and employees' organisations, sometimes in the form of *Codes of Practice;*

- *conciliation* — intervenes in a dispute but only when invited to do so; the process of conciliation involves the parties to the dispute being helped to reach their own agreement. ACAS conciliators do not have the power to recommend or impose settlements; and
- *arbitration* — intervenes in a dispute when invited to do so, usually where earlier conciliation has not produced a settlement. An independent arbitrator or board of arbitration will examine the case for each side and make an award. The arbitration award is binding on the parties. Sometimes an independent third party is needed and ACAS can help in selection.

ACAS also has a rôle in individual grievances, as opposed to collective disputes. Whenever anyone starts an action in an employment tribunal (previously called industrial tribunal) (alleging unfair dismissal, sex or racial discrimination — there are over 100,000 each year), an ACAS conciliation officer will be assigned to try to broker a binding settlement between the parties and manages to do so, on average, in about 71% of all cases.

Health and safety

Industry will be more productive if there is a safe working environment and this is sufficiently important to have been made the subject of stringent statutory regulation, the main provision being the *Health and Safety at Work etc. Act 1974.*

The duties imposed by the 1974 Act itself affect everyone alike — employers, employees, self-employed and manufacturers and suppliers of work equipment. The 1974 Act has a series of subordinate statutory instruments or regulations, the most notable of which is the *Control of Substances Hazardous to Health (COSHH) Regulations 1999.* The 1999 Regulations constitute a systematic and comprehensive set of measures controlling exposure to virtually all of the substances known to be hazardous to health if they are not properly controlled in the workplace. Lead and asbestos are so dangerous that they are covered by their own regulations. COSHH substances are those which are either used directly (e.g. glues and paints), or generated by the work itself (e.g. fumes), or naturally occurring (e.g. dust and bacteria).

The *Health and Safety Commission* (HSC) has the job of developing policy on health and safety matters, including simplifying the statutory regulation regime. The HSC's responsibilities extend beyond the workplace, to include such matters as public safety in connection with gas, petroleum and the railway system, and it oversees the work of the HSE, whose website it shares. Its work is supported by a number of advisory committees, boards and councils; for example, toxic substances, genetic modification and nuclear installation safety. There are also advisory committees dealing with specific sectors of industry (e.g. ceramics).

The *Health and Safety Executive* (HSE) *(www.hse.gov.uk)* is the body responsible for enforcing health and safety legislation. The day-to-day work is carried out by the *Field Operations Division,* incorporating the Factory, Agricultural and Quarries inspectorates, together with regional staff from the *Employment Medical Advisory Service.* The continuing issue is the relatively small number of inspectors for the job in hand.

The enforcement of some health and safety legislation is the responsibility of local authorities — offices, shops, warehouses, restaurants and hotels — working under HSE general guidance.

In Northern Ireland there is a broadly similar system. The *Health and Safety Agency* is roughly equivalent to the HSC; enforcement is, however, split between the inspectorates of the *Department of Enterprise, Trade and Investment* and the *Department of Agriculture and Rural Development* within the Northern Ireland Executive.

The commercial context for industry

Industry does not operate in a vacuum. The aim of industry is to provide employment for people and to make profits for the benefit of the company and its shareholders and, indirectly, for the benefit of the UK economy as a whole. If the industrial and commercial base of the UK is strong, so will be its place in the world economic scene. The economy can be thought of as consisting of two sectors: the *public sector* (which covers all government-related activity, usually funded through taxation, public loans and gilt-edged securities and bonds) and the *private sector* (which covers activity by private — i.e. non-government — companies, bodies and individuals, usually through private resources, private loans or capital raised through the sale of shares and other securities).

Public Private Partnerships

There is an increasing trend for government to use companies from the private sector to finance, wholly or partly, major public capital works and then manage them, in return for an annual payment from the government — for example, the *Private Finance Initiative* (PFI). The financing of the controversial Skye Bridge and some new motorways are examples of the way the private sector is used to improve the infrastructure of the country without increasing the public sector borrowing requirement.

PFI was introduced by the Conservative government in 1992 and, to many people's surprise, was continued and developed by New Labour to form the basis for Public Private Partnerships (PPP). The attraction for government (even for New Labour) is that money spent under PFI/PPP does not count as public expenditure in the UK economy. However, this comes at a price.

PFI/PPP projects can only be financed by borrowing and the private sector generally has to pay higher interest rates than the government when borrowing money, because the government's borrowing is better secured by its ability to raise taxes. Private companies also exist to make a profit for their shareholders and will expect a good return on their investment. These factors mean that over the long term, PFI/PPP arrangements will almost always be ultimately more expensive for the public sector — it is just that the amount is less noticeable when spread over a number of years. Some commentators regard PFI/PPP as akin to the hire-purchase arrangements prevalent in the 1960s — the so-called 'never-never' — you never own it and you never stop paying for it!

When the New Labour government pulled the plug on Railtrack in October 2001, one consequence was to make the private sector more wary of becoming involved in the larger controversial PFI/PPP projects, such as the London Underground and the successor to Railtrack. The government may be obliged to provide (but without admitting to doing so) state guarantees to underpin the projects, in order to persuade the private sector to participate; if that is the case, it is difficult to see the benefits, beyond short-term bookkeeping, of PFI/PPP. For a detailed critique of the impact of PFI/PPP on the NHS, see the article *"Crisis-hit hospital finds that private finance for NHS comes at a price"* published in the *Guardian* on 23 July 2001. The government's perspective might be different.

Corporate structures — limiting liability

A person who carries on business on his or her own account does so at considerable personal financial risk. The individual is personally responsible for all the debts and liabilities of the business. The same is true if a group of people join together to run a business — a partnership. In the case of a partnership, each partner is jointly and severally liable with all the other partners for the debts of the whole business.

There will come a point in any business (including at the outset) where the decision is taken to limit the personal liability of the people running the business, and this is achieved by adopting a corporate form of organisation — a 'limited liability company'.

There are three broad types of limited liability company: a company limited by *guarantee*; a company limited by *shares*; and a *public limited company* (plc).

A *company limited by guarantee* is the form of organisation usually adopted by non-commercial organisations, such as theatre or voluntary trusts or charities. There is no share capital; instead, the liability of individuals connected with the organisation is limited to the amount (usually £1) which the initial 'subscribers' agreed when they signed the company's original memorandum and articles of association. A company's memorandum and articles of association are, in effect, its constitution, including a description of its powers and objectives. The voluntary organisation concerned, especially if it is a charity, can obtain a dispensation from the Secretary of State to omit the word 'limited' from its working title, although its formal stationery will indicate its corporate status.

A *company limited by shares* is the form usually adopted by small to medium sized businesses, especially those in private hands. The personal liability of the owners of the business is limited to the nominal value of the issued share capital. In the very smallest companies very few shares will have been issued and these will be retained by the original owners or their immediate family. The shares in companies as small as these will not usually be traded.

Limited companies can fail and be put into receivership or liquidation for legitimate reasons, because the people running them acted in good faith but the trading conditions were not in their favour. However, the concept of limited liability can be abused. Companies limited by shares can sometimes provide the opportunity for unscrupulous people to run up debts in the company's name and then evade responsibility by placing the company into liquidation. In a few cases, directors have been known to liquidate their company one day and then form a new company the next day, to which they have transferred the assets, but not the liabilities, of the old company. The creditors of the old company are left nursing bad debts which they can sometimes ill afford and can never recover. The new company then carries on trading and may even use a name which is similar to that used by the old company. Such companies are usually referred to as 'phoenix' companies, because they arise out of the ashes of the old company. In extreme cases, the DTI has powers to disqualify such people from holding directorships in future, but this seems to take some time and can easily be evaded by using nominees.

A *public limited company* (plc) is similar to a company limited by shares, but with one important difference — the company's operations will be very much larger and it will need to raise a larger amount of capital in order to fund its operations and development. That capital is initially raised by the plc selling its shares to members of the public and, if appropriate, those shares are subsequently traded on the London Stock Exchange. Further resources for the company's development are subsequently raised by a combination of: income generated by the business; loans and bonds; and the issue of additional shares which then are sold either to existing shareholders (a 'rights issue') or on the open market. The 'market capitalisation' of a company is the product of multiplying its current share price by the number of shares currently in issue. The market capitalisation is used as the basis for the FTSE Indices.

The larger companies are sometimes referred to as 'blue chip' companies. This phrase is used to describe the better known companies, with a good financial reputation.

The phrase has, it seems, its origins in the US and is derived from the colour of the highest value chip used in poker

London Stock Exchange

The London Stock Exchange (LSE) *(www.londonstockexchange.com)* was established in 1760 when "150 brokers [who were] kicked out of the Royal Exchange for rowdiness form[ed] a club at Jonathan's Coffee House to buy and sell shares". The LSE became a private limited company in 1986 and a plc in 2000. The main administrative base of the LSE is in London, with regional offices in Belfast, Birmingham, Glasgow, Leeds and Manchester.

There are about 2,600 UK and overseas companies listed on the LSE, although the rôle as UK Listing Authority with HM Treasury was transferred to the Financial Services Authority (FSA) in 2000. Company shares — 'equities' — are traded in the Exchange. The Exchange has moved away from traditional floor-based trading to screen-based trading. In July 1996, *CREST,* a new computerised settlement system for shares and other securities went live. CREST is run by CrestCo Ltd (owned by 96 users of the system) and has over 33,000 members, of whom over 31,000 are individuals who hold their shares in CREST 'personal membership'. The extension of CREST personal membership will eventually eliminate the need for share certificates — towards a paperless (or to use FSA terms, 'dematerialised') Exchange.

In 1995 the LSE set up the *Alternative Investment Market* (AIM) to provide a market for the shares in the smaller developing companies or, occasionally, companies whose market capitalisation has fallen so low that they have decided to move from FTSE to AIM listing.

FTSE

The advent of screen-based trading has enabled the performance of the securities traded on the LSE to be judged almost every second, although hourly and daily price movements are usually reported. The usual measures of the state of the UK Stock Market are the series of *FTSE Actuaries Share Indices* based on the market capitalisation of the companies concerned and produced by FTSE (Financial Times/London Stock Exchange) in collaboration with the Faculty and Institute of Actuaries. There are nine UK Indices, the most popular being the *FTSE 100* (the 100 largest UK companies) and the *FTSE All-Share*. The words 'FTSE' and 'Footsie' are registered trade marks of FTSE *(www.ftse.com)*. FTSE licenses the use of its Indices and describes itself as the "world's leading index calculation specialist" and creates Indices for use in stock markets in other countries.

Each quarter, FTSE reviews whether adjustments should be made to the list of companies in the FTSE 100 Index because of intervening changes in the market capitalisation of the constituent companies. The current numerical value of the Index is derived by applying a published formula and 'ground rules' to the total capitalisations of the companies involved. FTSE has a discretion to keep a company within the Index if it believes that the change in capitalisation is exceptional and temporary.

Due to a combination of the current fashion for telecoms/internet stocks (even after the dot.com bubble burst in 2001) and of mergers and acquisitions, the FTSE 100 Index is greatly affected by the prices of the shares in a small number of companies. Following Vodafone's hostile takeover of the German telecomms company Mannesman, the shares of BT, BP and the enlarged Vodafone accounted for about 30% of the FTSE 100 Index between them. Although BT has since fallen in value considerably, its relative influence on the Index remains significant. This may not seem very important, but pension funds and institutional investors tracking the FTSE 100 index are now vulnerable to adverse fluctuations in their underlying investments because of the relative proportions concentrated in too few companies (too many eggs in one basket). Indeed, a massive amount of money (estimated at £40bn) would have needed to move into Vodafone shares immediately following the Mannesman takeover, if the managers of FTSE 100 Index tracking funds decided to adjust their position in line with the Vodafone enlarged proportion (about 15%) of the FTSE 100 Index. That money could come from only one place — by selling the shares in other British companies, with an adverse effect on the companies whose shares were sold.

The position is now such that some commentators are seriously suggesting that the FTSE 100 Index should be abandoned, because it is now dominated by the performance of a small number of companies and is no longer an effective indicator of the financial health of the broad range of the companies quoted on the LSE.

The share price of a company which enters the FTSE 100 Index does rather well, at least for a short time, because, as explained in a previous paragraph, the managers of all the Index tracking funds may feel obliged to buy enough of the company's shares to bring their managed funds more in line with the composition of the Index itself. The reverse is also true — when a company's share price (and, therefore, its market capitalisation) falls so much that it drops from the FTSE 100 Index, the share price drops even more, as the fund managers sell the company's shares to adjust their fund's composition to match the Index.

Competition

An economy will work for the benefit of consumers if there is genuine competition, keeping prices down. Although the Conservative government was keen on deregulation of the marketplace, there were limits.

Any true monopoly will be in a position to charge what it likes for its goods and services. A small number of suppliers may not constitute a monopoly but may still be able to control prices by forming a cartel. Either of these situations is undesirable and there are mechanisms to prevent them, if they work against the public interest.

Overall competition policy is the responsibility of the *Department of Trade and Industry* (DTI) *(www.dti.gov.uk)* under the Secretary of State for Trade and Industry. Competition law is administered by a combination of the *Director General* within the *Office of Fair Trading (www.oft.gov.uk)*, the *Competition Commission* (CC) *(www.competition-commission.org.uk)* which replaced the Monopolies and Mergers Commission in 1999, and the *Restrictive Practices Court*. Apart from UK competition law, there is also the added dimension of EU rules, enforced by the EU Commission.

In UK competition law terms, a *monopoly* is where a single business supplies or purchases at least 25% of a particular product or service. A *complex monopoly* is where a group of companies jointly have 25% of the market or where they behave in a way which affects competition in the marketplace.

Sometimes *mergers* of companies could result in a monopoly situation and merger proposals are closely examined. Either the Director General or the Secretary of State can refer a proposed merger to the Competition Commission (CC) for detailed examination.

The CC investigation will either approve the merger (there may be a monopoly, but it is not one against the public interest); or reject it; or require *undertakings* to be given before it can proceed. For example, in the UK context, when brewery companies propose to merge, quite often they have to give undertakings to restructure their businesses and dispose of their tied public houses. Mergers are also examined at EU level and in the interests of EU or even global competition, parts of a global business might have to be sold as the price for approval of the overall merger.

A new Appeal Tribunals within the CC deals with appeals against decisions of the Director General or the various Regulators of Utilities about infringements of the rules in the Competition Act 1998, concerning anti-competitive agreements or abuse of a dominant position.

Sometimes, companies will reach agreements between themselves covering prices and areas in which each will trade — restrictive trade practices or resale price maintenance. Such agreements are normally registered with the Director General. Any such agreements which are thought to be contrary to the public interest can be referred to the Restrictive Practices Court by the Director General — with the result that the court will declare them illegal unless the parties to the agreement can convince it otherwise.

14 The Utilities

The supply and control of gas, electricity, water and sewerage, telecommunications and railways

Public to Private

All of the utilities about which this Chapter is written were once part of the public sector. The successive Conservative Thatcher and Major governments changed all that, through their privatisation programmes. As each utility was privatised, money was raised from the flotation for the Treasury to help the public finances.

The last big privatisation was the railways, because it was the most difficult to achieve. Rather surprisingly, when it came into office in 1997, New Labour did not prevent this particular privatisation from proceeding. Perhaps when it was forced to pull the plug on Railtrack in 2001 (see the later section on *Railways*), New Labour might have regretted its ready acceptance of the poisoned chalice handed to it by the outgoing Major government. However, New Labour also proceeded with further privatisations which were not universally popular: for example, the air traffic control system; and would have privatised the Royal Mail had this been possible. New Labour's continuing endorsement of the principle of privatisation must have come as a surprise to the more left-wing members of the Labour Party.

One of the consequences of the successive privatisations was that large numbers of the population became shareholders for the first time, possibly with the government of the day hoping that this would make them more inclined to vote Conservative next time. People also often made a quick profit from state utilities sold at much less than their true market value (the people who applied for shares were called 'Sids', from the publicity for the British Gas privatisation) — also making them more in tune with Conservative philosophy. On the other hand, Railtrack shareholders cannot have been pleased to see the value of their shares nosedive when New Labour placed Railtrack in administration in 2001, effectively writing off the capital value of their personal investment. That, of course, has always been the risk associated with share investments.

After a certain interval, the Conservative government removed its control over the future ownership of the utilities, with the result that many are now wholly or partly in foreign hands — usually French, American or Canadian.

Each privatised utility was given its own Regulator, charged with protecting the public interest, since in most cases the utility would remain a monopoly supplier, but now privately-owned and more concerned with the interests of its shareholders than its customers. The gas and electricity Regulators were combined in 1999.

The Regulators also have to authorise any price rises, using a formula linked to the rate of inflation. With the exception of water, all price rises have to be below the rate of inflation. In the case of water, price limits take into account the greater financial demands on the water companies to improve their infrastructure to meet the requirements of the 1990 EU Waste Water Treatment Directive — pumping raw sewage into the sea is no longer an option. As a welcome consequence, UK beaches and rivers are becoming cleaner year on year.

For its part, the Conservative government would have had an interest in ensuring that the privatisation programme was seen to succeed and may not have expected too great an imposition on the new privatised utilities by the Regulators.

The New Labour government realised that the privatisation process as a whole could not be reversed (it could not afford to do so anyway), so instead it limited the ability of the privatised utilities to make excess profits from charges, by imposing a one-off 'windfall tax'. The Regulators are also increasingly more stringent in the way in which they supervise the activities of the utilities.

Gas Supply

Originally, gas was generated from coal and supplied by municipal authorities in the larger towns — so-called 'Town Gas'. The discovery of Natural Gas and its increasing availability led to the consolidation of the gas industry on a national basis; Natural Gas gradually replaced Town Gas throughout the UK. This consolidated gas industry became the sole responsibility of the State-run British Gas Board.

The British Gas Board was privatised in 1986. For a time, British Gas plc continued to be in a monopoly position, having control over both the means of distribution and the product being supplied. That changed as a result of the Gas Act 1995.

British Gas plc had to restructure itself in 1997 (into BG plc and Centrica plc) to meet the challenge of competition — a single company could not own the pipeline and be a gas supplier at the same time. It also sought to minimise the commercial impact on the more profitable parts of its business from some much earlier fixed-price 'take-or-pay' gas contracts. Over the years since those contracts were first negotiated, the open market price of gas from the producers had dropped but British Gas was still contracted to buy gas from producers at much greater prices than the current open-market price then being paid by its new gas supplier competitors.

Competition had been introduced earlier into that part of the gas supply market which involved the supply of over 2,500 therms to the larger commercial/industrial consumers. The 1995 Act extended competition in gas supply to residential customers on a phased basis: south-west England in 1996; south-east England in 1997; and the rest of England and Scotland in 1998. There were difficulties experienced by some customers when they switched away from BG to an alternative supplier — with BG continuing to bill them for gas!

The 1995 Act also introduced a new licensing regime (operated by the Regulator):

- *Public Gas Transporters* (PGT) — companies (such as the BG plc subsidiary, TransCo) operating a pipeline system; and
- *Gas Shippers* — companies who contract with a PGT for their gas to travel through the PGT's pipeline to reach the Gas Suppliers; and
- *Gas Suppliers* — companies (such as BG) who sell gas to consumers.

The whole privatised industry was originally overseen by the Regulator, the Office of Gas Supply (Ofgas). However, as some companies increasingly supplied both gas and electricity, it made more sense to regard gas and electricity as just different aspects of energy supply which required a single regime of regulation (see later section on *Energy Regulation*).

Electricity generation and supply

When the electricity industry was State-owned, both generation and high-voltage transmission through the National Grid was managed by the Central Electricity Generating Board (CEGB) which had responsibility for ensuring that there was sufficient electricity to meet peak demand, especially in winter. Medium- and low-voltage distribution was handled by a series of regional electricity boards, passing electricity from the National Grid to consumers through their own local networks.

Electricity was privatised in 1989 (or some of it was) forming National Power plc and PowerGen plc as *conventional* Generators and a series of privatised regional electricity companies (RECs — based on the regional electricity boards) as Distributors. The RECs also initially owned part of the privatised National Grid but they later passed their interests over to their shareholders in the form of a free distribution of National Grid shares.

The electricity supply system in England and Wales is now in three stages:

- *Generation* — National Power plc, PowerGen plc, British Energy, BNFL and some independent Generators which use gas-fired and combined heat and power stations;
- *Transmission* — National Grid Company (NGC); and
- *Distribution* — Regional Electricity Companies (REC), independent supply companies and Generating companies.

The position in Scotland is that ScottishPower plc and Scottish Hydro-Electric generate, transmit and distribute electricity. There is a similar arrangement in Northern Ireland, with Northern Ireland Electricity plc, privatised in 1993, undertaking all three rôles.

Electricity is imported by England from Scotland through the National Grid and from France through a cross-Channel cable jointly managed by NGC and Electricité de France.

The distinction between Generator and Distributor has become blurred. In 1998, RECs lost their monopoly to distribute electricity to franchise customers (using less than 100kW) — from that date, such customers were able to buy their electricity from their own REC, another REC, a new independent supplier, or even a Generator! At least one REC (East Midlands Electricity before — now part of PowerGen) also supplies gas through a subsidiary (Sterling Gas).

Prior to October 2000, the process of supply involved the Generators selling their electricity to NGC through a market known as the *'Electricity Pool of England and Wales'*. The Pool involved a measure of competition in that Generators indicated at the beginning of each day the amount of electricity which they were prepared to offer next day in each of 30 minute periods and at what price. NGC produced its own estimate of projected demand and the supply and demand were then matched by NGC at the lowest cost through a computer program called Generator Ordering and Loading (GOAL). NGC then supplied electricity in bulk to Distributors across the National Grid.

In recent winters, there have been fears that the new contract-based system, involving a limited range of Generators, has put the system in danger of voltage reduction ('brown-out') when demand has exceeded expectations. During two weeks in July 1999, there was an 80% increase in the wholesale price of electricity offered to the Pool, due to some Generators deciding to take a significant amount of their generation capacity off-line at the same time. This unusual price-sensitive activity stimulated the interest of the Regulator, who decided to impose 'good market behaviour' licence conditions on seven Generators, with the possibility of fines of up to 10% of turnover for breaches.

The system for the wholesale trade in electricity was reviewed and the Pool was replaced by NETA (New Electricity Trading Arrangements in England and Wales) on 27 March 2001. NETA involves bilateral trading between generators, suppliers, traders and customers. This trading includes forwards and futures under which contracts for electricity can be made over timescales ranging from several years ahead to on-the-day. NGC, as the system operator, 'balances' supply and demand by accepting offers of and bids for electricity. The 'good market behaviour' licence conditions are likely to continue under NETA. More information on the operation of NETA can be found at *www.ofgem.gov.uk*.

Electricity generated from nuclear and renewable sources

The *nuclear* power generation part of the industry initially remained in State ownership since it was thought to be unsaleable, because of uncertainty about future decommissioning costs. To make them more palatable for eventual privatisation, in 1996 Nuclear Electric and Scottish Nuclear, which ran the more modern Advanced Gas-Cooled (AGC) and Pressurised Water (PWR) nuclear stations, became subsidiaries of British Energy — the two companies are now consolidated as *British Energy plc*.

The older Magnox (from Magnesium oxide — describing the metallic material used to contain the nuclear fuel) nuclear stations were transferred to Magnox Electric, destined to remain in the public sector and, in January 1998, were further transferred when Magnox Electric itself became a wholly-owned subsidiary of British Nuclear Fuels Limited (BNFL) *(www.bnfl.com)* which is still State-owned. In the year 2000, about 30% of the UK's electricity was generated by nuclear stations.

The 'fast breeder' reactor at Dounreay (constructed to develop military and civil nuclear energy) continued to be the responsibility of the United Kingdom Atomic Energy Authority (UKAEA) *(www.ukaea.org.uk)*. The UKAEA was established as a statutory corporation in 1954 to pioneer the development of nuclear energy. Its rôle has now changed completely — to responsibility for managing the decommissioning of nuclear power stations and the restoration of their sites to conventional use (the plan is that all existing nuclear stations will be decommissioned by 2023).

British Energy *(www.british-energy.com)* currently runs seven AGC stations: Heysham 1 & 2; Hinkley Point B; Dungeness B; Hunterston B; Hartlepool; and Torness; and one PWR station: Sizewell B.

The seven older Magnox stations currently run by BNFL/Magnox Electric are Calder Hall; Chapelcross; Bradwell; Dungeness A; Oldbury; Sizewell A; and Wylfa. The future of the Magnox stations is problematic because of their age and their non-compliance with modern design standards — they are licensed to operate for between 33 and 50 years. Four other Magnox stations have already been closed and are being decommissioned; Bradwell is due to cease generating in 2002.

From a safety point of view, the whole nuclear power industry is subject to supervision by the *Nuclear Safety Directorate* (NSD) of the Health and Safety Executive (HSE) *(www.hse.gov.uk)*. Inspections of nuclear sites to ensure compliance with NSD licence conditions are undertaken by the *Nuclear Installations Inspectorate* (NII). The NSD advises the Secretary of State for Trade and Industry in England and Wales and the Secretary of State for Scotland on nuclear safety. NSD consists of four divisions dealing with: British Energy plc; BNFL/Magnox Electric; UKAEA, Ministry of Defence and other sites; and Nuclear Safety Research and Strategy. Over recent years, British Energy, in an effort to cut costs, progressively switched from retaining its skilled in-house workforce to employing cheaper contractors and this caused the NII to issue a highly critical report on safety at some British Energy nuclear plants.

In the 1980s, with the agreement of the government at that time, the nuclear industry itself set up *Nirex (www.nirex.co.uk)* to examine safe, environmental and economic aspects of the deep geological disposal of radioactive waste. However, at the end of November 2001, the real cost of electricity generated from nuclear sources finally became clear. For years, BNFL had claimed that nuclear electricity was both cheaper and cleaner than electricity generated from fossil fuels, but it was generally believed that in arriving at the claim about relative prices, the true costs of the safe storage of nuclear waste had been consistently underestimated. At the end of November 2001, BNFL had to take full account of the true costs of repackaging some inadequately stored waste at Sellafield. On the basis of that episode alone, BNFL's liabilities exceeded its assets by £1.7bn — it was technically insolvent. The government's immediate solution was to announce that a new *Liabilities Management Authority* (yet another quango) should be created, to assume responsibility for all nuclear waste, including that belonging to BNFL and the UKAEA. This proposal would need to feature in a White Paper, followed by the necessary legislation, in 2002.

Prior to this, BNFL had been pressing the government to build yet more nuclear power stations to replace the existing 15 reactors, as they were progressively decommissioned over the period to 2023. In view of the BNFL insolvency, this now seems less likely, since apart from public concern about safe waste storage and disposal, the risk from accidents and terrorist activity can no longer be regarded as theoretical. On the other hand, it remains to be seen whether it will be possible to replace the declining nuclear generating capacity with new gas-fired stations and wind power. Interestingly enough, the other (privatised) nuclear generator, British Energy plc, has set its future sights in an entirely different direction — wind power — picking up on the outcome of the government's review of future energy policy.

The government aims to produce at least 10% of electricity from renewable sources (wind and wave power) by 2010. The largest existing wind farm is at Blyth in Northumberland, but it generates less than 50 megawatts. In November 2001, the government announced that a new wind farm of 39 turbines would be built at Cefn Croes near

Aberystwyth — at a cost of £35m and able to supply more than 40,000 homes. In December 2001, British Energy and Amec announced that they were undertaking a study of the feasibility of building a wind farm of 300 turbines near Stornaway on the Isle of Lewis in the Hebrides, at a cost of £600m and able to generate 2,000 megawatts — this would be equivalent to two nuclear stations. One possibility would be to link the farm up to the National Grid through a new 350 mile cable laid under the Irish Sea and coming ashore at Merseyside or North Wales.

Practical considerations aside, the problem for any major wind farm development is obtaining planning permission — keeping noisy wind farms away from residential areas necessarily means that they have to be located in countryside areas where intrusive development is discouraged. Perhaps, in the future, wind farms will become as ubiquitous as electricity pylons have become — such that people will no longer mind?

Energy Regulation

As already explained, the increase in the number of companies distributing both gas and electricity led to a review of the arrangements for the regulation of the energy industry. The separate Regulators — the Office of Gas Supply (Ofgas) and the Office of Electricity Regulation (Offer) — were replaced by a single regulation regime under the Utilities Act 2000.

The Utilities Act 2000 created the Gas and Electricity Markets Authority, which determines the regulation strategy and major policy, and issues licences. The actual work of regulation is undertaken by the *Director General of Gas and Electricity Markets* in the *Office of Gas and Electricity Markets* (Ofgem) *(www.ofgem.gov.uk)*. The 2000 Act also established the *Gas and Electricity Consumers Council* (aka 'energywatch') to represent the interests of all gas and electricity consumers. Ofgem and energywatch have reached a memorandum of understanding on how the two organisations should work together.

Water

Before privatisation, water supply and quality was the responsibility of a range of statutory boards and companies. The government departments involved in overseeing the now privatised water industry are the Department for Environment, Food and Rural Affairs (DEFRA) *(www.defra.gov.uk)* and the Welsh Assembly.

The DEFRA/Welsh Assembly carry out their part of the statutory structure through three bodies: *Office of Water Services (www.ofwat.gov.uk)*, the *Environment Agency (www.environment-agency.gov.uk)* and the *Drinking Water Inspectorate (www.dwi.gov.uk)*.

The *Director General of Water Services* (in the *Office of Water Services,* Ofwat) regulates the *economic* aspects of the water industry — the level of infrastructure development and the charges to customers. OFWAT will take account of the need for the service /

supply companies to be able to make sufficient profits from charges for reinvestment and to pay dividends to shareholders, but the Regulator's prime responsibilities lie with the customers. Even so, the Regulator has permitted charges above the rate of inflation because of the costs of compliance with the EU Urban Waste Water Treatment Directive and related sewerage infrastructure. The recent fairly dramatic improvement in the quality of UK beaches is one of the benefits of this.

Water customers' interests at national and European levels are represented by the *OFWAT National Customer Council* (ONCC) which consists of the chairmen of the 10 regional Customer Service Committees (CSC) established by Ofwat.

The *Environment Agency* (EA)(which took over the functions of the National Rivers Authority (NRA) in April 1996) regulates and enforces water *quality* in inland, estuarial and coastal waters — the management of water resources and pollution control; recreation and conservation. The consent of the Environment Agency is needed for the abstraction of water and the discharge of effluent.

The *Drinking Water Inspectorate* (DWI) regulates and enforces *drinking* water quality.

The DEFRA/Welsh Assembly is responsible for policy relating to land drainage, flood protection, sea defence and the protection and defence of inland and coastal fisheries and oversees the work of the Environment Agency in these activities.

There are 10 water service companies which have statutory responsibilities for the quality and sufficiency of water supply and for sewerage and sewage treatment. There are 19 (originally 29 prior to mergers) supply-only companies, supplying water to nearly 25% of the population.

Water supplied to domestic premises is charged for either on a basis similar to the old rating system (the value of the property) or by metering. Supplies to commercial or industrial premises are metered.

In Scotland, three water authorities (North, West and East of Scotland Water Authorities) are responsible for public water supply, sewerage and sewage disposal. The interests of consumers are protected by the Scottish Water and Sewerage Customers Council. In April 1996, the Scottish Environment Protection Agency (which now reports to the Scottish Executive) took over responsibility for water pollution control from the Scottish river purification authorities.

The Department of the Environment of the Northern Ireland Executive is now responsible for public water supply, sewerage, conservation and river cleanliness throughout Northern Ireland.

Telecommunications

Before privatisation, telecommunications were originally the responsibility of the Post Office (Post Office Telephones) and later a State-owned monopoly British Telecommunications plc (British Telecom — BT). BT was privatised in 1984.

Until 1991, only two companies, BT and Mercury Communications Ltd (then part of the Cable and Wireless Group and 20% owned by Bell Canada Enterprises) were permitted to operate telecommunication systems — a so-called 'duopoly'. Mercury constructed its own long-distance all-digital network, which now links 90 cities and towns across the UK and can provide a service to the whole population, using BT's local line network.

There are now about 150 licensed telecommunications operators in the UK — including 125 cable operators, 19 regional and national public telecommunications operators and four mobile operators, Vodafone, mmO2 (formerly BT Cellnet), Orange and One to One. The greatest increase in telecommunications activity is in mobiles and accessing the internet.

In spite of this increased competition, BT is still by far the largest operator, with 27 million residential and business lines, handling over 103 million local, national and international calls a day. In addition, most of the other operators require to use BT lines to supply their services to customers and BT still benefits from the use of its network.

The industry is regulated under the Telecommunications Act 1984 by the *Director General of Telecommunications* in the *Office of Telecommunications* (Oftel) *(www.oftel.gov.uk)* who: checks that licence conditions are followed; ensures that operators (especially BT with its pre-eminent position in respect of the 'local loop') behave fairly in the competitive regime; deals with complaints; administers the UK telephone numbering system; and provides advice to the Secretary of State (DTI). In 1998 a *Calls and Access* system was introduced under which competitor telephone companies were given rights to use BT's network and provide their own prices and billing — with Oftel adjudicating on disputes. One of the major complaints was BT dragging its feet in 'unbundling' its 'local loop' to maintain its competitive advantage, despite continual pressure from the Director General to make faster progress.

Railways

The railways system in the UK, which began in 1825 with the Stockton and Darlington Railway, was developed by a series of independent companies — that is why St. Pancras and Kings Cross stations in London are adjacent, because they were the termini of rival railways. By the Second World War, the companies had merged to form four large companies: Great Western (GW); London, Midland and Scottish (LMS); London and North Eastern Railway (LNER); and Southern. In 1948, the system was nationalised, to be co-ordinated and controlled by the State-owned British Railways Board (BRB).

Although some rationalisation of the system took place in the 1960s (the then Chairman of British Rail (BR), Dr. Beeching, used his 'Axe' to close many small branch-lines), it still remained a single integrated system — until recently.

Under the Railways Act 1993, the Conservative government set about privatising the system against a background of widespread concern about the results which might ensue from the fragmentation of the system. For many years, pursuing its aim of reducing public expenditure, the government had deprived BR of the capital investment needed for track and rolling stock replacement and development — the consequences of this chronic under-investment are still being felt today.

The process of privatisation was much more complex than earlier privatisations of the other utilities and involved a staged process:

- splitting track and signalling infrastructure from train operations;
- making a new company, Railtrack, responsible for infrastructure;
- retaining train operations with BR until they could be sold off or franchised;
- privatising Railtrack;
- selling off BR's freight and parcels operations to the private sector;
- franchising BR's passenger services, on a piecemeal basis, to the private sector;
- following the complete disposal of BR operations, retaining the British Railways Board (BRB) to manage and dispose of non-operational railway land and to manage the British Transport Police;
- leasing some stations to private companies;
- appointing a Rail Regulator in the Office of the Rail Regulator (ORR) to supervise access to Railtrack's infrastructure; and
- appointing a Franchising Director in the Office of Passenger Rail Franchising (Opraf), to negotiate, award and monitor the franchises and to pay public subsidies.

BR restructured its passenger services into 25 train operating units, to facilitate privatisation through franchises. Railtrack was privatised in May 1996. BR's freight and parcels operations Transrail, Mainline and Loadhaul (trainload freight); Red Star (parcels); Rail Express Systems (Royal Mail trains); and Freightliner (containers) — were sold to private sector companies.

In the first few years of privatisation, some of the issues which emerged were:

- some inflexible and, at times, bizarre pricing and ticketing arrangements, especially affecting through-ticketing;
- when an accident happens, a process akin to 'pass the parcel' appears to operate between the various companies now involved;
- rail franchises were sold to bus companies, raising questions about true commitment to developing rail services;
- some franchise companies have reduced their costs by cutting

staff, which results in large-scale cancellations and poor performance;
- the franchise companies receive such large State subsidies that the fines imposed by Opraf did not really hurt the companies involved; and
- integrating public transport in urban areas to reduce car -usage is harder to achieve.

To address some of these concerns, when it came into office, the New Labour government gave BRB new responsibility for advising the government on railway policy, including suggesting ways in which the system could be improved and integrated with other methods of transport. The New Labour government followed this with an announcement in September 1998 that it intended to establish a new *Strategic Rail Authority* (SRA). The SRA operated as *Shadow Strategic Rail Authority* after Spring 1999, prior to the implementation of the necessary amendment of the Railways Act 1993.

The SRA *(www.sra.gov.uk)* assumed Opraf's responsibilities, together with those of the BRB, the consumer protection functions of the ORR and freight grant functions of the DETR. The ORR *(www.rail-reg.gov.uk)* retained its functions for regulating the activities of Railtrack *(www.railtrack.co.uk)*, and issuing licences to operate trains, networks and stations.

Then everything started to go wrong. Three rail disasters in as many years (Southall 1997; Ladbroke Grove 1999; and Hatfield 2000) were not a good testimony either to Railtrack's management or to the poor rate of public investment in the system over the previous twenty years. At the same time, Railtrack was claiming massive subsidies to keep it afloat, while using part of those subsidies to continue paying dividends to its shareholders. The disruption to the railways after the Hatfield rail disaster, coupled with the ever-spiralling cost of the improvement of the West Coast Main Line, caused the Secretary of State, Stephen Byers, to decide to put Railtrack into administration and went to court to obtain the necessary order. In the circumstances, there seemed to be little else that he could do to achieve any sort of improvement on the railway system.

Having put Railtrack into administration, Stephen Byers' problems took a different turn: threats of legal action from a variety of sources; conditions on the railways becoming worse as the Railtrack 'in administration' situation drifted; the possibility that financial institutions would be more reluctant to contribute to future PPP/PFI projects for the railways, unless there were appropriate inducements and guarantees from the government; and uncertainty about the best form of legal organisation for the future running of the railways — is the idea of a not-for-profit company the best option? There is even speculation that the SRA and the ORR should be combined. All of this will take some time to resolve. In the meantime, the major issue will be how

228

the badly-needed improvement in the railway infrastructure is to be funded — the extent to which the private sector can be persuaded to buy into something which was sold by the government in 1997 and then taken back by the government in 2000; and the extent to which the government can afford to pick up the balance, without an adverse effect on the public sector part of the UK economy.

The future of the system looks to change back: partly to the way the rail system was run prior to privatisation. As the different franchises fall in, the aim may well be to create 'super' railway companies which will control each major terminus, thus creating more capacity by reducing conflict between companies. The point was well illustrated by Richard Bowker (the new SRA Chairman) reported in the *Times* of 20 December 2001 as saying *"Liverpool Street trains are trying to get into the station and the signalman has to have regard for which train belongs to which company and where it has to go. The platform you are allowed to use may be full, while the next one is empty. What bonkers is this?"*

The ultimate aim could be to reduce the number of train operating companies from 25 to less than 20 by 2005, and possibly to less than 10 by 2010. In the meantime, companies will be encouraged to work together in anticipation of the later fusion of franchises. For example, in the case of Wales, the present franchise arrangement under which four overlapping companies currently run the trains, will be replaced in 2003 by a new single franchise, Wales and Borders. At the time of writing this (February 2002), the SRA appears to have no intention of going further and permitting train companies to run their tracks in place of Railtrack (or whatever replaces it).

15 The Treasury

The Treasury — the regulation of investment services — the Bank of England — the annual budget process — basic financial terms

The Treasury

Her Majesty's Treasury *(www.hm-treasury.gov.uk)* is one of the Great Offices of State — its importance is emphasised by the fact that the Prime Minister is *First Lord of the Treasury.* The Treasury has the primary responsibility for formulating and implementing national economic policy. However, there are others involved — the Bank of England and some other government departments, notably the Department of Trade and Industry; and other bodies such as the Office of Fair Trading and the Competition Commission (formerly the Monopolies and Mergers Commission (MMC)).

The economy is complex and the government keeps in touch with developments through informal links with the industrial, commercial and financial sectors. Apart from any other sources of advice, the Chancellor of the Exchequer receives a twice-yearly report from the Panel of Independent Forecasters on the current state of the economy and its future prospects.

Final responsibility for the broad thrust of economic policy rests, like other aspects of major government policy, with the Cabinet.

The Treasury is also responsible for legislation which regulates banks, building societies, friendly societies and investment business generally.

The regulation of investment business

The Treasury supervises the *Financial Services Authority* (FSA) *(www.fsa.gov.uk)* which

230

has statutory responsibilities for the regulation of all types of investment business. With the demutualisation of some building societies and insurance companies and the complexity of some modern financial products (hybrids between insurance, investment and banking), the earlier financial regulation regime was falling behind the sectors it was designed to regulate. In addition, there had been a series of scandals (the mis-selling of pensions was one) which had called into question the efficacy of the then existing regulation arrangements under the Securities and Investments Board (SIB) and the other regulators.

The New Labour government decided to simplify the regulation scene — by increasing SIB's own powers at the expense of the other regulatory bodies — creating a 'Super-SIB': the FSA. In addition, FSA later (1998) assumed responsibility from the Bank of England for regulating the banking sector. The FSA's rôle is to strengthen (but not guarantee) the protection of investors and it does this through authorisation and supervision. Under the Banking Act 1987 no person or body can accept deposits from the public unless authorised to do so by the FSA. The FSA does not become involved in handling complaints between banks and their customers — these are dealt with by the *Financial Services Ombudsman (www.financial-ombudsman.org.uk)*. Building Societies are similarly regulated by the *Building Societies Commission*.

Furthermore, as a consequence of the Financial Services and Markets Act 2000, on 1 December 2000 the FSA became the single Regulator for all financial services in the UK — an even more powerful position.

The more powerful FSA has the following objectives:

- maintaining confidence in the UK financial system;
- promoting public understanding of the financial system;
- securing the right degree of protection for consumers; and
- contributing to the reduction in financial crime.

The FSA carries out its regulatory rôle in one of several ways. The 'frontline' regulation is not carried out directly by the FSA but by a number of specialist bodies specifically *recognised* by the FSA. The recognised body then has the power to authorise firms to conduct investment business in the UK and (under the EU Investment Services Directive) in the European Economic Area. The FSA monitors the performance of the recognised bodies. The four types of recognised body are:

Self-Regulating Organisations (SROs) vet firms to ensure that they are 'fit and proper' to conduct investment business; monitor approved firms to ensure that their financial resources are adequate; supervise firm's dealings with investors; arrange for complaints against firms to be dealt with, including access to an Ombudsman scheme; and disciplining, fining and expelling firms which have broken the SRO's rules. The Personal Investment Authority (PIA) is an example of an SRO.

Recognised Professional Bodies (RPBs) operate in much the same way as SROs but they firms which they regulate are in professions which are not primarily involved in the conduct of investment business although they may conduct some investment business collateral to the main professional activity. An example of an RPB is the Law Society which regulates the investment aspects of solicitors' practices as well as the professional solicitor activity itself.

Recognised Investment Exchanges (RIEs) are the six organised markets recognised in the UK for trading investments, ranging from equities to derivatives. RIEs are obliged to ensure that exchange business is conducted "in an orderly manner and so as to afford proper protection to investors". The London Stock Exchange (LSE) is an RIE.

Recognised Clearing Houses (RCHs) are the two bodies recognised in the UK for settling transactions on the RIEs. The two RCHs are the London Clearing House (LCH) and CrestCo. LCH guarantees and clears transactions on markets such as LIFFE (futures and options) and LME (base non-ferrous metals) and guarantees transactions on Tradepoint (an order-driven exchange). CrestCo is unusual in that it operates as a 'dematerialised settlement system' — in other words, a largely paperless computer system. CrestCo clears and settles transactions on LSE and Tradepoint and some transactions on LIFFE.

The Bank of England

The Bank of England ('The Old Lady of Threadneedle Street') *(www.bankofengland.co.uk)* was founded in 1694 by Royal Charter and Act of Parliament. Its capital stock was acquired by the government in 1946 and it is, in effect, the UK Central Bank. As such, the Bank is also represented on the General Council of the European Central Bank (ECB), although, since the UK has not yet joined the euro, its rôle is less significant than that of the Central Banks of the other EU countries which are in membership of the euro. The Bank is managed by the Court of Directors.

The rôle of the Bank of England is to maintain a stable and efficient monetary and financial framework within which the UK economy can operate. In doing so, the Bank acts as the Treasury's agent in managing the 'Exchange and Equalisation Account' which holds the UK gold and foreign exchange reserves. The Bank *issues* short-term 'Treasury Bills' and *buys* and *sells* long-term 'gilt-edged' government stock in the money markets. The Bank no longer *issues* 'gilts', which are now issued by an executive agency of the Treasury, the *Debt Management Office* (DMO), which as its name suggests, now (since 1 April 1998) manages debt and cash on behalf of the government.

The Bank also has the sole right in England and Wales to issue banknotes, backed by the government. In Scotland there are three banks which issue banknotes and four such banks in Northern Ireland.

It used to be the case that the Chancellor of the Exchequer took decisions about interest rates, as a political issue, which the Bank then implemented. Shortly after the

New Labour government came into power, the Chancellor of the Exchequer announced that, in future, responsibility for deciding interest rates would be a technical rather than a political one and would, instead, rest with the Governor of the Bank of England and a special *Monetary Policy Committee*.

However, things did not go all in the Bank's favour — as a result of some previous spectacular bank scandals, notably Barings Bank, the Chancellor announced shortly afterwards that the Bank would lose some of its existing responsibilities to supervise the UK retail and wholesale banking system under the then Banking Act 1967 — these became the responsibility of the FSA as mentioned in the previous section.

The annual budget process

The UK budget system changed in November 1993 when a unified Budget arrangement was introduced — under which the government presents to Parliament its taxation proposals for the next financial year beginning 5 April and its spending proposals for the next three years. The system was further changed in May 1997 when the New Labour government came into office and now involves an autumn *pre-Budget Report* and a spring *Budget Speech*.

The pre-Budget Report is, in essence, a progress report on the UK economic position and government finances and describes the approach which the government is likely to take in the following Spring when the Chancellor presents the Budget to Parliament. This broad brush approach of the pre-Budget Speech can change if circumstances require it — the 2000 pre-Budget Report was used by the Chancellor to announce a £4.5bn cut in fuel taxes, to placate the fuel protestors.

The convention is that the Chancellor's Spring Budget Speech covers fiscal matters, that is about taxation, rather than spending proposals, which again by convention are regarded as the province of the relevant Secretary of State to announce later. However the Chancellor might choose to stray into the area of spending proposals, if only to soften the blow when taxes are to be increased or where there is a need to make a big impact, especially with one eye on the next General Election.

The modern trend is for increases or decreases in taxes, benefits or pensions to be announced for the next-but-one tax year — so any evaluation of the impact of a particular Budget Speech needs to take into account what was said in last year's Speech and which may be about to come into effect. Strictly speaking, the proposals in the Budget Speech need to be authorised by a subsequent Finance Act before they can be implemented. However, some of the tax changes (such as excise, vehicle licence and other duties) can take effect immediately the Chancellor announces them, in advance of the Finance Bill, as authorised by the Provisional Collection of Taxes Act 1968. Some taxes are permanent (indirect taxes such as VAT), whereas other taxes (direct taxes such as income tax) are annual and need to be renewed by Parliament each year. These days, most tax allowances are indexed to the *Retail Prices Index* and will be adjusted automatically in line with inflation — such allowances will only be mentioned in the Budget Speech if the Chancellor decides to adjust them otherwise than by reference to inflation.

On the day that the Chancellor makes the Budget Speech, the detailed government Budget is also published in the *Financial Statement and Budget Report* (FSBR) — more usually referred to as the *Red Book* or the *Budget Report*. It is the detail in the FSBR which is studied by accountants over the days following the Budget Speech — to find out where the real pain is hidden and which the Chancellor did not mention in the Speech itself!

Some basic terms defined

The UK economy is *market-based,* involving the buying and selling of goods and services within the UK and the rest of the World. The concept of a market is based upon supply and demand — ideally, the most stable market is where the supply of goods matches the demand for them. The present approach to economic policy in the UK is to expose as much of the economy as possible to market-forces, avoiding the use of direct controls on pay, prices, foreign exchange and commercial credit.

The ideal balance is never achieved. If supply exceeds demand, then prices will generally fall — good news for the consumer in the short-term, but bad news for the supplier/manufacturer who might go out of business. If demand exceeds supply, then there will be too much money chasing too few goods and prices will tend to rise — good news for the supplier (who will try to raise production) but bad news for the consumer, because increased prices also means inflation in the economy.

Inflation in the economy is expressed in terms of the percentage rise in the *Retail Prices Index* (RPI), which records the price of goods and services purchased by households. A variant of the RPI is one which excludes mortgage payments — called *underlying inflation*. The rate of inflation is one of the key indicators to the health of the economy — so key, in fact, that the Bank of England produces a *Quarterly Inflation Report* which is used as a basis for monetary control and interest rates.

All developed economies involve trade with other countries — exporting and importing goods and services. The EU is now the UK's most important trading partner. There will always be some difference between the value of goods and services exported and those imported — the *Balance of Payments*. Goods are not the only commodity exported — exports also include services, the so-called *invisible exports,* such as financial and insurance services and investment income transactions. Invisible exports are always in surplus and are an important component in calculating the net position on the *Balance of Trade* with the rest of the World.

If the value of exports exceeds imports, then the Balance of Payments are said to

234

be *in surplus*; if imports exceed exports, then there is said to be a Balance of Payments *deficit*. The Balance of Payments is usually expressed as a *current account* position. The current account basis includes trade in goods and services, including finance, tourism, transport and transactions in investment income and transfers. Less often, a *capital account* position is quoted — this includes inward and outward investment in the UK, external borrowing and lending by UK residents and changes in the UK official reserves. At present the UK Balance of Payments is in deficit and although the figures look enormous, they represent less than 1% of the GDP.

Gross Domestic Product (GDP) is the value of all goods and services produced in the UK economy, after offsetting the cost of imported goods and services. *Gross National Product* (GNP) is the GDP plus net property income from overseas investments. GDP and GNP can be expressed in more than one way: either in terms of market prices (the prices actually paid by people for goods and services) or at factor cost (the cost of goods and services before adding taxes and deducting subsidies). *National Income* is the GNP at factor cost, minus capital consumption. The figures can also be expressed at different price bases: current prices or constant prices (removing the effect of inflation).

General Government Expenditure (GGE) is the total of central and local government expenditure, including support for nationalised industries and other public corporations. Government expenditure is financed through taxation and borrowing. If the economy is performing well (that is, not in recession), then more of government expenditure can be financed through taxation, reducing the need to borrow to make up the shortfall. The amount which the government needs to borrow is expressed as the *Public Sector Borrowing Requirement* (PSBR).

The taxation levied by government can be of two kinds — direct and indirect. Direct taxation is levied 'directly' on an individual's or body's *income* — such as Income Tax or Corporation Tax — the individual pays the tax directly to the taxing authority. *Indirect Taxation* is paid 'indirectly' on *expenditure* by an individual when, for example, purchasing goods — such as Value Added Tax (VAT) or Customs and Excise duties, which are paid directly by the retailer and indirectly by the consumer.

Taxes are regarded as more fair, *'progressive'*, if they are linked in some way to the individual's ability to pay them — such as Income Tax, which takes an increasing (or progressive) proportion of the subject's income as that income rises. Taxes which are not so linked to ability to pay are likely to have harsh consequences for the less well-off and are criticised as being *'regressive'*. For example, low-income smokers pay a higher rate of taxation (tobacco tax) in terms of their income than high-income smokers do.

16 The Home Office

The rôle of the Home Office — the criminal justice system — the treatment of offenders — immigration and asylum

The Home Office

The *Home Department* (the Home Office) *(www.homeoffice.gov.uk)* is supervised by the *Secretary of State for the Home Department* (the Home Secretary). Like the Treasury and the Foreign and Commonwealth Office, it is one of the Great Offices of State. Apart from other responsibilities, the Home Secretary advises the Sovereign on the exercise of the Royal Prerogative of Mercy.

Although the main responsibilities of the Home Office are to do with the criminal justice system, it has other responsibilities such as elections, race relations, immigration and asylum.

As far as *elections* are concerned, the rôle of the Home Office is almost entirely one of overall supervision, since the various aspects of the electoral system are dealt with by others — electoral registration and the conduct of elections are the responsibility of local authorities and electoral boundary review is the responsibility of the Boundary Commissions (ultimately to be transferred to the Electoral Commission).

As far as *race relations* are concerned, previous legislation was strengthened by the Race Relations Act 1976, which outlawed various forms of racial discrimination and gave access to various forms of redress. The Public Order Act 1986 made the incitement of racial hatred a criminal offence. A quango, the *Commission for Racial Equality* (CRE) *(www.cre.gov.uk)*, investigates alleged unlawful racial discrimination and can issue formal *Non-discrimination Notices* to stop discriminatory practices. The CRE also issues *Codes of Practice* aimed at promoting good practice.

The criminal justice system

The criminal justice system has two aspects — the courts and the treatment of offenders sentenced by the courts. The Home Office is concerned with the treatment of offenders.

The court system is overseen by the Lord Chancellor *(www.lcd.gov.uk)*, who is head of the judiciary and a senior member of the Cabinet — with the day-to-day work being undertaken for the Lord Chancellor's Department by the *Court Service,* an executive agency. The Lord Chancellor has responsibility for promoting any general reforms of the *civil* law and for the legal aid system.

The Attorney-General and the Solicitor-General are the government's main legal advisers and they can represent the Crown in the more important domestic and international cases. They are members of the Commons and their posts carry Ministerial status. The Lord Advocate and Solicitor General for Scotland perform similar rôles in devolved Scotland. The Attorney-General also has ultimate responsibility for *enforcing* the criminal law, with the Solicitor-General effectively acting as his deputy. The Attorney-General also supervises: the Director of Public Prosecutions (DPP), who runs the *Crown Prosecution Service* (CPS); the Director of the Serious Fraud Office (SFO); and the DPP for Northern Ireland.

The Home Secretary has overall responsibility for *criminal* law and will introduce any Bills required to change it. The police service, the probation service and the prison system are all services under the overall supervision of the Home Office.

The Home Secretary used to be the Police Authority for London, supervising the Metropolitan Police Commissioner, but this changed when the Greater London Authority came into existence in July 2000. Outside the metropolis, the police service is managed by a series of Chief Constables, reporting to their local Police Authority (as described in *Essential Local Government*).

The *National Probation Service* is managed by a series of Chief Probation Officers, who used to report to their local Probation Committee, but who, since April 2001, now form part of the National Probation Service under the *National Probation Directorate* within the Home Office. There are 42 Probation Services in England and Wales, which match police force area boundaries. The National Probation Service is subject to supervision by the independent HM Inspectorate of Probation.

The 135 prisons in England and Wales are not managed directly by the Home Office, but through the *Prison Service Agency,* an executive agency of the Home Office, with its own Chief Executive. Similar executive agencies exist in Scotland and Northern Ireland. The use of an executive agency means that it is the Prison Service Chief

Executive who is responsible for administrative mistakes, rather than the Home Secretary (see section on *Ministerial responsibility* in Chapter 6). In Scotland, the Deputy First Minister is responsible for criminal law, crime prevention, police, prisons and legal aid.

Consistent with the Conservative government's policy of privatising as much of the public services as possible, the Criminal Justice Act 1991 authorised the Home Secretary to contract out to the private sector the management of prisons and the escort of prisoners outside prison. The prison escort services were privatised with initial criticism of the quality of their service — including the loss of some prisoners. Four new prisons, as they were completed (The Wolds, Humberside; Blakenhurst, Worcestershire; Doncaster; and Buckley Hall, Rochdale) were put out to private sector management, but are still part of the Prison Service.

In addition, the *Private Finance Initiative* (PFI) has been used for financing, designing, building and managing three new prisons in England and Wales (Merseyside, Nottinghamshire and South Wales) and one in Scotland (Kilmarnock) — opened 1998-99.

Both the probation and prisons services are subject to a single complaints process. The independent Prisons and Probation Ombudsman is appointed by the Home Secretary to investigate complaints from prisoners, and from people who are subject to probation supervision in the community or about whom reports have been written by the National Probation Service.

Treatment of offenders

Offenders, if convicted, receive either a non-custodial or a custodial sentence.

Non-custodial sentences include: fines, compensation orders, probation orders, supervision orders, community service orders, and combination orders (elements of probation and community service). In England and Wales, the *Probation Service* will be involved in monitoring non-custodial offenders during the life of a probation, supervision or community service order. In Scotland, similar work is undertaken by local authority social work departments.

Custodial sentences will be served in prison — with varying degrees of security ranging from an open prison to a high security prison — or in a young offender institution.

Early release of prisoners — England and Wales

The Criminal Justice Act 1991 reformed the sentence remission and parole arrangements in England and Wales, with the Parole Board advising the Home Secretary on the early release of long-term prisoners.

The arrangements involved the early release of prisoners sentenced to less than four years, after they had served half of their sentence. Prisoners serving four years or more could be released early after serving half of their sentence, if approved by the Parole Board, and automatically after serving two-thirds of their sentence. The Parole Board had the final decision on prisoners serving more than four but less than seven years; and made recommendations to the Home Secretary on those serving longer sentences. All prisoners on parole and who were originally sentenced to one year or more, were let out of prison on licence (under supervision by the Probation Service) until the three-quarters point of their sentence.

Prisoners sentenced to life imprisonment for certain kinds of murder — murder of police and prison officers; terrorist murder; murder in the course of robbery using firearms, and sadistic murder of children — usually have to serve at least 20 years. The release of mandatory life prisoners on licence is authorised only by the Home Secretary on the recommendation of the Parole Board and after the judiciary have been consulted.

Prisoners sentenced to life imprisonment for offences other than murder would be released by the Home Secretary (if directed by the Parole Board to do so) after a period set by the judge at the trial. The Parole Board has to decide whether or not continued confinement in prison is needed to protect the public.

If a prisoner who has been released early commits another offence while on parole, the trial judge at the subsequent trial may order the offender to serve all or part of the outstanding original sentence as well.

The purpose of parole is to give prisoners something to look forward to and to encourage good behaviour in prison by paroling those with a good record of conduct.

However, in April 1996, the Conservative government under Home Secretary Michael Howard decided to issue a White Paper *Protecting the Public* as part of its 'get tough with crime' policy — possibly with the forthcoming General Election in mind. The proposals in that White Paper were:

- an automatic life sentence would be imposed on an offender convicted for a second time of a serious sexual or violent offence;
- mandatory minimum prison sentences would be imposed on drug dealers and burglars for repeat offences; and
- automatic early release and parole would be abolished, with prisoners serving the full term of their sentence, unless they earned up to 20% off their sentence for good behaviour; those sentenced to one year or more and released early would be supervised by the Probation Service for a period equal to 15% of their original sentence.

These proposals attracted much criticism — especially from all parts of the criminal justice system, including the judiciary — not least because the same Conservative government in an earlier 1990 White Paper had said "nobody now regards imprisonment *as an effective means of reform...* ". The prison population was already high, with adverse conditions in overcrowded prisons leading to more internal disturbances and with the need to build ever more new prisons. The Home Office even imported a prison ship from the USA at great expense because it could not build new prisons fast enough. The new policy would increase the number of prisoners retained in the prison system, leading to yet more demand for additional prison places.

In the event, most of these changes were included in the Crime (Sentences) Act 1997. All prisoners have to serve the full sentence. However, those serving less than three years could gain, and lose, 'early release days'. Those serving three years or more could be released on Parole Board recommendation after serving five-sixths of the sentence. The New Labour Home Secretaries have not shown much inclination to be less tough on crime.

Early release of prisoners — Scotland and Northern Ireland

The arrangements in Scotland are broadly similar, but there are differences. The Parole Board can release prisoners serving between four and 10 years, after they have served half of their sentence. The early release of those serving more than 10 years needs the consent of the Secretary of State. Those released early from sentences of four years or more are supervised to the end of their sentence. Parolees are supervised by local authority social work departments.

In Northern Ireland, special arrangements are in place for terrorist offences. Terrorists sentenced to five years or more can usually be paroled only after serving two-thirds of their sentence — but this was changed in November 1995 to bring it in line with the rest of the UK; parole after serving half of the sentence. If a terrorist is convicted of another terrorist offence before the expiry of the original sentence, then the original sentence has to be completed before the next one starts. The whole issue of the early release of terrorist prisoners was revised as part of the process which led to the Anglo-Irish Agreement — with the result that most of the inmates of the Maze prison, including those serving life sentences, were allowed home on licence for Christmas 1999 and New Year 2000.

Oversight of the prison system

Each prison and young offender institution has a *Board of Visitors* — volunteers from the local community appointed by the Home Secretary. A similar arrangement, involving a visiting committee reporting to the Secretary of State operates in Scotland. The Board of Visitors visits prisons and hears complaints from prisoners.

There are independent *HM Prisons Inspectorates,* reporting to the Home Secretary and the Scottish First Minister, which visit each prison about every three years to report on prison conditions and the treatment of prisoners.

As already explained, complaints are dealt with by the independent Prisons and Probation Ombudsman.

Immigration and Asylum

This area of activity is undertaken by the *Immigration and Nationality Directorate* of the Home Office. The immigration of people into the UK was originally regulated by the Immigration Act 1971 and the statutory Rules made under it. British citizens and those Commonwealth citizens who had the right of abode before January 1983, retained the right of abode in the UK and are not subject to immigration control. Nationals of the European Economic Area (EEA), which is the EU plus Iceland, Liechtenstein and Norway, are not subject to significant immigration control. They may work in the UK and, if able to support themselves, also have the right to reside in the UK. Nationals of other, specified, countries require a *visa* before they may enter the UK. All other nationals subject to immigration control need *entry clearance* before coming to the UK to work or live.

People fleeing from persecution or refugees can seek asylum in the UK — in accordance with the United Nations Protocol on the Status of Refugees. The Conservative government decided that too many people were trying to enter the UK as 'refugees' — many were called 'economic refugees' after a better lifestyle, to suggest that they were not real refugees. So, the Asylum and Immigration Act 1996 was passed — enabling the government to designate countries as not giving rise to a serious risk of persecution and, therefore, people coming from those countries could not be refugees; some of the government's designations brought criticism about what factors had been taken into account.

The former two-tier appeal system against a decision of an immigration officer on behalf of the Home Office was derived from the recommendations of the Wilson Committee. The first appeal stage was to an *Adjudicator* who sat alone, usually in public, to decide the appeal. *Special Adjudicators* sat to hear asylum appeals; this stage of the appeal system was supervised by the *Chief Adjudicator*. Either party (the appellant or the Home Office) could appeal against the Adjudicator's decision to the Immigration Appeal Tribunal (IAT), but only if the IAT agreed that there was an arguable point of law. The IAT consisted of three people — a legally qualified chairman and two lay members. Under the Asylum and Immigration Appeals Act 1993, there was a further right of appeal to the Court of Appeal (England and Wales) or the Court of Session (Scotland), but only if the superior court agreed that there was, again, an arguable point of law. The Secretary of State also had the discretion to refer cases back to the Adjudicator or IAT where a first appeal had been dismissed.

A consultative paper was issued by the Home Office in 1999 on streamlining the present appeal system, which had become bogged down with the number of appeals awaiting determination and overcrowded detention centres. The suggested solution to the problem was to reduce the grounds and circumstances under which an appeal could be made and to reduce access to an 'in-country' appeal — that is, by deporting ('administrative removal') various categories of illegal entrant back to their country of origin, from where they could make a proper application for entry and appeal against any refusal there. The present two-tier system of hearing the remaining 'in-country' appeals would be simplified into a single tier-system, involving either a single adjudicator or panel, at the discretion of the Chief Adjudicator.

Illegal entrants who claimed refugee status and those who claimed a right to remain under the provisions of European Commission of Human Rights would, if their applications were refused, be given an 'in-country' right of appeal before deportation. Given the nature of the asylum claim, a right of appeal after deportation was not regarded as an effective remedy. A proposal to return a person to a country in which he claimed to have a well-founded fear of persecution without a right of appeal would almost certainly be inconsistent with the UK's international obligations.

The Immigration and Asylum Act 1999 introduced, from October 2000, a new *One Stop Appeal* system. This Act also had to take into account the provisions of the Human Rights Act. Under the new system, there should be one application, one decision and one appeal. Applicants are required to disclose all of their reasons for staying in the UK when they first apply. If their application is refused, they cannot then raise new reasons without a reasonable excuse for failing to disclose them before.

The precise nature of the immigration appeal process depends upon where and at what stage the decision being appealed was made. Where the application for entry was made abroad at a British Embassy or High Commission, the appeal is dealt with in the UK; however, the applicant cannot enter the UK for the appeal, but can be represented. If the applicant is in the UK, then appeals can be either an 'on-entry appeal' or an 'after-entry appeal'. The appeal is intended to be the final outcome and there should be nothing to prevent deportation in that event. The right of appeal is only available to a person with a valid entry clearance or who claims 'the right of abode' and even then does not arise in all cases; in some instances the appeal can only be made after leaving the UK. All applicants can assert a 'human rights appeal' if they believe that refusal of entry breaches their human rights — but this must be raised at the same time as they exercise any other right of appeal, if they have one. In very rare special cases, involving removal from the UK for reasons involving national security or the public interest, the right of appeal is under a different legislative provision, to the Special Immigration Appeals Commission.

Asylum appeals are handled differently. Anyone can allege that they should stay in the UK on asylum grounds, but they must raise these grounds at the earliest opportunity if they wish to pursue an asylum appeal. If they have immigration rights of appeal, they cannot later raise asylum grounds if they lose their immigration appeal, just to delay their removal from the UK. An applicant may be given 'exceptional leave to remain' if he or she does not strictly qualify under the 1951 Refugee Convention but should still not be returned to his or her own country. An unsuccessful applicant is not always deported to his or her own country — if they have attempted entry to the UK from a 'safe third country' they can be sent back to that country and be required to argue their case from there.

Where a right of appeal against a decision made by the Home Secretary and his officials exists, the appeal must be claimed within 10 days of receipt of a 'one-stop' notice, indicating refusal of entry, served on the individual and is heard by an individual Adjudicator. There can be a further appeal, but only with permission; any such appeals are heard by the Immigration Appeal Tribunal, consisting of a legally-qualified chairman and two lay members. Appeals are heard in nine centres: London, Hatton Cross, Birmingham, Leeds, Manchester, Glasgow, Havant, Cardiff and Belfast. The process is supervised by the Immigration Appeals Authority. The Authority is part of the Tribunals Group of the Court Service, which is an executive agency of the Lord Chancellor's Department.

17 Culture, Media and Sport

The rôle of the Department of Culture, Media and Sport — the arts — media — National Lottery — heritage — sport

The Department of Culture, Media and Sport

The Secretary of State for Culture. Media and Sport is a member of the Cabinet. The Department's *(www.culture.gov.uk)* responsibilities include support for the arts, heritage and sport and the regulation of the film industry, broadcasting, the press, the National Lottery and the export licensing of antiques. The department was previously called the Department of National Heritage. The devolved institutions for Scotland, Wales and Northern Ireland have similar responsibilities in their respective countries.

Arts

The department determines government policy on support for the arts and supervises expenditure on national museums and art galleries, by the *Arts Council of England* and by the *National Library.*

Central government expenditure on the arts is mostly spent on supporting the performing and visual arts. Grants are made to the *British Film Institute,* the *Crafts Council* and to the *National Heritage Memorial Fund* — the aim of the Fund is to help bodies who want to buy (for the public benefit) land, buildings, works of art and other objects connected with the national heritage. Quite often a grant from the Fund helps to keep a particularly important work of art in the UK when it would otherwise have been exported.

The *Arts Council (www.artscouncil.org.uk)* is a quango and aims: to develop and improve the knowledge, understanding and practice of the arts; to make the arts more accessible; and to advise and co-operate with central and local government and other organisations. Direct financial support and advice is given to major arts centres and opera, drama and dance companies (such as Royal Opera, Royal Ballet, English National Opera and the Royal Shakespeare Company) — and to touring companies as well. Individual creative artists and writers are also supported.

The 10 *Regional Arts Boards* also offer similar support to the arts, but on a regional basis — complementing the support from the Arts Council itself.

Broadcast media

In relation to the broadcast media, the rôle of the department is essentially one of overall policy and supervision of the broadcasting *system*. However, the Broadcasting Acts 1990 and 1996 enable the government to intervene when programme content issues such as taste and decency are involved. Unacceptable foreign satellite services receivable in the UK can be (and have been) banned by the government — anyone supporting such services in the UK can be prosecuted for a criminal offence.

In the case of television and radio, three public bodies work to broad requirements and objectives approved by Parliament:

- *British Broadcasting Corporation* (BBC) *(www.bbc.co.uk)* — the UK's main public service broadcaster in television and radio, under its latest Royal Charter granted in 1996, funded by the annual licence fee collected by TV Licensing, a subsidiary of the Post Office;
- *Independent Television Commission* (ITC) *(www.itc.org.uk)* — licensing and regulating commercial television services, including cable and satellite, analogue or digital; and
- *Radio Authority (www.radioauthority.org.uk)* — starting in 1991, licensing and regulating commercial radio services, including cable, satellite and digital.

Through the Broadcasting Act 1996, the government introduced a new regulatory framework for digital (as opposed to analogue) terrestrial broadcasting for both commercial and public service broadcasting.

Change is in the air. In December 2000, New Labour published a White Paper *A New Future for Communications*. That White Paper raised a number of issues, including media ownership. Another issue was the creation of a new single Regulator, *Ofcom* (Office of Communications). Earlier proposals for the regulation of communications had been removed from the Utilities Bill, which, as the Utilities Act 2000, established the single energy Regulator, Ofgem. The creation of a single Regulator of Communications requires primary legislation — a Communications Bill, which has yet to be published. What has been published is a Bill (the Office of Communications Bill) to create the Regulator, without defining precisely what that Regulator should do — this will be left to the Communications Bill when the government decides to publish it and when it makes it through Parliament. The idea is that Ofcom will replace the five existing regulators dealing with economics (Oftel), content (Independent Television Commission, Broadcasting Standards Commission, and Radio Authority) and radio spectrum allocations (Radiocommunications Agency). At the time of writing this (February 2002), those proposals are still out for consultation.

Press media

The regulation of the press media is still voluntary — through the *Press Complaints Commission (www.pcc.org.uk)* set up in 1991 by the newspaper and periodical industry. The Commission replaced the Press Council established in 1953 and consists of newspaper and magazine representatives and people from outside the industry.

The Commission deals with complaints by members of the public about the content and conduct of newspapers and magazines; and operates an ethical Code of Practice agreed with editors concerning respect for privacy, opportunity to reply, corrections, journalist behaviour, references to race and religion, payments to criminals for articles, and protection of confidential sources.

The Commission is a good example of the advantages and disadvantages of 'self-regulation'. The Code of Practice was drafted by editors and other people in the press media industry — with the expectation that, because of its authorship, the Code of Practice would be more likely to be respected within the industry. Even so, there were breaches of the Code (sometimes stories which might increase circulation being run thinly disguised as being 'in the public interest') for which no real sanction was (or could be) imposed.

The government published a White Paper *Privacy and Media Intrusion: the Government's Response* in 1995 — explicitly rejecting calls for the statutory regulation of the press.

Media ownership

The Broadcasting Acts 1990 and 1996 provided a detailed framework under which the regulatory bodies (the ITC and the Radio Authority) could keep ownership of the broadcasting media dispersed — and prevent undue concentrations of single and cross-media ownership, especially by companies based outside the EU.

The Broadcasting Act 1996 relaxed the media ownership rules within, and across, different media sectors. There is now a set of 'public interest' criteria which enable the regulatory bodies to allow or reject mergers or acquisitions between newspapers and television and radio companies.

The previous two-licence limit on ITV licences has been replaced by a 'television ownership limit' of a 15% share of the total television audience. In addition, local newspapers with more than a 50% share of their market can now own a local radio station, but only if there is at least one other independent radio station operating in that area.

The National Lottery

The National Lottery was launched in November 1994 and is run by a private company, *Camelot Group plc*, who won the contract. The Lottery was originally regulated by the *Director-General of the National Lottery* in the *Office of the National Lottery* (Oflot) but as a consequence of the National Lottery Act 1998, Oflot was replaced in April 1999 by a new five member *National Lottery Commission (www.natlotcomm.gov.uk)*.

There has been criticism of the way in which the Lottery is run and the level of the profits made by Camelot plc. Camelot plc said that it would co-operate with suggestions from the New Labour government that the Lottery should be run on a non-profit-making basis in the future. The National Lottery Commission's first major task was to award the operator's licence to run after the expiration of Camelot's licence in September 2001. The nature of the lottery (for profit or not for profit) became a key feature because there were only two runners in the final shortlist for the new licence: Camelot plc and Richard Branson's 'People's Lottery'. However, the Commission managed to make a mess of the selection process, with Camelot plc successfully challenging the Commission in the High Court for the way in which the Commission had rejected Camelot's bid as being unsatisfactory but yet giving Richard Branson more time to sort out the 'People's Lottery' bid which was also regarded by the Commission as unsatisfactory. Camelot plc retained the contract.

Voluntary organisations and charities also complained that the level of donations which they would normally expect to receive dropped significantly, because people were spending their money on lottery tickets instead, in the belief that the money would find its way to the charities through the Lottery's 'good causes'. Evidence has been produced that grants from the National Lotteries Charities Board have not made up the shortfall.

There have also been criticisms that in most regions of the country there is little correlation between the amount spent on the lottery and the amount returned on 'good causes' within the region. The South East has benefited particularly generously, with large grants being made to prestigious arts venues for which most ordinary people could not afford to buy tickets.

The money which goes into the National Lottery emerges as follows:

Prizes	50%
'Good causes'	28%
Tax	12%
Retailer Commission	5%
Operating Costs and Camelot plc profit	5%

The 28% 'good causes' proceeds were originally divided equally between five 'good causes': the arts, sport, heritage, charities and projects to mark the millennium. The National Lottery Act 1998 introduced a sixth 'good cause': health, education and the environment. In the first year of the Lottery's operation, £1.2bn was awarded to 'good causes' and by April 1999 this had risen to £6.3bn. Since April 1996, National Lottery funds can be spent not only on buildings and equipment but also on projects which develop people's talents and potential. Since 1998, National Lottery funds an also be spent on people. When the National Lottery was introduced the then government promised that the 'good causes' money would not be used to replace public expenditure. Non-compliance with this promise would be difficult to prove. The addition of the sixth 'good cause', health, education and the environment, caused cynics to wonder whether the New Labour government was demonstrably replacing public expenditure with National Lottery money.

Camelot plc pays the 'good causes' money to the National Lottery Distribution Fund (NLDF) which then pays it to applicants approved by the distributing organisations:

- *arts* — the Arts Councils of England, Wales and Northern Ireland and the Scottish Arts Council;
- *sports* — Sport England, the Sports Councils of Wales, Northern Ireland and Scotland;
- *heritage* — the Heritage Lottery Fund;
- *charities* — the National Lottery Charities Board;
- *projects to mark the millennium* — the Millennium Commission; and
- *health, education and the environment* — the New Opportunities Fund.

Heritage

The department has responsibility for the maintenance of the royal palaces and parks open to the public — which is carried out by two executive agencies: *Historic Royal Palaces* and the *Royal Parks Agency*.

The department maintains the statutory list of buildings of special architectural and historical interest — see the section on *Buildings of architectural or historic interest* in *Essential Local Government* for more information about the listing of buildings.

The department also has responsibility for the care of over 400 properties of special architectural or historic interest or which are ancient monuments. Again, the responsibilities are carried out by an executive agency — English Heritage. English Heritage *(www.english-heritage.org.uk)* also provides advice to the department on how to deal with applications to demolish or alter scheduled monuments or listed buildings. In Scotland, the executive agency Historic Scotland provides a similar service to the Scottish Executive. In Wales, the executive agency Cadw is responsible to the National Assembly.

The *Heritage Lottery Fund,* as a grant-aiding body and as a distributor of the heritage share of the Lottery proceeds, has already been mentioned.

Sport

The Secretary of State is responsible for government policy on sport and recreation in England. The relevant Minister or Secretary of the devolved bodies for Scotland, Wales and Northern Ireland has similar responsibilities. National sports policy is led by the Secretary of State, in association with the relevant Minister or Secretary.

Sports policy and advice is delivered through the five quangos appointed by the relevant Secretaries of State — the Sports Councils: the *English Sport* (previously the English Sports Council), the *Sports Council of Wales,* the *Sports Council of Scotland,* the *Sports Council of Northern Ireland* and the *United Kingdom Sports Council* (UKSC). The rôle of UKSC is strategic planning and co-ordination — including representing UK interests overseas and trying to bring major sporting events to the UK.

The *National Sports Medicine Institute,* based at the medical college at St Bart's Hospital in London is jointly funded by UKSC and English Sport.

Finally, spectator safety is the responsibility of the department, which jointly with the Scottish Office, published its *'Guide to Safety at Sports Grounds'* which is used by local authorities when issuing safety certificates to licensed sports grounds.

18 International Relations and Defence

The rôle of the Foreign and Commonwealth Office — the Secretary of State for International Development — UN — NATO — UK defence strategy — the Ministry of Defence

The Foreign and Commonwealth Office

The Foreign and Commonwealth Office (FCO) *(www.fco.gov.uk)* is the government department in charge of the UK's overall foreign policy and is headed by the Foreign and Commonwealth Secretary (the Foreign Secretary), who is a senior member of the Cabinet.

Before the New Labour government, the Foreign Secretary was assisted by five Ministers, none of whom had Cabinet rank, and one of whom was the *Minister for Overseas Development*, responsible for the *Overseas Development Administration* (ODA), part of the FCO. When New Labour came into power that changed — there is now a *Secretary of State for International Development,* with Cabinet rank, turning the ODA into a new *Department for International Development* (DfID) *(www.dfid.gov.uk)* and the number of FCO Ministers has dropped to four.

The *Diplomatic Service* within the FCO is headed by a career civil servant, the Permanent Under Secretary of State at the FCO, who also provides foreign policy advice to the Foreign Secretary.

The FCO maintains diplomatic or consular relations with 188 countries and has diplomatic missions at nine international organisations or conferences (such as the UN). The main rôle of UK embassies abroad is to act as a local point of contact in the formal diplomatic relations between the UK and that country. However, the embassy also provides a range of consular services, aimed at protecting the interests of UK citizens within that country, especially when they encounter difficulties. There is also a significant emphasis on the promotion of the UK as a trading partner and some embassy staff — commercial attachés based in more than 200 Diplomatic Posts — are devoted to this activity.

People seeking entry into the UK and who are subject to immigration control and require pre-entry clearance, obtain that clearance from the visa section or consulate of the local FCO mission in their country.

The FCO has one executive agency — *Wilton Park International Conference Centre*, West Sussex — which organises conferences on international problems, involving politicians, academics, professionals and business people, often from abroad.

Other government departments and bodies

The FCO and DfID are not the only government departments interested in international relations. The *Ministry of Defence* (MoD) obviously maintains the UK armed forces, but it is also responsible for military liaison with the UK's allies — in NATO and elsewhere.

The *Department of Trade and Industry* (DTI) influences international trade policy and commercial relations with other countries. The FCO and DTI jointly run an export promotion body — *British Trade International* (BTI) (formerly *Overseas Trade Services*) *(www.tradepartners.gov.uk)* — with staff based overseas in FCO diplomatic missions and in the UK at the DTI in London, in regional offices and in Business Links (a DTI programme aimed at supporting the development of small firms). The activities of BTI in England are matched by those of *Scottish Trade International (*STI), the National Assembly for Wales and *Trade International Northern Ireland* (TINI).

In relation to Europe, the FCO co-ordinates UK EU policy through the *Cabinet Office European Secretariat.*

The *British Council (www.britishcouncil.org)* is a registered charity which receives its core grant-aid from the FCO but also earns about half of its total income from teaching English, running British examinations and managing training and development contracts. The Council is the UK's principal agency for cultural relations, having 254 offices and teaching centres in 110 overseas countries and territories. The British Council's aims are to promote a wider knowledge of the UK and the English language, thus enhancing the UK's reputation as a valued partner. The Council does this through encouraging, and in some cases financing, cultural, scientific, technological and educational co-operation between the UK and other countries. One of the more significant activities of the Council is supporting educational exchanges, especially in Europe, through its *Central Bureau for Educational Visits and Exchanges.*

The UK aid programme — the D/ID

The principal rôle of the D*f*ID is the delivery of the UK international aid programme, which is the sixth largest in the world — details can be obtained from the current edition of *Statistics on International Development*. Most of the countries receiving aid are not only the poorest 'developing countries' in Asia and Sub-Saharan Africa but also middle-income countries elsewhere with the aim of eliminating poverty and encouraging sustainable development. In addition, there is now a special category — 'countries in transition' — which covers the emerging democracies in Central and Eastern Europe and the former USSR whose economies are in transition from centrally-managed to market-based.

The UK aid is either given directly by the D*f*ID or is allocated through international bodies such as the Commonwealth, EU, UN or the World Bank. Local private sector investment in developing countries is encouraged by the D*f*ID itself and through another government agency, the *Commonwealth Development Corporation* (CDC). The CDC provides loans, equity funds and management services for viable local enterprises in such things as agriculture, industry, transport and housing in over 50 such countries. Some of the D*f*ID aid is applied through programmes administered by the British Council and a variety of UK charities, such as Oxfam and Save the Children Fund.

At the same time as it created the D*f*ID, New Labour published its White Paper, *Eliminating World Poverty: A Challenge for the 21st Century,* which described the UK's overseas aid objectives, with a switch in emphasis towards the elimination of poverty:

- *Economic well-being* — a reduction by 50% in the proportion of people living in extreme poverty by 2015;
- *Human development* — universal primary education in all countries by 2015; progress towards gender equality and the empowerment of women by 2005, as agreed by the Fourth World Conference on Women in Peking in 1995; a reduction by two-thirds in the mortality rates for infants and children under age five and a reduction by three-fourths in maternal mortality, all by 2015; and access through the primary health care system to reproductive health services as soon as possible and no later than the year 2015, as agreed by the International Conference on Population and Development in Cairo in 1994;
- *Environmental sustainability and regeneration* — the implementation of national strategies for sustainable development in all countries by 2005, so as to ensure that current trends in the loss of environmental resources are effectively reversed at both global and national levels by 2015 — consistent

with the Convention on Climate Change at the 1992 Earth Summit (limiting the emission of greenhouse gases), the Montreal Protocol Multilateral Fund (phasing out ozone-depleting substances) and the Rio Biodiversity Convention (halting the loss of animal and plant species and the preservation of genetic resources). The DfID's scientific executive agency, the *Natural Resources Institute*, provides a multi-disciplinary centre of expert advice.

The DfID continues to provide humanitarian aid to meet local emergencies and for disaster relief — co-ordinated through the DfID's *Disaster Unit*.

The Commonwealth

The Commonwealth is of special importance to the UK. It is a voluntary association of 53 Member States most of which were previously UK territories. Mozambique, a former Portuguese colony, was permitted to join in November 1995 because it was effectively surrounded by Commonwealth states and wished to join them in membership. South Africa rejoined in 1994, after 33 years of absence. Pakistan was expelled in 1999, following the military coup there.

The Queen is Head of the Commonwealth and is Head of State of 15 of the Member States, besides the UK.

The organisation carries out its work through: a biennial *Meeting of Heads of Government* held at different locations throughout the Commonwealth (the UK hosted the 1997 Meeting — for the first time in 20 years); special conferences of Ministers and officials; and diplomatic representatives known as 'High Commissioners'.

The *Commonwealth Secretariat (www.thecommonwealth.org)* is based in London and effectively administers the various Commonwealth meetings and conferences, including the *Commonwealth Fund for Technical Co-operation* which arranges consultancy services and training awards for developing countries within the Commonwealth.

The *Commonwealth Games* are not only the most important sporting event taking place within the ambit of the Commonwealth, but also symbolise its qualities as an international organisation for mutual co-operation and development.

United Nations

The UK is a founder member of the United Nations (UN) *(un.org)*, which was set up by 51 countries in October 1945, in place of the League of Nations formed after the First World War. The UK contributes to the UN budget and provides assistance in UN peacekeeping activities. The UN's headquarters are in New York and at present practically every nation in the world is a member of the UN — 185 countries, all of whom agree to accept the obligations of the UN Charter. New member countries can be admitted on a two-thirds vote by the General Assembly, on a recommendation of the Security Council. All member countries are sovereign states and the UN is neither a form of government nor a legislative body.

The UN's *Charter* includes a set of principles and purposes, including: the maintenance of international peace and security; the development of friendly relations among nations; the achievement of international co-operation on economic, social, cultural and humanitarian issues; and the protection of human rights and fundamental freedoms.

The main elements of the UN are the General Assembly, the Security Council, the Economic and Social Council, the Trusteeship Council and the UN Secretariat (all based in New York) and the International Court of Justice (based in the Hague).

The *General Assembly* is the main deliberative body, where each member state has one vote. On issues such as peace, security and the budget, decisions require a two-thirds majority — other decisions require a simple majority. Recently, attempts have been made to reach decisions by consensus, without a formal vote.

The General Assembly also sets up agencies and programmes to carry its recommendations, especially on humanitarian issues — *UN Conference on Trade and Development* (UNCTAD), *UN International Children's Emergency Fund* (UNICEF), *the UN High Commissioner for Refugees* (UNHCR) and *UN Development Programme* (UNDP). UNICEF is probably the most widely-known and was set up in 1946, as a temporary measure only. Since that time UNICEF has proved its worth and is now a permanent organisation with a much wider brief — covering nutrition; drinking water; sanitation; health and welfare; education, training and literacy; and children's rights.

The *Security Council* has the principal task of maintaining peace and security, which it does through a combination of mediation and intervention — peacekeeping effort; peacekeeping operations (usually multinational); and economic sanctions. For example, the multinational force which carried out *Operation Desert Shield* and *Operation Desert Storm* against Iraq operated under a UN mandate.

The Security Council has 15 members, five permanent and 10 elected by the General Assembly for a period of two years. The UK is one of the five permanent members of the Security Council — the other four being China, France, the Russian Federation and the USA. Important decisions require nine out of the 15 votes — and all five permanent members must support the decision, giving each permanent member an effective veto.

The 54 members of the *Economic and Social Council* (ECOSOC) meet annually to co-ordinate the work of the UN and related agencies such as the World Health Organisation (WHO) and UNESCO, which promotes educational, cultural and social links between nations.

The *UN Secretariat* is headed by the *Secretary-General*, appointed by the General

Assembly, on the recommendation of the Security Council. The *Trusteeship Council* was set up to provide supervision for 11 *Trust Territories* with a view to their transition to self-government or independence either by becoming a separate State or joining neighbouring independent countries. In 1994 the Trust Territory of the Pacific Islands (Palau) previously administered by the USA became the 185th member of the UN. At that point, membership of the Trusteeship Council was reduced to the five permanent members of the Security Council and it only meets as and when required.

The *International Court of Justice (www.icj-cij.org)* sits in the Hague and consists of 15 judges elected for nine years, with no nation appointing more than one judge at any one time. Its purpose is to hear cases referred to it by member nations and to adjudicate in disputes between nations. Since some countries have said that they will not regard themselves as bound by its decisions (including China, France, Germany and the USA), its real effectiveness is questionable.

World Health Organisation

The *World Health Organisation (www.who.int)* is based in Geneva and its work is overseen by the *World Health Assembly* on which all 190 member states are represented. Its work is concerned with providing technical advice and training and implementing programmes in countries on such issues as disease and population control and nutrition.

The Group of Seven (G7)

The Group of Seven Leading Industrialised Countries (known as G7) was established in 1975 to discuss purely economic issues. The organisation is an informal one and has no secretariat. Over the years this informality has led to its discussions broadening to cover political as well as economic issues — such as international terrorism and crime.

The members of G7 are Canada, France, Germany, Italy, Japan, the UK and the USA. There is an Annual Summit of Heads of Government and the Presidency rotates round the Member States. The informality of the organisation has enabled Russia to take part in the political discussions since 1994 — when Russia is involved, the label 'G8' is used.

Other international financial organisations

To complete the international economic picture on an even broader scale, mention should be made of the International Monetary Fund, the World Bank, the Organisation for Economic Co-operation and Development, the World Trade Organisation and the World Economic Forum.

The *International Monetary Fund* (IMF) *(www.imf.org)* was set up in December 1945 by 29 countries signing its Articles of Government agreed at a conference the previous year at Bretton Woods in the USA; the IMF started its financial operations in March 1947. The IMF has its headquarters in Washington DC and its current member nations (182 in 1999) each have a representative on the IMF Board of Governors which meets annually. The IMF exists to administer a Code of Conduct on exchange rate policies; to provide a source of credit for member countries who are facing problems with their balance of payments; and to provide a forum where Member States can discuss international monetary problems.

The *International Bank for Reconstruction and Development* (aka the *World Bank*) *(www.worldbank.org)*, which also has its headquarters in Washington DC, was founded in 1944. The Bank is the source of loans to UN Member States to finance economic and social projects in developing countries, although the main thrust of its operations immediately after the Second World War was the reconstruction of Europe.

The *Organisation for Economic Co-operation and Development* (OECD) *(www.oecd.org)* consists of 29 industrialised countries (including the UK) and is based in Paris. OECD membership is open to any country which supports a market economy and a pluralist democracy. The aim of OECD is to promote economic growth generally, support less developed countries in particular, and promote the expansion of trade throughout the world.

The *World Trade Organisation* (WTO) *(www.wto.org)* was established in 1995, replacing the earlier General Agreement on Tariffs and Trade (GATT) set up after the Second World War. The system of multilateral trading was developed through a series of trade negotiations, or 'rounds', under the auspices of GATT. The last round of GATT negotiations, Uruguay from 1986 to 1994, led to the WTO's creation. In February 1997, agreement was reached between 69 governments on telecommunication services; later that year 70 governments reached agreement on financial services covering more than 95% of world trade in banking, insurance, securities and financial information.

Although the WTO has lofty ideals about promoting the economic health of nations, the reality is rather different. Cynics believe that the US government's idea of Free Trade is trade which protects US interests. Cynics also believe that, in the last analysis, the WTO does the bidding of the US government which, in turn, protects the interests of US Multinationals. One recent trade dispute on which the WTO arbitrated illustrates why people think this way: the UK/EU wished to protect the economies of small Caribbean States by supporting the price of their bananas in UK/EU markets; the US multinationals engaged in the banana business in other countries on mainland South America ('banana republics'?) did not like this and arranged for a complaint to be made to the WTO; the WTO decided against the UK/EU. This widespread perception of the WTO was evidenced, graphically, at the Third WTO Ministerial Conference in Seattle in November/December 1999 — which was so disrupted by demonstrators (on a multiplicity of issues) that the Director-General of the WTO had to put a brave face on what turned out to be a PR disaster for the WTO.

The *World Economic Forum* (a not-for-profit foundation based in Geneva) *(www.weforum.org)* aims to improve the state of the world through interaction between leaders from government, business, academic institutions and the arts. Its members meet annually at the Davos Symposium, in Switzerland, involving over 200 government leaders, 800 chief executives, 300 experts, scientists, artists and media representatives, and officials from regional and international organisations. In addition to the annual Davos meeting, the World Economic Forum arranges regional summits around the world. The Davos 2000 meeting, like the WTO Seattle 1999 conference, attracted the attention of demonstrators. Previous Davos meetings have provided an opportunity for international diplomacy: Davos 1988 produced the 'Davos Declaration' enabling Greece and Turkey to avoid conflict and Davos 1994 enabled Israel's Foreign Minister, Shimon Peres, and PLO Chairman, Yasser Arafat, to draft an agreement on Gaza and Jericho.

NATO and the Western European Union

The *North Atlantic Treaty Organisation* (NATO) *(www.nato.int)* was founded in 1949 in the aftermath of the Second World War and following the emergence of the post-War communist states in the Warsaw Pact. Its *raison d'être* is the collective security of its Member States, by deterring aggression, by defending Member States against any aggression and by providing a forum for trans-Atlantic allied consultation. In other words, it is a military, rather than a political, organisation.

NATO is important to the UK because the UK's membership of NATO provides the foundation for its defence. Much of the UK's armed forces are committed to NATO.

At the beginning of 1997, there were 16 states in membership of NATO: Belgium, Canada, Denmark, France, Germany, Greece, Iceland, Italy, Luxembourg, the Netherlands, Norway, Portugal, Spain, Turkey, the UK and the USA. Each had a permanent representative in Brussels at the NATO headquarters there. Although a member of NATO, France is not part of the NATO military command structure because President de Gaul pulled France out of that structure in 1966 and it has been slow to rejoin.

Given the basis for the existence of NATO, the political issue likely to continue over the next few years is the extent to which membership of NATO itself will be extended to the Baltic and Central European states, most of which were part of the former USSR or the Warsaw Pact, but who now want to join NATO.

The problem with admitting former Warsaw Pact and, even more so, the Baltic States, is that their armed forces are, from a purely military point of view, relatively incompetent as individual forces without the central direction and support of the former USSR (and thus of little real immediate value to NATO). Their bases are in the wrong place for their new rôle within NATO. The cost of bringing their forces up to NATO standard would be a considerable burden on the other NATO members or on the new entrants' emerging market-based economies

In May 1997, NATO signed an Accord with Russia, the *Founding Act on Mutual Relations, Cooperation and Security between NATO and the Russian Federation,* which reassured its concerns over the expansion of NATO in that direction, by establishing the *NATO/Russia Permanent Joint Council.* The existence of the Founding Act and the Permanent Joint Council underpinned NATO and Russian activities in Bosnia, Herzegovina and in the Kosovo crisis.

In July 1997, the NATO Summit in Madrid agreed, after significant internal dispute, the admission of Poland, Hungary and the Czech Republic — who became full members in 1999, increasing the NATO membership to 19 plus the Russian Federation ('19+1'). Some NATO members would have liked Romania and Slovenia included as well, that time around. However, the 1997 Summit did issue an 'open door' statement, making it clear that other states could be invited to join later, provided that they made the right kind of progress. The next membership review took place at the NATO Summit in Washington DC in April 1999, coinciding with the 50th anniversary of the foundation of NATO. Although no new members were admitted to NATO, the Washington Summit confirmed developments through the NATO-Ukraine Commission and the Mediterranean Dialogue and approved a Membership Action Plan for the nine countries (Albania, Bulgaria, Estonia, Former Yugoslav Republic of Macedonia, Latvia, Lithuania, Romania, Slovakia and Slovenia) seeking membership of NATO, with their progress being reviewed at the next Summit in 2002.

The *North Atlantic Council* is the main decision-making body and meets at least twice annually at foreign Minister level. The permanent representatives meet weekly. There are many NATO committees at which detailed internal arrangements are discussed.

The NATO military command structure is headed by a *Military Committee* (on which the member countries' Chiefs of Staff sit) under the direction of the North Atlantic Council. Under the Military Committee the command structure divides into: Allied Command Europe, Allied Command Atlantic, Allied Command Channel, Regional Planning Group (for North America) — each with their respective Supreme Commanders (e.g. Supreme Allied Commander, Europe is designated as SACEUR). The forces available to NATO fall into three categories: immediate and rapid reaction, main defence and augmentation forces.

NATO's European members form the *Western European Union,* which is a forum for consultation and co-operation on defence issues. Of the European countries in membership of NATO mentioned earlier, Iceland, Norway and Turkey are 'associate members'.

Austria, Denmark, Finland, the Irish Republic and Sweden have 'observer' status. A new class of membership, 'associate partnership', has recently been created and accorded to 10 Central European and Baltic states.

The Organisation for Security and Co-operation in Europe (OSCE)

Despite its name, OSCE *(www.osce.org)* is not limited to Europe and it has no legal status under international law — its decisions are only politically, as opposed to legally, binding. OSCE is intended to promote co-operation between Member States on security, human rights and economic matters — refined in 1990 to democracy, human rights and market economies. OSCE now has 55 members, covering the world, as OSCE says, from 'Vancouver to Vladivostok' — every state in Europe, the states of the former USSR, Canada and the USA are members. The former federal republic of Yugoslavia was suspended from membership in 1992.

The OSCE arose from a Conference on Security and Cooperation in Europe (CSCE) which, in turn, had its roots in an idea originally floated by Russia in 1954 for a 50 year treaty on pan-European security. However, there were political difficulties with the detail of the Russian proposals and the idea was shelved. Over the following years, the East-West situation became more relaxed and Finland offered to host informal talks leading to a full conference (CSCE) which started in 1973 with foreign Ministers from 35 states. These talks continued in Geneva and returned to Helsinki in 1975, resulting in the 1975 *Helsinki Final Act*. The collapse of communism in Europe changed the political scene in Europe and it was felt that it was time for a new start — which was reflected in the *Charter of Paris* signed in November 1990. The original Helsinki arrangements (the 'Blue Book') are reviewed at further conferences at regular intervals.

The *Permanent Council*, supported by a Secretariat meets in Vienna and takes decisions by consensus. There is an OSCE *High Commissioner on National Minorities*. The officials meet twice each year at conferences organised by the OSCE office in Prague. Advice on democracy, human rights and law is provided by the OSCE *Office for Democratic Institutions and Human Rights,* based in Warsaw.

UK defence strategy

The UK's defence strategy has three broad objectives:

- to deter any threats to and, if necessary, defend the freedom and territorial integrity of the UK and its Dependent Territories, including assistance to the civil authority in countering terrorism;
- to contribute to the promotion of the UK's wider security interests, including the protection of freedom, democratic institutions and free trade; and

- to promote peace and help maximise the international prestige and influence of the UK.

The then Secretary of State for Defence, George Robertson, presented his Strategic Defence Review (SDR) to the Commons in July 1998. The SDR examined the UK's security priorities and revised the broad Defence Missions and Tasks, switching emphasis towards building international trust and preventing conflict and forming closer links with NATO and the UN.

The *UK Dependent Territories* (following the return of Hong Kong to China in July 1997) are the Falkland Islands (subject to a territorial claim by Argentina), Gibraltar (subject to a territorial claim by Spain), the Caribbean Dependent Territories and a range of small islands elsewhere.

The UK defence strategy is implemented by its three armed forces, listed in the order of their creation — the Royal Navy (RN — the 'Senior Service' whose flag always flies slightly higher than the other two!), the British Army and the Royal Air Force (RAF).

The UK has its own independent nuclear deterrent which is said to "provide the ultimate guarantee of national security". The present form of that deterrent is within the RN — three Vanguard class nuclear ballistic missile submarines (*Vanguard, Victorious* and *Vigilant*), built in the UK, carrying US Trident D5 missiles with UK nuclear warheads — in fact, the missiles are jointly owned by the US and the UK. A fourth such submarine *(Vengeance)* is undergoing sea trials. With four submarines it should be possible to keep up a permanent patrol of one submarine at sea while the others are in for service. Because of the present relatively relaxed international situation, the missiles are untargeted and the alert time is no longer measured in minutes.

The other form of nuclear deterrent was the free-fall air bomb, delivered by the RAF. With the collapse of the former USSR and the apparent end of the Cold War, these bombs were phased out by the end of 1998 — leaving Trident as the sole deterrent.

The Ministry of Defence (MoD)

The Ministry of Defence (MoD) *(www.mod.uk)* has two rôles — a Department of State (headed by the Secretary of State for Defence) and the highest military HQ of the UK armed forces. Each armed service has its own *Chief of Staff* who is responsible for the fighting effectiveness, efficiency and morale of that particular service. That responsibility is co-ordinated through the *Chief of the Defence Staff* and the Secretary of State for Defence.

The *Defence Council* which runs the armed forces, is chaired by the Secretary of State. The Council consists of the Chief of the Defence Staff, various Chiefs of Staff and the more senior officers and the civilian officials heading the main departments of the MoD.

Support services are provided by the *Procurement Executive*, the *Defence Intelligence Service*, the *Defence Estates Organisation* and the *Defence Exports Services Organisation*.

The *Defence Costs Study* examined all aspects of MoD activity, except the frontline, with a view to achieving greater value for money and clearer direction and account-ability. As a consequence, the Defence Budget is expected to fall, in real terms, over the next few years.

Appendix A
Election Results

The 1997 UK General Election (659 seats)
1 May 1997 (turnout 71%) electoral system: *first past the post*

party	seats	seats	vote
Labour	419	64%	44%
Conservative	165	25%	31%
Liberal Democrat	46	7%	17%
Others	29	4%	8%

The 1999 Elections for the Scottish Parliament (129 seats)
6 May 1999 electoral system: *proportional representation – additional member*

party	constituency	region	total	vote*
Labour	53	3	56	37%
SNP	7	28	35	30%
Conservative	0	18	18	15%
Liberal Democrat	12	5	17	15%
Scottish Socialist Party	0	1	1	]
Green Party	0	1	1	] 3%
Independent	1	0	1	]
total	73	56	129	

*average over both constituency and regional list ballots

LGC Information

The 1999 Elections for the Welsh Assembly (60 seats)
6 May 1999 electoral system: *proportional representation – additional member*

party	constituency	region	total
Labour	27	1	28
Plaid Cymru	9	8	17
Conservative	1	8	9
Liberal Democrat	3	3	6
total	40	20	60

The 1998 Elections for the New Northern Ireland Assembly (108 seats)
25 June 1998 – with subsequent changes of allegiance
electoral system: *proportional representation – single transferable vote*

party	seats
Ulster Unionist Party (UUP)	28
Social Democratic and Labour Party (SDLP)	24
Democratic Unionist Party (DUP)	20
Sinn Féin (SF)	18
The Alliance Party (All)	6
Northern Ireland Unionist Party (NIUP)*+	3
United Unionist Assembly Party (UUAP)**	3
Northern Ireland Women's Coalition (NIWC)	2
Progressive Unionist Party (PUP)	2
UK Unionist Party (UKUP)	1
Independent Unionist+	1

* elected as UK Unionist Party, resigned and formed NIUP w.e.f. 15 January 1999
** elected as Independent Candidates, formed UUAP w.e.f. 21 September 1998
+ Roger Hutchinson was expelled from the NIUP w.e.f. 2 December 1999.

The 1999 UK Elections for the European Parliament (87 seats)
10 June 1999 (turnout 24%)
electoral system: Northern Ireland: *proportional representation – single transferable vote*
remainder of UK: *proportional representation – regional lists*

party	seats	vote
Conservative	36	34%
Labour	29	26%
Liberal Democrat	10	12%
UK Independence	3	7%
Green	2	6%
SNP	2	2%
Plaid Cymru	2	2%
Democratic Unionist	1	2%
SDLP	1	2%
Ulster Unionist	1	1%
Others	0	7%

The 2001 UK General Election (659 seats)
7 June 2001 (turnout 59%) electoral system: *first past the post*

party	seats	seats	vote
Labour	412	63%	41%
Conservative	166	25%	32%
Liberal Democrat	52	8%	18%
Others	29	5%	10%

Appendix B
Government — UK and devolved

Her Majesty's Government

(as at February 2002 — current position at *www.cabinet-office.gov.uk*)
The portal to government websites has changed from *open.gov.uk* to *ukonline.gov.uk*

The June 2001 Shuffle

The aftermath of the June 2001 General Election brought with it not only the usual shuffle of personnel but also a substantial change in some departmental responsibilities and names.

The Ministry of Agriculture, Fisheries and Food (MAFF) and the Environmental responsibilities of the Department for the Environment, Transport and the Regions (DETR) were combined to form a new Department for Environment, Food and Rural Affairs (DEFRA). The name of the DETR was also changed to reflect this shift in responsibilities, becoming the Department for Transport, Local Government and the Regions (DTLR).

For a government which, according to its Manifesto, was apparently enthusiastic about some sort of regional devolution in England, it was strange that responsibility for regional issues (previously the sole responsibility of the DETR) was split three ways (DTLR, DfES and DEFRA), with co-ordination by the Deputy Prime Minister, John Prescott.

The Department of Social Security (DSS) took on the employment-related responsibilities of the Department for Education and Employment (DfEE), including the Employment Service, and changed its name to the Department for Work and Pensions (DWP). As a consequence, the DfEE changed its name, to become the Department for Education and Skills (DfES).

The Home Office lost Elections and the Fire Service to the DTLR; and Freedom of Information, Citizenship and Immigration to the Lord Chancellor's Department.

The increase in the power at the centre (the creation of the Office for the Deputy Prime Minister, placed with the Prime Minister's Office and the Cabinet Office, supported by a number of Ministers) tended to confirm some commentators' view that Tony Blair was, in reality, now heading a Prime Minister's Department in all but name. The reference in the following list to 'The Prime Minister's Department' is intended to be slightly facetious. Nonetheless, this accretion of power might, rightly or wrongly, lend credence to the view that this was further evidence of a more Presidential style of Prime Ministerial activity. The Prime Minister appears twice in this list, correctly reflecting his formal responsibilities within HM Treasury.

In the case of the Northern Ireland Office, Scottish Office and Wales Office the Ministerial responsibilities are subject to the devolution arrangements in those countries.

Where there is a number of Ministers of a similar rank within a department and their official title is unspecific, the *italic text* in square brackets [ ] indicates their principal area of responsibility, although they may have others within that department. This approach is also used where it would be useful to give some idea of how responsibilities are split within a department. The symbol + indicates a member of the Cabinet.

'The Prime Minister's Department'
[www.number10.gov.uk and www.cabinet-office.gov.uk]
Prime Minister, First Lord of the Treasury and Minister for the Civil Service +
Deputy Prime Minister and First Secretary of State +
Minister of State for the Cabinet Office (and Chancellor of the Duchy of Lancaster)
Minister of State *[Regions, Social Exclusion and Business Co-ordination]*
Minister of State *[Women and Equality]*
Minister without Portfolio and Party Chair + *
Parliamentary Secretary *[Civil Service]*
* *it seems that the Chair of the Labour Party is now appointed by the Prime Minister rather than the Party's National Executive! Has no departmental responsibilities but sits on a number of Ministerial Committees, presumably as the 'eyes and ears' of the Prime Minister.*

Department for Culture, Media and Sport (DCMS)
[www.culture.gov.uk]
Secretary of State for Culture, Media and Sport +
Minister of State for the Arts
Minister of State for Sport
Parliamentary Under-Secretary of State (Minister for Tourism, Film and Broadcasting)

Ministry of Defence (MOD)

[www.mod.uk] [sic]
Secretary of State for Defence +
Minister of State for the Armed Forces
Parliamentary Under-Secretary of State (Minister for Defence Procurement)
Parliamentary Under-Secretary of State (Minister for Veterans)

Department for Education and Skills (DfES)

[www.dfes.gov.uk]
Secretary of State for Education and Skills +
Minister of State for School Standards
Minister of State for Lifelong Learning and Higher Education *[plus Regional and Regeneration Policy]*
Parliamentary Under-Secretary of State for Early Years and School Standards
Parliamentary Under-Secretary of State for Adult Skills
Parliamentary Under-Secretary of State for Young People and Learning

Department for Environment, Food and Rural Affairs (DEFRA)

[www.defra.gov.uk]
Secretary of State + *
Minister of State (Environment)
Minister of State (Rural Affairs)
Parliamentary Under-Secretary (Commons) *[Animal health, fisheries, forestry and coastal defence]*
Parliamentary Under-Secretary (Lords) *[Food and farming, departmental science and inland waterways]*
* *also appointed as Minister for Agriculture, Fisheries and Food*

Foreign and Commonwealth Office (FCO)

[www.fco.gov.uk]
Secretary of State for Foreign and Commonwealth Affairs +
Minister of State (Trade) *
Minister of State *[Relations with EU and Central and NW Europe]*
Parliamentary Under-Secretary of State *[Counter-Terrorism, Drugs and relations with Middle East, North Africa and South East Asia]*
Parliamentary Under-Secretary of State *[Cultural Relations, relations with Eastern Adriatic, Latin America, North East Asia and China, and internal departmental administration]*
Parliamentary Under-Secretary of State *[Commonwealth, relations with South and Equatorial Africa, and the Caribbean, and consular activity]*
* *also appointed to the Department of Trade and Industry*

Department of Health (DH)

[www.doh.gov.uk]
Secretary of State for Health +
Minister of State for Health *[NHS and delivery]*
Minister of State (Commons) *[Social Care, long term care, disability and mental health]*
Parliamentary Under-Secretary of State (Lords) *[Performance and quality]*
Parliamentary Under-Secretary of State *[Public health and Embryology]*
Parliamentary Under-Secretary of State *[Emergency Care and public involvement]*

Home Office

[www.homeoffice.gov.uk]
Secretary of State for the Home Department +
Minister of State for Crime Reduction
Minister of State for the Criminal Justice System
Minister of State for Citizenship and Immigration
Parliamentary Under-Secretary of State *[support for Crime Reduction]*
Parliamentary Under-Secretary of State *[support for Criminal Justice System]*
Parliamentary Under-Secretary of State *[support for Citizenship and Immigration]*

Department for International Development (DFID)

[www.dfid.gov.uk]
Secretary of State for International Development +
Parliamentary Under-Secretary of State *[support for Secretary of State]*

Law Officers

Attorney General *[Treasury Solicitor, Director of Public Prosecutions and the Crown Prosecution Service, and Serious Fraud Office]*
Solicitor General *[support for Attorney General]*

Leader of the House of Lords

Leader of the House of Lords (and Lord Privy Seal) + *
* no departmental responsibilities; responsible for the organisation of government business in the House of Lords

Lord Chancellor's Department (LCD)

[www.lcd.gov.uk]
Lord Chancellor +
Parliamentary Secretary *[Courts, EU, Human Rights, Freedom of Information, and Land Registry]*

Parliamentary Secretary *[Tribunals, Social Exclusion and Public Record Office]*
Parliamentary Secretary *[Legal Aid, Civil Justice, Legal services and Law Commission]*

Northern Ireland Office (NIO)
[www.nio.gov.uk]
Secretary of State for Northern Ireland + *
Minister of State *[Security, policing and prisons]*
Parliamentary Under-Secretary of State *[Good Friday Agreement, criminal justice and victims]*
* *subject to devolution under the Good Friday Agreement*

Privy Council Office
President of the Council and Leader of the House of Commons + *
Parliamentary Secretary, Privy Council Office *[support for Leader of the House of Commons]*
* *as President of the Council, responsible for the Privy Council Office; as Leader of the House of Commons, responsible for the organisation of government business in the House of Commons.*

Scotland Office
[www.scottishsecretary.gov.uk]
Secretary of State for Scotland + *
Minister of State *[support for Secretary of State]*
Advocate General for Scotland *[Constitutional and legal advice to HM government on Scottish affairs]* **
* *subject to devolution arrangements; responsible for matters reserved to UK Parliament; the Scottish Executive and Scottish Parliament are responsible for other functions in Scotland*
** *Scotland has its own legal system*

Department of Trade and Industry (DTI)
[www.dti.gov.uk]
Secretary of State for Trade and Industry +
Minister for Industry, Energy and the Environment
Minister for Employment Relations and the Regions
Minister for E-Commerce
Minister for Trade (and Deputy Leader of the House of Lords) *
Parliamentary Under-Secretary of State for Competition, Consumers and Markets
Parliamentary Under-Secretary of State for Small Business
Parliamentary Under-Secretary of State for Science and Innovation
* *also appointed to the Foreign and Commonwealth Office*

Department for Transport, Local Government and the Regions (DTLR)
[www.dtlr.gov.uk]
Secretary of State for Transport, Local Government and the Regions +
Minister of State (Minister for Transport) *
Minister of State (Minister for Local Government and the Regions)
Minister of State (Minister for Housing, Planning and Regeneration)
Parliamentary Under-Secretary of State *[Railways, roads, maritime and aviation]*
Parliamentary Under-Secretary of State *[Housing, planning and regeneration]*
Parliamentary Under-Secretary of State *[Local Government, regions, elections and fire service]*
* *attends, but is not a member of, the Cabinet*

HM Treasury
[www.hm-treasury.gov.uk]
Prime Minister (and First Lord of the Treasury) +
Chancellor of the Exchequer (and Second Lord and Ministerial Head) +
Chief Secretary to the Treasury *[Public expenditure and procurement]* +
Paymaster General *[Taxation and Inland Revenue]*
Financial Secretary *[VAT and Customs and Excise]*
Economic Secretary *[Banking, foreign exchange, EU and National Savings]*

Wales Office (Office of the Secretary of State for Wales)
[www.ossw.wales.gov.uk]
Secretary of State for Wales + *
Parliamentary Under-Secretary of State *[support for Secretary of State]*
* *subject to devolution arrangements; former Welsh Office executive functions now the respon-sibility of the National Assembly for Wales*

Department for Work and Pensions (DWP)
[www.dwp.gov.uk]
Secretary of State for Work and Pensions +
Minister of State for Work *
Minister of State for Pensions
Parliamentary Under-Secretary of State (Lords) *[Children and the Family]*
Parliamentary Under-Secretary of State (Minister for Disabled People)
Parliamentary Under-Secretary (Commons) *[Work and Social Security Benefits]*
* *attends, but is not a member of, the Cabinet*

Government Whips (House of Commons)

Chief Whip and Parliamentary Secretary to the Treasury +
Deputy Chief Whip and Treasurer of HM Household
Comptroller of HM Household
Vice-Chamberlain of HM Household
Lord Commissioner of HM Treasury x 5
Assistant Whip x 7

Government Whips (House of Lords)

Captain of the Honourable Corps of the Gentlemen-at-Arms (Chief Whip) *
Captain of The Queen's Bodyguard of the Yeomen of the Guard (Deputy Chief Whip)
Lords in Waiting x 4
Baroness in Waiting
* *attends, but is not a member of, the Cabinet*

Executive Agencies and Units

(as at February 2002 — current position at *www.cabinet-office.gov.uk*)

The Executive Agencies are concerned with the delivery of executive functions which formerly were integral within the relevant government department. The significance for the government of those particular executive functions means that they have been 'externalised' only to the extent of placing them within an Executive Agency under the fairly direct supervision of a responsible Minister within the relevant department.

Those functions which the government wished to 'externalise' to a greater extent have been placed with *Non-Departmental Public Bodies* (NDPBs), otherwise referred to as *quangos*. No attempt has been made to list the NDPBs here because their numbers are legion and ever-increasing.

For the sake of completeness, the growing number of 'Units' within the Cabinet Office are also listed here, to show the extent to which activities based within the Cabinet Office have increased in recent years.

'The Prime Minister's Department'
Units within the Cabinet Office:
  Social Exclusion Unit
  Regional Co-ordination Unit
  International Public Service Unit
  Business Co-ordination Unit
  Women and Equality Unit
  Delivery Unit
  Regulatory Impact Unit
  Performance and Innovation Unit
  Forward Strategy Unit
Office for Public Services Reform
Central Office of Information
Government Car and Despatch Agency

Department for Culture, Media and Sport
Royal Parks Agency

Ministry of Defence
Armed Forces Personnel Administration Agency
Army Base Repair Organisation
Army Personnel Centre
Army Training and Recruiting Agency
British Forces Post Office
Defence Analytical Services Agency
Defence Aviation Repair Agency
Defence Bills Agency
Defence Communications Services Agency
Defence Dental Agency
Defence Estates Agency
Defence Geographic and Imagery Intelligence Agency
Defence Housing Executive
Defence Intelligence and Security Centre
Defence Medical Training Organisation
Defence Procurement Agency
Defence Science and Technology Laboratory
Defence Secondary Care Agency
Defence Storage and Distribution Agency
Defence Transport and Movements Agency

Defence Vetting Agency
Disposal Sales Agency
Duke of York's Royal Military School
Medical Supplies Agency
Meteorological Office
Ministry of Defence Police
Naval Manning Agency
Naval Recruiting and Training Agency
Pay and Personnel Agency
Queen Victoria School
RAF Personnel Management Agency
RAF Training Group Defence Agency
Service Children's Education
War Pensions Agency
Warship Support Agency
UK Hydrographic Office

Department for Environment, Food and Rural Affairs
Centre for Environment, Fisheries and Aquaculture Science
Central Science Laboratory
Pesticides Safety Directorate
Veterinary Laboratories Agency
Veterinary Medicines Directorate
Rural Payments Agency

Foreign and Commonwealth Office
Wilton Park

Department of Health
Medical Devices Agency
Medicines Control Agency
NHS Estates
NHS Pensions Agency
NHS Purchasing and Supply Agency

Home Office
Forensic Science Service
United Kingdom Passport Service
HM Prison Service

Attorney General
Treasury Solicitor's Department

Lord Chancellor's Department
HM Land Registry
Public Record Office
Court Service
Public Guardianship Office

Northern Ireland Office
Compensation Agency
Forensic Science Agency of Northern Ireland
Northern Ireland Prison Service

Department of Trade and Industry
Companies House
Employment Tribunals Service
Insolvency Service
National Weights and Measures Laboratory
Patent Office
Radiocommunications Agency

Department for Transport, Local Government and the Regions
Driver & Vehicle Licensing Agency
Driving Standards Agency
Fire Service College
Highways Agency
Maritime and Coastguard Agency
Planning Inspectorate*
Queen Elizabeth II Conference Centre
The Rent Service
Vehicle Certification Agency
Vehicle Inspectorate
the Secretary of State for Wales is responsible for the Planning Inspectorate in Wales

HM Treasury
Debt Management Office
National Savings*
Office for National Statistics*

Royal Mint*
Valuation Office**
separate government department reporting to the Chancellor of the Exchequer
**Executive Agency within the Inland Revenue*

Department for Work and Pensions
Appeals Service
Benefits Agency
Child Support Agency
Employment Service

The Civil Service Senior Grades

new	old	example of responsibility
1	Permanent Secretary	heads a major department
1A	Second Permanent Secretary	heads a smaller department / policy unit
2	Deputy Secretary	directs a large executive agency
3	Under Secretary	heads a functional division
4	[professional title]	holds a senior professional office
5	Assistant Secretary	heads a policy programme section
6	Senior Principal	heads a regional office
7	Principal	heads a local service office

Scotland Government

Scottish Parliament

(as at February 2002 — current position found at *www.scottish.parliament.uk*)
Presiding Officer of the Scottish Parliament
Deputy Presiding Officers

Main devolved responsibilities of Scottish Parliament:
- Health
- Education
- Transport
- Housing
- Training
- Economic development
- Agriculture
- Environment

Main reserved responsibilities retained by Westminster:
- Constitutional
- Foreign Policy and Defence
- most Economic Policy
- Social Security
- Medical ethics

The Scottish Executive

consists of the First Minister, Scottish Law Officers and the Scottish Ministers
(as at February 2002 — current position found at *www.scotland.gov.uk*)

First Minister

Scottish Law Officers
Lord Advocate
Solicitor General for Scotland

The Scottish Ministers
Deputy First Minister and Minister for Justice
Deputy Minister for Justice
Minister for Finance and Public Services
Deputy Minister for Finance and Public Services

Minister for Health and Community Care
Deputy Minister for Health and Community Care (1)
Deputy Minister for Health and Community Care (2)
Minister for Social Justice
Deputy Minister for Social Justice
Minister for Environment and Rural Development
Deputy Minister for Environment and Rural Development
Minister for Enterprise, Transport and Lifelong Learning
Deputy Minister for Enterprise, Transport and Lifelong Learning
Minister for Tourism, Culture and Sport
Deputy Minister for Tourism, Culture and Sport
Minister for Education and Young People
Deputy Minister for Education and Young People
Minister for Parliamentary Business
Deputy Minister for Parliamentary Business

Departments of the Scottish Executive
Justice Department
Health Department
Finance and Central Services Department
Development Department
Education Department
Enterprise and Lifelong Learning Department
Environment and Rural Affairs Department
Corporate Services

Scottish Executive Agencies
- Fisheries Research Service
- Scottish Agricultural Science Agency
- Scottish Prison Service
- Historic Scotland
- Scottish Public Pensions Agency
- Student Awards Agency for Scotland
- Scottish Courts
- Scottish Fisheries Protection Agency
- National Archives of Scotland
- HM Inspectorate of Education

Wales Government
(as at February 2002 — current position found at *www.wales.gov.uk*)

The National Assembly for Wales
Presiding Officer of the National Assembly for Wales
Deputy Presiding Officer of the National Assembly for Wales

Subject Committees
Agriculture and Rural Development
Culture
Economic Development
Environment, Planning and Transport
Health and Social Services
Local Government and Housing
Post 16 Education and Training
Pre 16 Education, Schools and Early Learning

Standing Committees
Audit
Business
Equality of Opportunity
European Affairs
Standards of Conduct

Regional Committees
Mid Wales
North Wales
South East Wales
South West Wales

Cabinet of the National Assembly for Wales
[originally called 'Secretary', now called 'Minister']
First Minister
Deputy First Minister
Minister for Culture, Sports and Welsh Language
Minister for Education and Lifelong Learning
Minister for Assembly Business
Minister for the Environment
Minister for Finance, Local Government and Communities

Minister for Health and Social Services
Minister for Rural Affairs

Executive Agency
● Cadw: Welsh Historic Monuments Executive Agency

Northern Ireland Government

Following the devolution of power to the New Northern Ireland Executive on 2 December 1999 under the terms of the Anglo-Irish Agreement, the Secretary of State for Northern Ireland still retained responsibility for constitutional, financial and security issues relating to Northern Ireland — including international relations, defence, taxation, law and order, police and criminal justice policy. There is also a number of agencies retained within the Northern Ireland Office at Whitehall, including the Northern Ireland Prison Service, the Compensation Agency and the Forensic Agency of Northern Ireland. Apart from the reserved matters, full legislative and executive power is transferred to the Assembly.

Note: due to the political volatility of Northern Ireland, the Northern Ireland Executive and cross-border bodies may be suspended. If they are not suspended then the arrangements described below are likely to apply. The current position can be checked on the Northern Ireland Office website (www.nio.gov.uk), the Northern Ireland Assembly website (www.ni-assembly.gov.uk) or the Northern Ireland Executive website (www.nics.gov.uk). The Northern Ireland Executive is drawn from the Northern Ireland Assembly, which has its own Presiding Officer.

Northern Ireland Executive — Ministers

First Minister
Deputy First Minister
Note: the occupants of the following posts claim them after the Assembly elections, in order of d'Hondt nomination:
Minister for Enterprise, Trade and Investment
Minister of Finance and Personnel
Minister for Regional Development
Minister for Education
Minister for the Environment

Minister for Employment and Learning
Minister of Social Development
Minister of Culture, Arts and Leisure
Minister of Health, Social Services and Public Safety
Minister of Agriculture and Rural Development

Northern Ireland Executive — Departments

Office of the First Minister and Deputy First Minister
Department of Agriculture and Rural Development
Department of Culture, Arts and Leisure
Department of Education
Department of Enterprise, Trade and Investment
Department of the Environment
Department of Finance and Personnel
Department of Health, Social Services and Public Safety
Department of Employment and Learning
Department for Regional Development
Department for Social Development

North-South Co-operation

The *North South Ministerial Council* brings together Ministers from Northern Ireland and the Irish government, under the authority of the Northern Ireland assembly and the Oireachtas (the Irish Parliament) for regular meetings to develop consultation co-operation and action on an all-island and cross-border basis on matters of mutual interest.

The arrangements for co-operation, established on 2 December 1999 under the *Anglo-Irish Agreement*, include six new bodies: Waterways Ireland; the Food Safety Promotion Board; the Trade and Business Development Body; the Special EU Programmes Body; the North-South Language Body (*An Foras Teanga* in Irish or *Boord o Leid* in Ulster Scots); and the Foyle, Carlingford and Irish Lights Commission.

British-Irish Co-operation

The *British-Irish Council* (aka the *Council of the Isles*) has the objective of promoting the harmonious and mutually beneficial development of the totality of relationships among the people of 'the islands'. The Ulster Unionists insisted on a British-Irish Council as one of their conditions for supporting the Good Friday Agreement, as a means of maintaining close links with the UK — to counter the emphasis on north-south co-operation by introducing the idea of east-west co-operation. In fact it has the potential to have a wider significance.

At the first meeting at Lancaster House, in London on 17 December 1999, four languages were heard at various times: English, Irish, Welsh and Manx. Contributions were made by Prime Minister Tony Blair; Taoiseach Bertie Ahern; First Minister Donald Dewar; First Secretary Alan Michael; First Minister David Trimble; Senator Pierre Horsfall of Jersey; Conseiller Laurie Morgan of Guernsey; and Chief Minister Donald Gelling of the Isle of Man. Five policy areas were chosen for further joint debate: drugs, social inclusion, environment, transport and e-commerce. Because of the continuing political difficulties in Northern Ireland, during which the Assembly was suspended on several occasions, the next meeting of the Council did not take place until November 2001.

The *British-Irish Inter-Governmental Conference* replaced the Anglo-Irish Inter-Governmental Conference previously established under the 1985 Anglo-Irish Agreement.

Appendix C
Treaty of Nice 2000

The Treaty of Nice 2000 provided for the following:

	now		*when enlarged to 27*		
	votes	*MEP*	*votes*	*pop*	*MEP*
Germany	10	99	29	2.83	99
France	10	87	29	2.03	74
UK	10	87	29	2.04	74
Italy	10	87	29	1.99	74
Spain	8	64	27	1.46	52
Poland	-	-	27	1.43	52
Romania	-	-	14	1.50	35
Netherlands	5	31	13	1.21	25
Belgium	5	25	12	0.85	20
Greece	5	25	12	0.87	20
Portugal	5	25	12	0.83	20
Hungary	-	-	12	0.84	20
Czech Republic	-	-	12	0.86	20
Sweden	4	22	10	0.86	18
Austria	4	21	10	0.81	17
Bulgaria	-	-	10	0.82	17
Denmark	3	16	7	0.76	13
Finland	3	16	7	0.74	13
Ireland	3	15	7	0.53	12
Slovakia	-	-	7	0.77	13
Lithuania	-	-	7	0.53	12
Luxembourg	2	6	4	0.11	6
Cyprus	-	-	4	0.19	6
Estonia	-	-	4	0.36	6
Latvia	-	-	4	0.60	8
Slovenia	-	-	4	0.49	7
Malta	-	-	3	0.12	5
totals	87	626	342		738

In the table above, 'votes' means votes in the Council of Ministers; 'pop' means the population per vote, in millions. The Qualified Majority would be 258 (73%) votes and would need to represent a minimum of 62% of the population. This would mean that three large and one small Member States could block developments and Germany's 80m population would give it the edge over the UK and France, with 60m each.

Index

LGC Information

Notes

LGC Information

Notes

LGC Information

LGC Information